Voices from the Bottom of the South China Sea

The Untold Story of America's Largest Chinese Emigrant Disaster

Robert S. Wells

FⴲRTIS

A NONFICTION IMPRINT FROM ADDUCENT

www.Adducent.co

Titles Distributed In
North America
United Kingdom
Western Europe
South America
Australia

Voices from the Bottom of the South China Sea

By Robert S. Wells

ISBN 9781937592431

Published by Adducent (under its *Fortis* nonfiction imprint)
Jacksonville, Florida
www.Adducent.Co

Published in the United States of America

Dedicated to my wife, Christine... still the most beautiful flower in the garden.

Table of Contents

Illustrations

Note on Chinese Spellings

This book makes references to Chinese names and terms based on the two fundamental methods of transliterating Chinese characters into the Roman alphabet.

The *Wades-Giles* method was used throughout the 19th and 20th Century until 1979 when the People's Republic of China adopted the *Pinyin* method.

In an attempt to maintain as much authenticity as possible with the geographic and nautical references used by diplomats serving at the U.S. Consulates, the *Wades-Giles* pronunciation of Canton, Swatow and Hong Kong remained as cited from the primary sources in order to align with the critically important references of the mariners of the Pacific Mail Steamship service and U.S. Navy and their role in helping piece together the story and locate the final resting places of the *Japan* wreck.

Kwangtung Province in southeast China, the origin of almost 100% of the Chinese emigrants to California, uses the *Pinyin* translation of Guangdong in order help communicate the story to the modern day descendants of the lost emigrants in the waters of the South China Sea.

Wreck Discovery and Salvage Operations 1874-1878
South China Sea
Southwest Monsoon Season: March-October

Salvage and Underwriters: The Stakeholders

Captain John Pratt Roberts: CMSNC; Russell & Co.
Captain Holcomb: S.S. *Scotland*
CMSNC: S.S. *Rajah*
CMSNC: S.S. *Aden*
Augustine Heard (U.S.):   S.S. *Little Orphan*

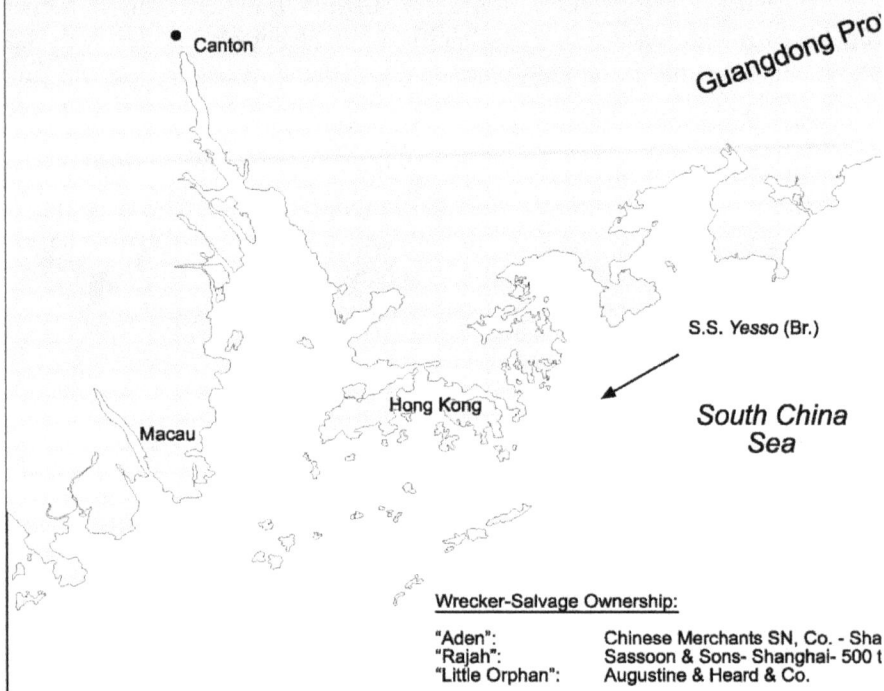

• Canton

Guangdong Pro

S.S. *Yesso* (Br.)

Hong Kong

Macau

South China Sea

Wrecker-Salvage Ownership:

"Aden":   Chinese Merchants SN, Co. - Sha
"Rajah":   Sassoon & Sons- Shanghai- 500 t
"Little Orphan":   Augustine & Heard & Co.

N

20 miles

Shantou

USS *Ashuelot*
(Aug-Sept 75)
"Piracy Patrol"

Tungao Bay

Yantic
Saco S.S. *Yettung*

Province

Scotland (Mar 75)
Saco (Dec 74)
Aden (Jan-Feb 75)
Yantic (Dec 74)
Scotland (May 75)
Aden *Little Orphan* (Jun 75)
Badigs *Loitens* (Jun 75)
(17 Feb 75) *Divers* (Oct 75)

Rajah (Jun 76)
English Divers (Mar 76-77)

Key	U.S. Navy Asiatic Fleet	Wreckers Salvage
1874	Yantic Saco	Aden
1875	Yantic Ashuelot	Aden Scotland Loitens Little Orphan
1876	Monocacy	Rajah

Captain J. P. Roberts
worked for CMSN

inghai
ton

S.S. *Japan* wreck sites

Starboard sternwheel site
discovered Feb 27, 1875

Main body of wreck
discovered July 31, 1875

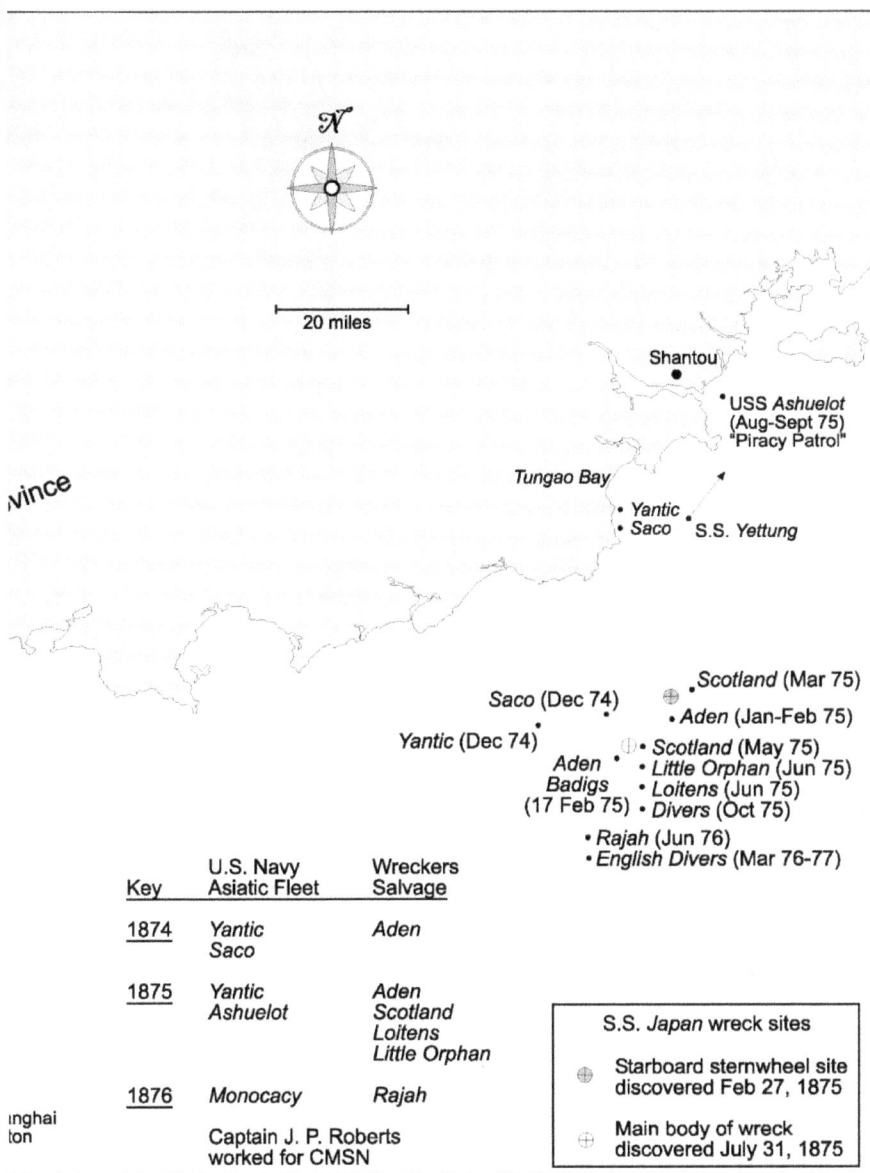

Charles David Grear

iv

Final S.S. *Japan* Wreck Sites
Burned at Sea and Sank
December 17-18, 1874

Total Aboard: 557

128 Crew
2 Cabin passengers
2 Europeans, steerage
425 Chinese, steerage

Saved: 151

114 Crew
2 Cabin passengers
1 European, steerage
34 Chinese, steerage

Lost: 406

14 Crew
1 European, steerage
391 Chinese, steerage

Guangdong
Province

China

Charles David Grear

American Chinese Emigration 1867-1875

100,000 Departures
40,000 Returnees

Chinese Consolidated Benevolent Association
"Huigan"
"The Six Companies"

Huigan	Year Formed	Region	District	SF Population
1. Ning Yeung	1853	Taishan	Siyi	75,000
2. Hop Wo	1862	Kaiping-Eping	Siyi	34,000
3. Kong Chow	1851	Xinhui	Siyi	15,000
4. Yeong Wo	1852	Zhongshan	Delta	12,000
5. Sam Yup	1851	Canton, Guangzhou Panyu, Nanhai, Shunde	Sanyi	11,000
6. Yan Wo	1852	Hakka	Han	4,300

Siyi Districts
Farmers
Fishermen
Peasants
Craftsmen
Agriculturalists
Railroad Labor
Dialect: Taishan/Local

Yangjiang
(Maritime Silk Road Museum)

Enping
Kaiping (2)
Taishan (1)
Xinhui (3)
Zhongshan (4)
Sacramento Delta
Rice
Shunde
Nanhai
Panyu (5)
Guangzhou (Canton)- Treaty Port

US flagged transports to Hong Kong after Canton clearance by British Q'ing authorities

Pearl River

Macau "Coolie Labor" Institution 1850s

South China Sea

Sanyi Districts
Merchants
Artisans
Merchandising/ Garment Manufacturing
Urban Entrepreneur (SF, AZ, WA, Boston)
Dialect: Cantonese

Guangdong Province
The "Sojourners," "Wild Geese," emigrants of the Sanyi and Siyi Districts represented almost 100% of 19th century emigration to the U.S.

Guangdong Province is China's 2nd Largest Province
Population: 96 million
GDP: 3 Trillion Remindi ($494B)

Shantou

Pacific Mail
Steamship Company
Sidewheel
Steamers Arrivals
1867 **8,287** 1879
3,357 tons 17/16
1868 **6,743** 1879
3,881 tons 25/25
1868 **14,198** 1880
3,386 tons 25/25
1868 **9,935** 1874
4,351 tons 25/24
1869 **1,929** 1872
4,454 tons 11/9
1868 **4,476** 1885
4,011 tons 12/9
S.S. Colorado
S.S. Great Republic
S.S. China
S.S. Japan
S.S. America
S.S. Alaska

Charles David Grear

San Francisco Customs House

	Arrived	De-parted	Female Arrivals
1867	4.29	4.475	N/A
1868	11,081	4,210	256
1869	14,990	4,895	1,540
1870	10,870	4,230	645
1871	5,540	3,260	100
1872	9,770	4,890	565
1873	17,075	6,805	516
1874	16,085	7,710	307
1875	18,021	6,305	358

Legal Transit to US via SF
Average Transit 34 days

Steamer Anchorage
Hong Kong, BCC Treaty Port
"Credit Ticket" System
for "Free Will" passage
Six company, Labor Agent
PMSSC Contract

* From 1848-1867 there were 108,470 arrivals on clipper & 45,160 departures> cargo vessels. Approximately 63,000 Chinese were in San Francisco when steam sidewheel transport began when S.S. Colorado on Jan 1, 1867

Hong Kong

20 miles

Authors Note: From all of my research, believe this chart matches for the first time in U.S. history the Chinese emigrants by their Guangdong region with the ships that brought them to America. Almost 100% of Chinese immigrants to U.S. emigrated through Hong Kong from Guangdong province. The bold black numbers represent the total number of emigrants transported on each ship (1868-75).

vi

Prologue

Voices From the Bottom of the South China Sea is a gripping, never-been-told story that weaves together the beginnings of the modern U.S. and China relationship, post–Civil War trans-Pacific sea commerce, a Chinese emigrant disaster, and the remnants of a treasure still buried at sea.

It takes place in 1868, at the dawn of the bilateral relations between two great world powers, the U.S. and China. Both countries are in significant periods of transition. The United States is coming to grips with a growing industrial revolution and its future after the Civil War. In the South, Reconstruction is beginning its third year, as federal political authority attempts to manage the Confederate planter culture and economy in the wake of the collapse of slavery and the slaveholder class. In Washington, D.C., a reunited nation is facing a political crisis—growing prospects of the first-ever impeachment of President Andrew Johnson in the House of Representatives. This would build momentum at the Republican convention in Chicago to draft General Ulysses S. Grant as the party's nominee for President, to place the country on a firmer path towards prosperity.

In the Northeast, powerful financial interests continue to extend the tentacles of industry and commerce westward, motivated by the dream of building a railroad from the Mississippi to the Pacific Ocean. Backed by Northeast and Midwest businesses from Chicago, the Union Pacific railroad had started west from Omaha, Nebraska, passed through Nebraska into Wyoming, only to become bogged down in the Rockies by the worst winter storms of the century.

The Central Pacific railroad, a mostly western concern, had started its portion of the trans-Pacific railroad in Sacramento, California, at sea level. It was struggling to build a track eastward that would need to climb from sea level to seven thousand feet in the first hundred miles. At the beginning of 1868, the Central Pacific had finished only 131 miles of track, compared to Union Pacific's 500 miles of track westward. America's trans-continental railroad dream had yet to be realized.

In 1868, China is also in transition, as the northern Imperial Manchu or Qing Dynasty in Beijing entered a period of political decay and transformation. The Qing bureaucracies were using a combination of force and imperial edict to deal with the remnants of the Taiping Rebellion (1851-1864), whose army, estimated over 500,000 strong, had decimated the countryside and the river valleys of the Yangtze River valley in the north.

1

In the southern Guangdong Province, China's most populous province, the Pearl River valley around Guangzhou remained impoverished. The region was prone to strife between settlers (called pun-ti) and squatters (called hak-ka), resulting in occasional conflict and loss of life. A generation of Chinese inhabitants have been living in fear under imperial edicts. Facing the need for family survival, many of its citizens might have been willing to emigrate as laborers and merchants. But this was not allowed. Threatened with punishment if they even communicated with foreigners, the citizens of Guangdong had been discouraged to emigrate overseas. They remained in poverty-stricken villages, trying to till a land not blessed with an abundance of arable soil.

In 1868, however, a new treaty between China and the U.S. would allow the beginning of the largest migration of Chinese overseas in history. Representing the start of the modern U.S.-China relationship, the Burlingame Treaty established the "Most Favored Nation" policy for China in exchange for "free emigration" to the U.S. To escape their backdrop of poverty, the Chinese of Guangdong Province became overseas-minded. Canton (Guangzhou) and Hong Kong were the closest treaty ports for the emigration journey to the U.S. Southern China had access to the sea and were able to use the southern treaty ports, imposed after the Opium Wars in 1842 when Britain demanded that China cede away coastal ports to Britain for trade. These ports, in particular Hong Kong, would become the point of departure for tens of thousands of Chinese workers to depart China bound for California, also known as Gum Shan- or Gold Mountain. Chinese emigrants are recruited to make the treacherous journey across the Pacific Ocean and South China Sea, with promises of jobs that they might use to get rich enough to return home as prosperous citizens.

However, in a few short years, the economic situation would worsen in American, and American workers would look on the Chinese emigrants with suspicion, hate, and fear, and would ultimately seek to pass legislation to send the emigrant workers home unwillingly.

The story that follows is an important chapter in that emerging relationship.

It is written to hopefully rekindle interest in the beginnings of this important chapter at the dawn of the modern U.S.-China relationship, recalling the enormous contributions of the Chinese emigrant pioneers, initially welcomed for their labors but eventually excluded as a race from emigration to the U.S.

Within this fascinating story of railroads, financiers, emigrant workers, silver mines, and paddlewheel steamships, there is one central figure and one vessel whose fates were interlocked with all these remarkable events, but whose names are little known today. Captain Edward R. Warsaw was the master and commander of the S.S. *Japan*. Together, they played a significant role throughout this story, a story that unfortunately would end in great tragedy, with the loss of the *Japan* in the South China Sea and the deaths of hundreds of Chinese workers headed home.

The Call=Chronicle=Examiner

SAN FRANCISCO, THURSDAY, APRIL 19, 1906

EARTHQUAKE AND FIRE: SAN FRANCISCO IN RUINS

NO HOPE LEFT FOR SAFETY OF ANY BUILDINGS

BLOW BUILDINGS UP TO CHECK FLAMES

WHOLE CITY IS ABLAZE

CHURCH OF SAINT IGNATIUS IS DESTROYED

MAYOR CONFERS WITH MILITARY AND CITIZENS

Figure 1: The 1906 San Francisco Earthquake destroyed the records of the Pacific Mail Steamship Company. A major reason the story was lost to history.

3

Many of the details of the *Japan* disaster, however, were lost to history, literally destroyed in April 1906 during the San Francisco earthquake when all of the Pacific Mail Steamship Company records were destroyed by fire. That 1906 earthquake destroyed all of the company records kept in its office on Market Street. The files of employees, ship records, and priceless photographs from the heyday of the shipping enterprise in the last part of the 19th century were all lost.

This book, drawing on documents culled from many sources, seeks to piece together the strange fate of the *Japan*, her valiant captain, her shipload of Chinese steerage passengers, and the treasure that sank to the bottom when this vessel caught on fire and sank in the middle of a December night in 1874.

As 1868 begins, the story starts as the prospective Chinese emigrants are called to leave the villages of Guangdong and their small family businesses in Canton for a trans-Pacific journey. Employment recruitment messages are blanketing the province, proclaiming the need for Chinese labor to work on the trans-Continental railroad in America. The Central Pacific is striving to break through the high mountains of the Sierra Nevada. The American steamships of the Pacific Mail Steamship Company are arriving in Hong Kong, ready to pick up workers to return with them to California. In large numbers, Chinese workers would answer the call, leaving the villages and cities of Guangdong Province in search of prosperity abroad.

Chapter 1

The Central Pacific Railroad Needs Workers!

A lantern, held by a Chinese worker, illuminated the rock and a freshly drilled hole bored into the end wall of the dark cavern, the terminus of a long underground passageway stretching deep into a granite mountain high in the Sierra Nevada Mountains of California. Carefully, a second Chinese workman poured a small quantity of yellow, oily liquid—just enough nitroglycerin— into the burrow. After packing the hole with hay and black powder, an electric blasting-cap fuse was set into a handful of wet sand, molded over the hole to cap the charge. The Chinese packer and lantern tender then scurried quickly away toward a sheltered area to huddle and take cover.

The brief sound of a magneto switch preceded the subsequent deafening roar and blast. Choking smoke billowed outward and lingered for a few minutes, as the lantern's light bounced crazily off the swirling particles. Only when the acrid dust began to settle could the light illuminate the area ahead, shining on what had been the end of the cave, where the two Chinese teammates now could observe piles of rubble and broken rock. Glancing at the blast site, they could also see remarkable sight: another lantern shone from the other side of the newly opened gap in the wall of rock in front of them.

Eureka! They had finally broken through.

Within the depths of the Summit Tunnel, reaching east and west at an altitude of over 7,000 feet high, crossing under the inner sanctum of California's formidable Sierra Nevada Mountains, the once impenetrable barrier to rail travel had now been pierced in August 1867. The Summit Tunnel ran underneath the path taken just a few decades earlier by the ill-fated Donner Party, which had perished in the Sierras in 1846. Now, once the transcontinental railroad was built, passengers would be able to ride in luxury cars under those same mountains on a continuous route from the American eastern seaboard to the California coast.

The light ahead now provided a new urgency to proceed. As the news was shared, logistical minds of engineers and financiers and crew managers raced, sending a flurry of messages back and forth from the Summit Tunnel site to San Francisco. Ties could now again be put down in endless repetition; heavy rails could be lined up, levered into precise position, and spiked. In the closing days of August 1867, the Central Pacific Railroad could now plan on completing the California portion of the great trans-continental railroad route, and thus avoid falling further behind the Union Pacific railroad efforts, the rival company that was rapidly laying track westward from Wyoming. The plan was to meet the Central Pacific—somewhere in the middle of nowhere. Someday soon, the managers could dream, a final spike would be driven, a golden spike to unite the United States by rail.

The Central Pacific section of the trans-Continental railroad was directed by an elite group of powerful men of California commerce, the "Big Four," a San Francisco–based executive committee. Leland Stanford was the committee's president and chief politician. Collis P. Huntington was in charge of finances and Congressional lobbying. Mark Hopkins kept the financial books. Charles Crocker was the fourth man, the manager of the actual railroad-track construction project, including its massive labor needs.

Things were not going well for the Central Pacific. Beginning in January 1863, by the time two years had passed, the company had laid only fifty miles of track. The construction foreman, J. H. Strobridge, said he needed 5,000 laborers "for constant and permanent work." But by the spring of 1865, the most he had been provided at any one time was 800.

As an experiment, about 50 Chinese laborers were recruited from the surrounding area. At first, many, including Strobridge, had questioned the abilities of Chinese workers to do the jobs: building of tunnels and bridges, assembly of massive remaining walls, placement of ties and tracks. The first teams, though, had proved their mettle. The Chinese workers were hard-workers, well behaved, quick to learn. The Central Railroad scoured the silver and gold mining areas to hire as many Chinese workers as they could. Now, with the successful breakthrough at the Summit Tunnel, the "Big Four" contemplated a new bold labor strategy for the construction of the next sections of the Central Pacific railroad.

If only there were more such Chinese workers. The Central Pacific railroad planners were desperate for greater speed for the coming phase of the work; the hard granite, blizzards and cold, and high altitude of the Sierras had delayed them terribly. Accordingly, during the San Francisco summer of 1867, the Big Four committee determined that they would do well to recruit more Chinese laborers—many more—for the undertaking. Knowing that the streets of San Francisco and the surrounding mining areas would never yield enough men, they decided to dispatch agents armed with printed handbills and promises of good-paying work directly to China. There, especially in the Southern provinces of China, a region stricken with poverty and political turmoil, they expected to be able to recruit many thousands of laborers to journey across the South China Sea and Pacific Ocean. The immigrants would be able to travel on a set of four newly commissioned paddlewheel steamships run by the Pacific Mail company, to arrive at the San Francisco docks, ready to go to work on the railroad.

Figure 2: President Abraham Lincoln approved the construction of the four largest passenger steamers in the world two months before his assassination. They would transport over 100,000 Chinese emigrants to California and link the China trade with the new transcontinental railroad.

The number of cheap laborers the Big Four hoped to employ with this strategy was staggering. Collis Huntington wrote to Charles Crocker on October 3, 1867, "I like your idea of getting over more Chinamen. It would be all the better for us and the state if there should be a half million come over in 1868."[1]

Charles Crocker was now in full agreement. He directed his construction superintendent to "hire the Chinese." The Big Four knew that best strategy would be to work with networks that the sizable Chinese communities already in the San Francisco area had in place. The company agents approached the Chinese Consolidated Benevolent Association, known as the "Six Companies," that had representatives both in San Francisco and in home districts in Southern China.

The Six Companies began recruiting the Chinese right off incoming vessels, and they built up their overseas efforts in Guangdong Province. There they were joined by agents of the Central Pacific railroad who travelled to China on the new steamers to bolster the urgent recruitment effort in Hong Kong and Canton. Initial results were good, and the Central Railroad agents were able to return with good news to San Francisco on New Year's Day, 1868. In San Francisco, Charles Crocker, one of the "Big Four" was working

7

closely with his brother, Judge E.B. Crocker, who served on the labor-contracting firm of Sisson, Wallace and Company. During the first week of the New Year, E.B. Crocker relayed the good news to his brother Charles: "Right after the Chinese New Year (which is Feb. 5) every steamer which leaves China monthly will have 800 to 1,000 men and [they will all be sent] on to our work."[2]

The "half million" number was greatly exaggerated, but roughly 100,000 emigrants would make the trip from China as steerage passengers, and the Central Pacific railroad would ultimately employ at the high mark 12,000 to 15,000 of those Chinese laborers. With those workers, the company could now envision a goal of 400 miles of track to be laid in 1868, fulfilling a promise that Charles Crocker had confidently made on New Year's Day at the start of that year: that the Central Pacific could lay at least a mile per day."[3]

The need for Chinese labor wasn't the only landmark news impacting both China and the U.S. in 1868. On March 31, 1868, the Pacific Mail Steamship Company steamer, the *S.S. China,* brought almost 800 Chinese steerage passengers and China's first ambassador to the U.S.—an American named Anson Burlingame.

Figure 3: Presentation of Anson Burlingame and the attaches of the Chinese embassy to President Andrew Johnson. (1868) Courtesy N.Y. Public Library

8

Several years earlier, Burlingame had been appointed by President Abraham Lincoln as the U.S. Minister to China in 1862. Subsequently, in late 1867, while contemplating retirement, Burlingame was approached by the Chinese government to represent China as a special envoy to the U.S. and the other "treaty powers," including the United Kingdom and Europe. Burlingame pondered the request, and then accepted. In his official correspondence to the U.S. State Department, he said that "when the oldest nation of the world, containing one third of the human race, seeks for the first time to come into relations with the west and requests the youngest nation, through its representative, to act as a medium to such change, the mission is not to be solicited or rejected."[4]

As China's Special Envoy to the Treaty Powers, he would begin his mission in San Francisco. His mission as a diplomat was to gain "Most Favored Nation" trade status from the U.S. In exchange, the U.S. would press for China's recognition of the right of Chinese subjects to emigrate freely, allowing the influx of workers needed by companies like the Central Railroad involved in the nation's ambitious growth underway.

Accompanying Burlingame to San Francisco in March 1868 were members of China's first overseas embassy. The excitement in the political and business communities of the city, both American and Chinese, for the arrival of the new representatives of China was enormous. The festivities climaxed with a grand banquet in honor of Mr. Burlingame and the Chinese mission at the Lick Hotel. All of California's leaders, including Governor Henry H. Haight, were on hand for the event. The emerging relationship crowned at the grand banquet was considered a great step forward in international relations, as the first time that the youngest and the oldest of nations had been brought together "face-to-face" in America.

The banquet attendees were introduced to China's first national flag, the Imperial Flag of China, which would fly in America for the first time over the nearby Occidental Hotel, heralding the presence of the Chinese Embassy. Burlingame explained in the flowery language of diplomats that China's mission to the U.S. was of good will:

"This mission means progress. It means that China desires to come into warmer and more intimate relations with the west. It means that China, conscious of her own integrity, wishes to submit her questions to the general judgment of mankind. It means that she intends to come into the brotherhood of nations! It means commerce; it means peace; it means unification of its own interest of the whole human race. . . . It means that the fraternal feeling of 400,000,000 people has

9

commenced to flow, through the land of Washington, to the older nations of the west and it will flow forever."[5]

For his part, the Chinese Envoy and Minister to the U.S., Chih Tujen, addressed his countrymen and the Directors of the Six Companies:

"On leaving Peking I was charged by his majesty, our august Emperor [Qing Dynasty, Mandarin leader Tseng Kuo-fan], to assure you of its affectionate interest in your welfare and good name. . . . Be careful to obey the law and regulations of this nation in which you attend to your labors; while a contrary course will infallibly bring on you failure and misfortune. I feel confident that you will show yourselves by your good conduct, worthy of his majesty's affection."[6]

By June 1868, the components of a new and mutually beneficial U.S.-China relationship were in place. These included the demand for more Chinese labor for the Central Pacific railroad, the expanded overseas recruitment efforts by the Six Companies and labor groups, a new U.S.-China relationship forged on a "most favored nation" trade status and a free emigration policy for Chinese subjects.

The final piece of the puzzle was a reliable way to transport tens of thousands of Chinese emigrants to California. The solution came in the form of the sidewheel steamers of the Pacific Mail Steamship Company, operating from their San Francisco docks.

In post-Civil War America, the clipper ships of an earlier era of sail power had mostly been replaced with the new sidewheel steamers. With their reliable motive power, no longer dependent on the wind, steamship travel had shrunk the average trans-Pacific transit time between San Francisco and Hong Kong from 45 days to 33 days. The new vessels also had more room for steerage passengers.

Especially after the American Civil War, the steamships were also recognized as a more reliable means of transporting the mail. The Pacific Mail Steamship Company was first established mostly for this purpose, to service the New York to San Francisco route, which they came to dominate. But with the imminent development of the transcontinental railroad, on the route being rapidly completed from each end of the country, the company realized that the mail business and other cargoes would soon diminish greatly on that route, and they looked for expansion.

In 1866, the Pacific Mail was awarded a long-term contract by the U.S. Postmaster General to deliver the mail to Japan and China, with, initially

10

at least, required service to Hawaii en route. Besides the mail, the ships also typically carried cargoes such as tea and silk, the silver treasure used to pay for the China trade, plus the increasingly important human cargo: the Chinese labor urgently needed to complete the Central Pacific portion of the transcontinental railroad.

In the decade between 1867 and 1877, the first regular steamship service between the U.S. and China was established. The route ran from San Francisco and Hong Kong via Yokohama, Japan. During this period, almost 100,000 Chinese emigrants from Guangdong Province, China, would respond to these circulars. Seeing opportunities, throngs of Chinese men and women would leave their homes in the hills, valleys and areas surrounding Canton and make their way to gather at Hong Kong. There, they would board the paddlewheel-powered steamers for the trip across the Pacific, in search of the Promised Land where "money is in great plenty."

ROUTES OF THE PACIFIC MAIL STEAMSHIP COMPANY.

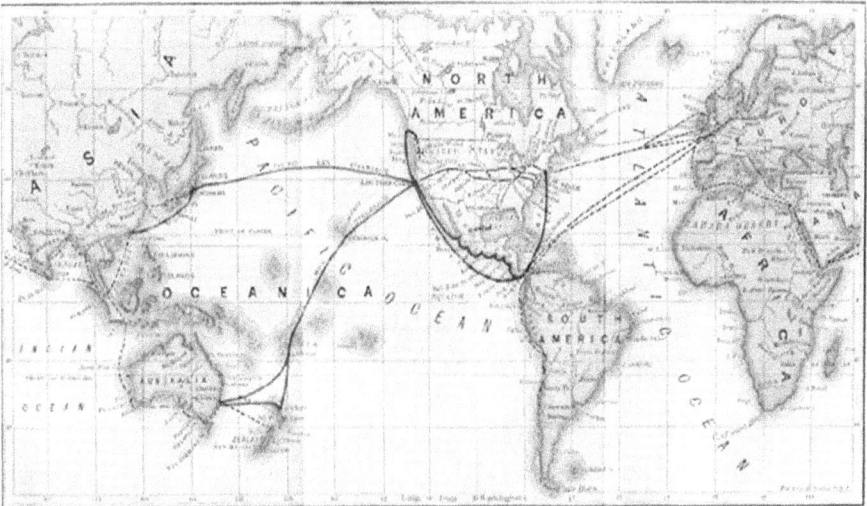

Figure 4: The Route of the Pacific Mail Steamship Company (1868.)

The "flowery-flag" ships, as the Chinese termed them, referring to the 37-star American flag of this period, were the four massive sidewheel steam ships (S.S.) of the Pacific Mail Steamship Company. They were the largest wooden sidewheel passenger vessels in the world, the grand culmination of the age of steam. Their names reflected their proud origins—the S.S. *Great Republic* and S.S. *America*—and in equal measure, the promising destinations so valuable to the trans-Pacific trade: the S.S. *China* and S.S. *Japan*.

11

Figure 5: Launch of the Sea Steamer GREAT REPUBLIC, Harpers Weekly, November 24, 1866 (Author's Collection)

The new China steamers cost, on average, one million dollars each. They were 4,000 gross tons in weight, 360 feet long, with a 49- to 50-foot beam drawing 23 feet of water. The ships were built between 1865–1868 at the Canal Street and Greenpoint Yards near Brooklyn, Long Island, New York, by shipbuilders William Henry Webb and Henry Steers. They were coal fired, consuming, on average, 40 to 45 tons of coal per day. They were had three masts with sails, which could be used to economize fuel on the voyage and could help make it to port if stranded in mid-ocean with a paddlewheel or rudder failure.

More than 100,000 Chinese emigrants would make the voyage as steerage passengers. As such, they were berthed well forward of the ship's lifeboats, deep in the hull in steerage, in numbers that could exceed 1,200 such travelers on a single vessel.

A booming San Francisco, a well-established Chinatown, and a call to work on the railroad would pull these emigrants from their poverty, but also from the tightly-knit web of their families, to brave the dangers of crossing the South China Sea and Pacific Ocean on wooden ships fired by coal. It could be a life or death journey, through monsoons, coastal pirates, disease, and the ever-present possibility of flooding, collision or coal fire aboard the ships.

The largest wave of Chinese emigration in history was ready to begin. The new emigrants from their Guangdong Province homes would respond to the call from the Six Companies and Central Railroad advertisements to gather near the coast, to travel to Hong Kong where they would climb on board the great sidewheel steamships to find their steerage berths. During the long passage, they would have plenty of time to eat, sleep, play games, tell stories, and dream of success to be found in a land they optimistically called Gum Shan, or New Gold Mountain.

On June 3, 1868, the first steamer to depart San Francisco after the Burlingame-Chinese Embassy Grand Banquet was the Pacific Mail's *Colorado*. It was bound for Chinese ports, soon to return with workers for the railroads.

13

Chapter 2

The Chinese Emigrants

"Americans a very rich people. They want the Chinamen to come and will make him very welcome. There you will have great pay, large houses, and food and clothing of the finest description. You can write to your friends and send them money at any time, and we will be responsible for safe delivery. It is a nice country, without Mandarins or soldiers. All alike; big man no larger than little man. There are a great many Chinamen there now, and it will not be a strange country. China God is there and the agents of this house. Never fear and you will be lucky. Come to Hong Kong, or to the sign of this house in Canton, and we will instruct you. Money is a great plenty and to spare in America, such as wish to have wages and labor guaranteed can obtain the surety by application at this office."
Chinese Broker Emigration Circular, Guangdong Province, 1870

The southwest monsoon winds come to China during the spring and summer months and, with the exception of an occasional typhoon during the summer, offer a speedy tailwind for the passage of sidewheel steamers bound up China coast and into the Pacific Ocean, bound for California. It was a good time to make the trip.

California was already ensconced in the imagination of the working classes of Guangdong province. When gold had been discovered at Sutter's Mill in 1848, stories about the fabled wealth of California quickly spread across the Pacific on American sailing ships and by a few letters sent home by Chinese workers in the gold fields in the early 1850s. California in the minds of the peasants and farmers of Guangdong became known as "Gum Shan" or Gold Mountain. According to historian Iris Chang, author of *The Chinese of America, A Narrative History*,

"A Cantonese nursery rhyme of the era...expressed the collective longings of entire families:

14

Swallows and magpies, flying in glee;
Greetings for New Year.
Daddy has gone to Gold Mountain
To earn money
He will earn gold and silver,
Ten thousand tales.
When he returns,
We will build a house and buy farmland."

During the spring of 1868, a new round of appealing stories of wealth to be made in America had been especially enticing, this time in the form of jobs. The Six Companies' agents circulated advertisements and flyers calling for labor needed by the American railroads. In China, letters that had been sent home earlier were confirmed by a wave of good news from more than 600 returning passengers of the Pacific Mail Steamship, the *China*. Returning to their Guangdong districts, these lucky, rich men each had $300–$400 dollars in gold to take care of their families, and they were telling stories of hard work and good fortune. They had been employed in California, in trades in San Francisco's Chinatown, in the wheat fields and fruit orchards of the Central Valley, in the mines and streams of El Dorado County, and as Central Pacific railroad workmen in the Sierra Nevada Mountains.

The stories of wealth and work in California proved irresistible especially for inhabitants of the province of Guangdong. The most populous and poorest province in China, its lack of sufficient arable soil and frequent upheaval by revolts made many of the Chinese men and women of the region "overseas minded." [7] In 1868, a veritable throng of Chinese men – and a few women – from the villages of Guangdong province and the city of Canton were willing to make the journey to California's Gum Shan, the "Gold Mountain." The would-be emigrants left the hills and Pearl River valleys to flock to Canton. From there, they would make a 90-mile journey downriver to Hong Kong. From that port, the new coal-powered steamers would take them across 7,000 miles of the South China Sea and Pacific Ocean to a new life.

Two primary areas in Guangdong Province, the Sze Yap districts west of Canton and the Sam Yup districts surrounding Canton and the Pearl River delta, were represented by the Six Companies. These benevolent societies organized and facilitated almost all of Chinese migration to California in the latter part of the 19th century.

"Emigration is never undertaken lightly, and the Chinese were like so many others who rarely abandoned one home to go in search of another overseas without great deliberation and high hopes. Especially for the Chinese workers, when they went abroad, they did so intending to come back. Wives

15

and children were left at home, but every man hoped to return as soon as possible and in a richer state, having improved his fortunes by laboring in foreign lands. The money brought back would allow him to then spend the rest of his life where generations of his family had lived, finally being laid to rest among the honored dead of a long ancestral line."[8]

It took the better part of a month to prepare. During that time, each emigrant had to raise the passage money. If his family was not able to come up with the required funds, he would need to make arrangements with his regional Six Company district house to secure a loan, with a labor payment agreement, to ensure passage and support upon arrival in San Francisco. Such an advance involved a lot of interest – and a commission for the agent. But the stories of the returnees were enticing, giving him the courage to see it through. Answering the labor circular, he would commit himself to one of the Six Companies to oversee his safe passage, food, clothing, San Francisco temporary housing, and contract with labor agents. If all went well, he would be gone, as had others, for three to five years, then to return to live prosperously with his family.

One by one, increasing numbers of Chinese from the counties of Guangdong and Canton came to the realization that this was to be their moment. Twenty years had passed since an earlier emigration surge, during the years following of gold rush fever of 1849.

Dissatisfied with the injustice and poverty of his surroundings, the emigrant was forced to accept many bargains in the quest for a better life. After deciding that it was time to take action, he mortgaged his meager resources, committing wife and family to debt, to receive the advance money needed to pay the Six Company fee to secure his passage on next ship, which was to be the *Colorado*. The *Colorado* would be returning to Hong Kong on July 3, 1868 to board its next batch of passengers. There would be much to do.

The key contact was with one of the Six Companies of the Chinese Consolidated Benevolent Association. Each regional company house was responsible for one of five districts or counties in the southwest parts of Guangdong Province. The five were of the Sze Yap (Siyi) district-Sunwui (Xinhui), Toishan (Taishan), Hoiping (Kai-ping), Yangping (Enping) and the Sam Yap (Sanyi) district- (Namhol, Punyo and Shuntak). These five were established to look after the welfare of the Guangdong emigrants and help them when they arrived in America. The sixth company was formed to look after the Hak-ka immigrants from other places in China.

For the new emigrant in the late 1860s, after a goodbye to his family and friends, he made his way from the fragrant hills and river valleys and the coastal villages and the streets of Canton to the emigration house on the docks of the Pearl River. They would need to travel on to Hong Kong in order to meet the steamship, but first the emigrant had to settle matters in Canton with the British and Chinese emigration authorities, with the Six Company agents, and with the Pacific Mail Steamship Company before his name was added to the Canton shipping manifest.

All of the emigration, transport, and financial arrangements with the British, Chinese and now the American Consul at Hong Kong took a month. If all went well, the emigrant's name was put on the *Colorado's* manifest for her July return voyage to California.

The growth of the steam-powered China fleet had been ushered in one year earlier with the first ever trans-Pacific passage in 1866 between San Francisco and Hong Kong by the Pacific Mail steamship *Colorado*, after the company won the U.S. mail service contract for the route, which included a $500,000 annual subsidy. She was now expected to return again to the Hong Kong port. The *Colorado* was considered a lucky ship by the Pacific Mail Company and by the Chinese steerage passengers, having already made a number of successive safe passages between China and the United States. She was slightly older than the newly introduced four new sidewheel steamers – the *Great Republic, China, Japan*, and the *America*, filling the gap until the larger ships were placed in service.

The *Colorado* was close to the specifications of the new China steamers. The vessel was 363 feet length, 45 feet in width, and 31 feet in depth, and weighed 3,600 tons. Unlike the larger China sidewheel steamers, the *Colorado* was built with two rather than three masts. She was also equipped to deal with any potential encounter with China pirates, presenting two twenty-pound iron-projectile field artillery pieces on her quarter, two twenty-pounders forward, and an assortment of Sharp rifles, muskets, revolvers, pikes and axes to ward off any foes that dared come closer.

When shipping day came in Canton, the American-flagged steamer *Kin-Shan* waited at the dock. Up to 300 steerage passengers were eligible for the twice-daily 90-mile downriver transport to Hong Kong. The Canton emigration house was filled with labor agents, officials from British emigration and the Chinese government, and hundreds of emigrants, each hoping to be one of the 300 on the manifest.

Figure 6: The American-shallow-draft steamer Kin-shan

After they signed up for the *Kin-Shan*, the register was reviewed by the Emigration Board members, who then examined their bona-fides. Of particular concern was whether those signing up were acting on free will. The authorities wanted to determine that none of the potential passengers were involved in the notorious "Coolie" trade that originated from Hong Kong's neighbor at the mouth of the Pearl River, Portugal's Macao Island.

"Coolie" is an Indian term for servant. It became a pejorative term for indentured servitude in post-slavery America. Contract laborers hired in Guangdong Province shipped abroad from either the Portuguese treaty port of Macao or the British treaty port of Hong Kong. In 1868, reports of the ill treatment and enslavement of contract Coolie labor coming though Macao to work on ships and at labor plantations in Cuba and Peru to incensed British and American public and political opinion. Passionate outbursts opposed to all "coolie" labor entering the U.S. caused the financial and business interests needing cheap labor in California to urge the Six Companies to contract only with Chinese "free will" emigrants.

The Burlingame Treaty agreement between China and the U.S. had just been negotiated in July 1868. It provided the legal basis for the free emigration of Chinese to California. This new framework meant that U.S. consulates in Canton and Hong Kong would monitor the Chinese emigration process to America to certify that steerage passengers travelling on the Pacific Mail steamships were not indentured "coolie" laborers, but were traveling of the own free-will.

A screening process was in effect for the *Colorado* passage. After being assembled in groups according to their labor interests, each emigrant was called before a Chinese clerk and asked a series of questions: Are you willing to go to California? Do you comprehend the terms of the contract? Once the terms of the labor agreement were validated by the candidate and his free will to emigrate affirmed, the candidate could sign the document, and the Chinese officials and British Consular officers would affix their official seals to it. With this approval, each emigrant became entitled to an advance of his future wages from his labor agent.

After the advances were received, the groups were gathered in the emigration house for departure and received a final feast, after which each man picked up his chest, with his clothing, food utensils, and mementos. If he did not have a chest, his simple alternative was a stick with a bundle of clothing. The passengers were then marched down to waiting boats along the bank for passage across the crowded Pearl River to the *Kin-Shan,* waiting at the steamer wharf.

If family or friends were present, firecrackers and pieces of bright paper might provide a bittersweet send-off. But many of the emigrants had left any relatives and sweethearts at home. They would travel alone, unless a friend had also decided to make the long journey.

On board the *Kin-Shan,* the emigrants were checked against the manifest, then directed to fill up the lower areas of the vessel. They were made comfortable and as soon as 300 were on board, the *Kin-Shan* loaded the waiting topside passengers and got underway down the Pearl River for Hong Kong. The topside passengers included European and American cabin passengers and Chinese traders who paid the purser the transit fare of one Mexican silver dollar, the world's most prominent trading currency, minted from Mexico's silver mines.

The *Kin-Shan* pushed through the brown water and slowly negotiated her way through the thousands of floating boats and a sea of human activity on the water. From the ship's bridge and top deck, one could see the city of Canton on the northern bank, branching out across the river. Watchful eyes of pagodas on the surrounding hills and valleys with their orange and banana groves and sugar plantations served up a tropical vista pleasing to the eye.

The *Kin-Shan* passed the famous Whampoa Roads, the original clipper-ship anchorage of the China-trade sailing ships of the 18th and 19th centuries. Many Yankee traders, including Robert Bennett Forbes and Samuel Russell, founder of America's pioneer Chinese trading firm, the Russell and

Company Trading House, greatly influenced the business of trade and the eventual U.S. Open Door trade policy with China.

Farther down river, the *Kin-Shan* passed the empty Bogue Forts that now marked, rather than protected, each side of a narrow entrance channel. The forts were once considered a reliable defense of Canton as China's southern capital, but were overcome by the British navy during the 1844 Opium War, leading to the establishment of the British treaty ports in China. Past the Bogue forts, the Pearl River widened. When she reached the mouth of the river the *Kin-Shan* entered the South China Sea, making the turn to port to begin her approach to Hong Kong Island.

The name Hong Kong (Heung Kong) means good harbor. In June 1868, Hong Kong was indeed a good harbor, a treaty port crowded with shipping-trade traffic. Ceded to Great Britain by the Chinese Government in 1841, it was beginning its 28th year as a British Crown Colony. The eleven-mile-long island included the port city of Victoria and one of the finest ports in the world.

The *Kin-Shan* had arrived into the beautiful harbor after a nine-hour passage from Canton. She slowed to approach her berth at the Clock Tower pier. At the foot of the ship's brow, agents from the Six Companies were assembled to greet the emigrants, feed them, and lodge them in Hong Kong living quarters, to prepare for their immigration depot processing the following week. Also on the pier, agents of the Pacific Mail Steamship Company observed the latest group of emigrants, confirming the expected number to manifest on board the *Colorado* when it arrived later that week.

Figure 7: The Colorado at Hong Kong after her 1867 maiden voyage (Author's Collection)

Hong Kong was the only port in China that had scheduled American steamship service to San Francisco, and so the Guangdong Province emigrants began their journey to California there. In addition to tea, sugar and textiles, one of the most important exports to the U.S. from Hong Kong was that of emigrant laborers, and almost 100% of the Chinese emigration to California between 1844 and 1875 was from Guangdong Province. Although freight and treasure transport, wheat, quicksilver were also important to the Pacific Mail Company's business, the most important revenue generator for the line was the transport of Chinese emigrants, traveling in the spacious forward berthing areas aboard the sidewheel steamers.

That was one reason the sidewheel steamer design had been chosen by the company, instead of more modern iron-screwed steamships, despite significant criticism. The steamer companies of Great Britain (Peninsula and Oriental among others) were operating iron-screw steamers regularly from the east; they were astounded that the Americans chose "such an outdated design for the long and treacherous trans-Pacific passage." That criticism was acknowledged by the executives of the Pacific Mail. However, with the Congressional subsidy to transport the mail, the revenue from Chinese freight, the need to transport of thousands of Chinese emigrants, and the political and economic strength of the New York shipbuilding lobby after the Civil War sealed the matter of design. The orders had been placed for the creation of the largest sidewheel steamers in the world, vessels specifically built for the China trade.

The prospects for growth when the new ships became available were impressive. The Pacific Mail agents in Hong Kong anticipated being able to accommodate about 650 emigrants for the July, 1868 passage, given the size of the *Colorado*. It was a profitable business. But the newer, larger sidewheel steamers soon to become active on the route would be able to carry more than 1,200 such passengers to America—at $45 dollars in gold per emigrant.

While the emigrants had high hopes for their journey, for success in America, and for their eventual return as richer men, they also had to face the matter of the risks involved. When an emigrant left home, all knew there was a chance he would never return. As with so much physical labor of the era, there were many injuries and untimely deaths due to poor working conditions, lack of safety equipment and protocols, and limited medical attention for sickness or injuries for the working poor. As well, the long journey at sea posed its own set of risks. Death aboard the ships was always a possibility.

For the Chinese emigrants, there was a heightened concern for death abroad. Some two thousand years before, the great philosopher, Confucius, had said: "The bones of every Chinese must eventually rest in China's soil."[9] The Six Companies took great lengths to ensure that the bodies of deceased emigrants would be returned to their Chinese homeland. If a Chinaman died on the voyage, wrote Ellen Walworth in *An Old World Seen Through Young Eyes*, "his body is being taken back to China by the next steamer. It is so with every Chinaman that dies abroad, for they believe they cannot go to heaven unless buried in China."[10]

On the eastward voyages, seasickness, dehydration and small pox were the most likely causes of death. On westward voyages, other dangers came from the use of opium on board in the ship's opium dens, or from those with terminal illnesses who had booked the passage hoping to get home in time before succumbing to their diseases.

"It was one of the duties of the ship's doctor to embalm them or preserve them by some corresponding process," wrote Thomas Hinchcliff in *Over the Sea and Far Away*. "They are then put into coffins and taken home comfortably to their friends. To throw one overboard would probably produce a mutiny, and as the crew are all Chinamen except the officers and quartermasters, it would perhaps be as well not to disregard their feelings in a matter which to them is one of sacred importance. A sick Chinaman will come onboard quite happy and fully prepared to die in a day or two, knowing he will be taken back to home and heaven; but the company would soon be deprived of their Celestial passengers if they thought there was any chance of their being pitched into the sea."[11]

"Celestials" was a favorite term given to the Chinese by literati of the day. The sobriquet was based on a direct translation of Chinese term Tien Chan, or heavenly dynasty of heaven, with the emperors the sons of the heaven. The colorful name was used in the 19th century by writers from Henry David Thoreau to travel writer Thomas W. Knox to signify the mystique of Chinese citizens, so exotic to Americans.

The return of the dead "Celestials" back to their home in China had all been arranged in advance as a sine qua non in the deal with the Pacific Mail Steamship Company. The Six Companies agents in San Francisco would only help the Pacific Mail make the arrangements for transporting the labor that was needed in California if they were assured of this one demand.

The Six Companies requested (through an interpreter) "a promise on the part of the Pacific Mail that they would transport back to China the bodies of all Chinese who died in America, for purpose of final interment in the land of their ancestors. It is not a request for free transportation; they stand ready to pay; but they want your promise that you will surely give these bones transport when the time arrives. Furthermore, it is only for the bones of their dead they ask for this solemn promise of transportation; skeletons packed in sanitary packages hermetically sealed."[12]

Iris Chang, in her narrative history *The Chinese in America*, noted that the commitment by the Six Companies to ship their bones on the Pacific Mail steamers back to Guangdong Province served as an act of patronage. The Six Companies would hold lavish, theatrical funeral processions from the store or home of the deceased, then head to the graveyard on Lone Mountain where each company had a separately fenced-off area.

"The entrance to the graveyard lot was usually marked by a canopy, beyond which lay a brick furnace, table, and headboard with Chinese characters. There, friends would burn paper near the body – Chinese messages, paper servants, and paper money – gifts for the deceased in the afterworld that disappeared with his spirit in flame and smoke. Instead of the corpse being buried, the flesh would later be scraped off and the bones laid out to dry in the sun before being bundled into white muslin and being shipped back to China."[13]

Such worrisome thoughts may have passed through the minds of many of the emigrants as they arrived in Hong Kong to contemplate the impending journey to a land thousands of miles away. The trans-Pacific voyage ahead was unlike any they had ever experienced. For weeks they would be confined to the steerage berths of a strange vessel, out on the deep waters, subject to the whims of storms, to diseases that could spread in a crowded situation, and to the special dangers inherent in traveling far in a wooden vessel powered by steam and fire.

After departing the *Kin-Shan* upon their arrival in Hong Kong, the Chinese emigrants passed the Pacific Mail offices at the Russell and Company building and got a good look at the waterfront area of Hong Kong and the Praya area. In one short week, they would walk back down to embark in the small boats that would take them to the lucky ship, the *Colorado*, when she returned to Hong Kong and dropped anchor, her steerage berths waiting just for them.

Chapter 3

Mark Twain and a Perfect Palace of a Ship

San Francisco, California July 1868

It had been a busy period of review and modification, but now Samuel Langhorne Clemens was preparing the letters he had sent to the *Daily Alta* newspaper for inclusion in his first book, a humorous travel narrative titled *The Innocents Abroad*. In May 1868, Clemens had rushed back to San Francisco for an in-person conference with the *Alta* publishers and had reached agreement with them to release their restrictions, secure his intellectual property, and allow him to publish the observations from his 1867 "Holy Land" tour on the S.S. *Quaker City*, which the *Daily Alta* had sponsored.

Figure 8: Samuel Clemens becoming "Mark Twain" 1867

The book would soon become a bestseller, establishing Sam Clemens – writing under the pseudonym of Mark Twain – as a prominent American writer. It featured his tongue-in-cheek voice, his wry and scathing wit, as he described his fellow travelers that began with a journey to the Mediterranean on the *Quaker City*, a retired Civil War steamship.

Now, after three months of manuscript revision of *The Innocents Abroad*, Clemens was ready to book passage on a Pacific Mail steamship for his return to the east coast.

Clemens had achieved considerable attention as a literary figure after he had moved to San Francisco in 1864, when he had selected his Mark Twain pen name after trying out some other less memorable choices, such as W. Epaminondas Adrastus Blab.

Twain worked at first for the *Call*, a local San Francisco rag, then for several other publications over the next few years. In 1865, Clemens/Twain rewrote a tale he had heard in the California gold fields. First titled "Jim Smiley and his Jumping Frog," the piece eventually was republished as "The Celebrated Jumping Frog of Calaveras County," a comic tale of a contest lost when a champion frog was filled with lead shot so he couldn't jump. Twain's short story became a national sensation which it ran in the *Saturday Press* of New York, and overnight Clemens was known as a gifted humorist with a knack for folksy speech and biting satire.

Samuel Clemens stayed in San Francisco for four years, writing commentary and travel writings. In 1866 he took a four-month trip to Hawaii, then known as the Sandwich Islands, as a correspondent for the *Sacramento Union*, producing a series of letters during his trip. The next year, he took the excursion to Europe and the Holy Land.

Now, he was ready to depart the West for the East coast. It was Friday, July 3, 1868 and that return passage to New York would be via Panama and Aspinwall. He was staying at the Occidental Hotel, just seven blocks up from the First and Brannon Street docks of the Pacific Mail Steamship Company, and had just earned some money after completing his last lecture ever in San Francisco the night before at the Mercantile Library.

Steamer Day in San Francisco meant that the China traders and merchants would all converge down at the docks in an excited atmosphere. Samuel Clemens joined the multitudes while securing a ticket for his return home to New York on the outbound steamer, the *Montana*. After bidding the Occidental Hotel staff farewell, he boarded a carriage which passed the Mercantile Library for one final nostalgic look before heading on to the docks of the Pacific Mail Steamship Company to purchase a ticket from the booking agent.

This particular San Francisco Steamer Day was for the July 3, 1868 arrival of the *S.S. Japan*. The ship had just arrived that afternoon, via Panama, after completing an 82-day trip inaugural voyage from New York through the

Straits of Magellan. Pacific Mail's veteran Captain George H. Bradbury commanded the ship, and J. Ross Browne, the new U.S. envoy to China, was also on board. Clemens walked into the Pacific Mail dock, greeted the booking agent, and began to pay for his July 6 ticket home on the steamer *Montana*.

The booking agent, however, would not accept Samuel Clemens' payment. The incident made such an impression on him that he recalled it in a subsequent letter to his mother, telling how he insisted on buying a steamer ticket from the booking agent, but the clerk wouldn't take his money.

Aboard the arriving *Japan* was the ship's First Assistant Jonathon Harris, an acquaintance of Mark Twain. Harris had served as the First Engineer on the *Quaker City* during Twain's 1867 "Holy Land" tour. Mr. Twain admired Harris' ability and future prospects with Pacific Mail, and now he had a chance to renew his acquaintance with Harris as well as admire the newest sidewheel steamship in the world.

Writing to his mother on the evening before his final departure, Clemens told her that he'd just seen "our engineer, Harris last night. He is just in, from around the Horn as 1st Assistant in Japan – the new steamer, & Oh such a perfect palace of a ship. I do want to sail in her so badly."[14]

Mark Twain made his way down to the Pacific Mail docks the next morning and boarded a different vessel, the *Montana*, never to return to San Francisco again. *The Innocents Abroad* was published the next year on July 20, 1869.

The *Japan*'s arrival represented a proud moment in San Francisco's history and commanded front-page attention. It also marked the first time in American history that monthly direct steamship service to Japan and China would be offered.

Figure 9: Mark Twain's possible view of the Pacific Mail docks from First Street, (1868) Courtesy Library of Congress

The *Japan* would now prepare for her inaugural voyage to China. En route, she would meet the *Colorado* at sea. The *Japan* was the second largest passenger sidewheel steamship ever built, with an extreme length of 375 feet; a width of 49 feet, 10 inches; and a tonnage that ranged from 4,350 tons to 5,500 tons fully loaded. She had six decks including a main deck, berthing deck, cargo deck, orlop deck, and a lower hold where the coal was loaded.

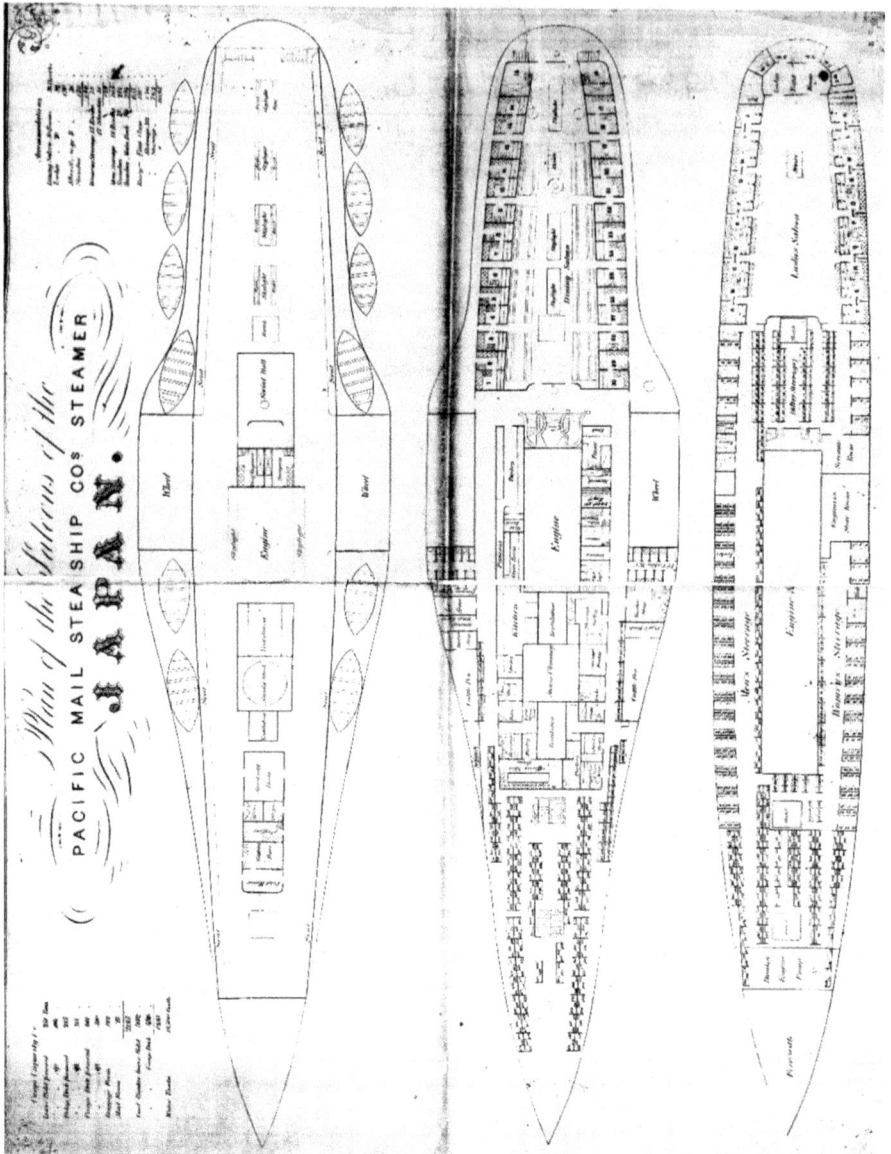

Figure 10: Saloon Plan of the Japan.
Courtesy San Francisco Public Library

The ship also had a solid oak frame from the bottom up to the water line and wheel housings. The frame inside and out was diagonally strapped with iron, which joined a 12- to 14-inch-thick yellow-pine ceiling. The bottom frame was three feet thick with sides that were 20 inches thick. Three masts

28

were provided for efficiency and emergency propulsion if the powerful engines or great sidewheels were damaged or unavailable on the Pacific or South China Sea crossing.

The *Japan*'s engineering plant and machinery had been constructed by the Novelty Iron Works. Her vertical beam engine could generate 1,500 horsepower and used a 105-inch cylinder with a 12-foot stroke of piston to generate the power necessary to turn the ship's massive sidewheels, 40 foot in diameter that pulled the ship through the water.

For comfort and relaxation of women crossing the Pacific, the *Japan* had a ladies' saloon, a dining hall, two bridal rooms, and twenty-six staterooms, single and double, furnished and fitted up in the most tasteful and substantial manner of late–19th century. The woodwork and furniture were black walnut, and the lounge and chair coverings were blue. The bridal room also had the finest carpet and the saloons the most durable oilcloth.

For the paying first-class passengers, each of their staterooms had two berths, a lounge, washstand, mirror, a window that measured 16 by 24 inches, and a fresh-air ventilator. The saloon and main entrance were also used as a social hall, decorated with frescos painted in peach-blossom, lavender, purple, and pea-green with gold ornamental trim.

The captain's quarters were on the upper deck. The living quarters and working spaces for officers and crew were located forward of the main saloon. These consisted of a purser's office, pantry, storeroom, post office, kitchen, officers' mess-room, engine-room, armory, bathrooms, and barber's shop. An ice house, cow house, water closets where the fresh meats and poultry were maintained within the sidewheel compartments on each side of the ship, along with wash rooms for the passengers.

Compared to the lives of the first-class passengers, the *Japan*'s forward areas were more crowded, intended to be occupied by third-class or steerage passengers. The berth deck had one hundred staterooms, single and double, with three to six berths each, with plenty of light and air, and properly fitted up. The rooms were designed for families and female passengers. The deck was designed for occupation by the steerage passengers with a total number of berths (stateroom and standee) coming in at 1,050. Standee berths were moveable berths set up in the forward steerage areas or in passageways leading to the other berthing areas. The standee berths would be removed during the day to make room for traffic and cleaning chores.

On the upper deck was a social hall, its entrance from the main stairway leading to the upper deck. The social hall was 35 by 20 feet in size, with an arched roof that was twelve feet high. It was lighted all round by ground glass. Its decorations were similar to the main saloon, however, its gold ornamental work was much more elaborate. People also needed a place to smoke on this all-wooden ship, and the smoking room was located topside on the main deck.

Modern lifesaving equipment was also a prominent feature of the *Japan*. It had to be. An all-wooden vessel fueled by the enormous amount of coal needed for a 7,000-mile crossing had to have a means for saving life in case of fire or shipwreck.

The *Japan* had twelve metal lifeboats with a crew, compass, chart, life preservers, and provisions for twelve days. The lifeboat capacity was between 100-120 passengers and crew.

For firefighting, the ships had two wrought-iron pipes that extended through the whole length of the ship on the berth deck. The larger 6-inch pipe was for water; it had twenty outlet valves with attached firefighting hoses. The smaller 4-inch pipe was for steam, which could be used to smother a fire in the hold and among the cargo.

The main engine pumped and furnished the steam for the pumps. As a last-resort in an emergency (for instance, if the middle- and after-parts of the ship were in flames and the engine room abandoned), an independent coal-fired "donkey boiler" steam-engine of twenty-five horsepower was located in the bow of the ship.

Finally, for protection against pirates, the armory was loaded with 50 Enfield rifles, 26 carbines, 25 revolvers, 25 cutlasses, 1 dozen boarding pikes, five rifle-cannons, and a special apparatus for throwing steam and hot water over and upon the decks.

As Mark Twain steamed through the Golden Gate Strait on the *Montana* for the final time and the *Japan* began her preparations for her inaugural voyage to China, on the far side of the Pacific, the *Colorado* had finally arrived in Hong Kong.

Chapter 4

Captain Warsaw and the S.S. *Colorado*

A trans-Pacific voyage in a wooden coal-fired sidewheel steamer was a test of a strength and faith. Hurricane-force monsoon winds and severe wind and sea conditions could be encountered in the Pacific Ocean and the South China Sea, threatening the existence of all aboard, challenging the seamanship and skill of the crews and their captains. These challenges and conditions were made for men like Edward R. Warsaw. Had you been a passenger on a long and perilous sea journey, you would pray for such a captain, with his experience and fearless character, to be at the helm of the ship.

Figure 11: Captain Edward R. Warsaw (April 1871)
Courtesy, UC Santa Barbara-Davidson Library
(Bernath-Shanghai Steam Navigation Company Album)

Captain Warsaw was born in Montgomery, Alabama, in 1827. He shipped out in a vessel engaged in the China trade from the Gulf Coast when he was fourteen, remaining at sea in the trade until the U.S.-Mexican War in 1846. He joined the Texas Rangers that year and participated in their 1846–1448 campaigns in Mexico. After the war he set out for California, arriving there in September 1849 in quest of a fortune. After failing to strike it rich, he moved to San Francisco in 1853 to try his hand at being a stock broker. A few years later, sometime in 1856, he made the decision to return to his initial calling: the sea.

Warsaw returned to the East Coast that year to command his first ship, which ran from New York to Valparaiso, Chile, and the Caribbean Indies. He achieved the status of master mariner in 1857.

During his time sailing from New York, he became friendly with ship captains from Boston and particularly Portsmouth, New Hampshire. It was a New Hampshire captain who introduced him to Miss Ann S. Weeks, the woman he would marry on January 29, 1861. Together, they established a home on State Street in Portsmouth, New Hampshire. A daughter, Hattie, was born two years later to the couple in September 1863. Soon, though, Warsaw returned to sea, commanding the clipper ship *Marmion,* sailing past Pier 19 on New York's East River en route to voyages to New Orleans from late 1865 until mid-1866.

Figure 12: Anna Weeks Warsaw
Courtesy, UC Santa Barbara-Davidson Library
(Bernath-Shanghai Steam Navigation Company Album)

Figure 13: Miss Hattie L Warsaw
Courtesy, UC Santa Barbara-Davidson Library
(Bernath-Shanghai Steam Navigation Company Album)

During this time, across the river at Brooklyn's Greenpoint Shipyard, the first of the four sidewheel steamers, the *Great Republic*, was being built. An adventurous, forward-looking individual, Warsaw began to contemplate the transition from the old sailing clipper ship trade to the new steam-powered China trade. With this in mind, in command of the extreme clipper-ship *Ocean Express* from New York, he modified his route to terminate in San Francisco, There, he established residence and began shipping California wheat from San Francisco to Liverpool, England, from February 1867 until January 1868.

Warsaw knew the clipper-ship era was in transition. The ships were slower than the newer technologies, and stiff competition from steamships and the emerging screw-propelled ship technologies were making the old-fashioned sailing voyages unprofitable. The owners of the *Ocean Express* decided to sell the clipper ship in February 1868. At the same time, the new steamship, the *Great Republic,* had just returned from her second voyage from China.

Warsaw applied and was accepted for service as part of the growing Pacific Mail Steamship trans-Pacific China trade. He left his wife and daughter in New Hampshire, maintaining his West Coast residence at the Occidental Hotel in San Francisco. In June 1868, Edward R. Warsaw, at 41 years of age, would become the *Colorado's* First Officer.

As the other ships of the Pacific Mail placed in operation in early 1868 – the *Colorado*, the *Great Republic,* and the newly arrived *China* – groups of captains were embarked on the inaugural voyages to receive navigation, seamanship, and engineering training. They were also able on these journeys to better understand the operations of the new cargo and the Chinese steerage passenger trade. With the July 1868 arrival of the *Japan* in San Francisco, and the *China* and *Great Republic* already in operation, the Pacific Mail now was able to offer the Congressionally-mandated monthly service between Hong Kong and San Francisco.

Warsaw would eventually become a captain of one of these mountains of a ship in due course. Strong willed, he wore a prominent beard symbolic of the sea captains of the 1860s and 1870s. His commanding nature was governed by his character of personal honor and his word. He knew his business and was a man, as later described by tourism pioneer Thomas Cook in his *Letters to the Sea and Foreign Lands* "that combined humanity with stern discipline. Another significant trait was his concern for all who traveled on his vessels, whether in first class or steerage; he was described by his Chinese passengers on one voyage as a "true and impartial lover of his fellow creatures."

His courage and ability as a mariner was sorely tested during his service as First Officer on the *Colorado's* June 1868 voyage. Commander E.W. Smith was completing his second *Colorado* voyage – his third passage from Hong Kong to San Francisco – when he fell ill and was confined to his cabin. A chronicle of the ship's voyage to Hong Kong chronicles Warsaw's ability as he stepped up to take charge.

"The Captain was taken seriously ill and was not able to get out of his room. On Captain Warsaw devolved the responsibility of life and property. He took the Colorado to Hong Kong and on the return, coming up the China Sea, she was struck by a hurricane, in the midst of which, a tremendous wave boarded her stern, threatening to engulf the ship and carried away her rudder. With nine hundred and fifteen passengers, and a full cargo of valuable goods, the ship was at the mercy of an angry sea. Here was the time for ability, courage, determination and prompt action. The noble craft was taken in hand, thus disabled, and skillfully carried through the storm, a jury-rudder rigged, and brought into port without the loss of a single life or damage to the cargo. This is the kind of timber that the officers of the Pacific Mail are made of."[15]

On July 6, 1868, the Chinese steerage passengers waiting in Hong Kong got their first glimpse of the ship that would take them to California. The *Colorado* was the workhorse of the Pacific Mail Company for the first eighteen months of the new contract for the U.S. mail service, carrying the load for the company while they waited the arrival of the larger sidewheel steamers. This would be the *Colorado*'s fourth and final trip across the Pacific, unless needed as an occasional spare vessel in rotation when critical repairs were needed on the other steamers.

Arriving in the Hong Kong harbor, the ship offloaded its contingent of returning Chinese passengers, along with her cargo of California wheat and silver treasure, which the trading companies involved were now able to exchange for silk, teas, and other Chinese products. Preparations for the July 13, 1868 scheduled departure for the return to California could then commence. Under the direction of Captain Smith and First Officer Warsaw, it would take a week to load more than 2,000 tons of cargo, including silk bales, 2,000 chests of tea, 600 bales of hemp, and other cargoes and mail valued at one to two million dollars. The crew of the *Colorado* also refreshed the berthing areas needed, to transport more than 800 Chinese steerage passengers, of which 30 were women, on the return trip to San Francisco.

Everyone's fondest hope was to have a voyage back across the Pacific that was free of the angry southwest monsoon and potential typhoon seas. A massive storm was one of the biggest risks for ships at sea and was always of great concern. With the primitive weather forecasting of the period, little advance warning was possible, and once a storm overtook a ship, the towering waves and mighty winds were impossible to avoid. The only course of action was generally to run with the storm winds, keeping the ship from being toppled sideways, and hope for the best.

The shipping-day arrived with not with a storm but with a bout of intense Hong Kong heat. In the hours just after dawn, the emigrants gathered their belongings and walked to the Hong Kong emigration depot. Like the departure process they had already endured upriver in Canton, the manifest clearance for final approval for emigration from in the Hong Kong port was conducted by a committee. This consisted of the British Hong Kong Consul, British and Chinese customs officials, and now the U.S. Consul. The passage manifest was then brokered by the agents of the labor guilds and the Six Companies, concluding with the Hong Kong magistrate at the Depot. The committee also double-checked for medical and legal issues and confirmed each individual's willingness and free will, as noted on his labor contract.

Figure 14: AMCONSUL Hong Kong Immigration Certificate certifying voluntary emigration
Courtesy U.S. National Archives (Archives II)

36

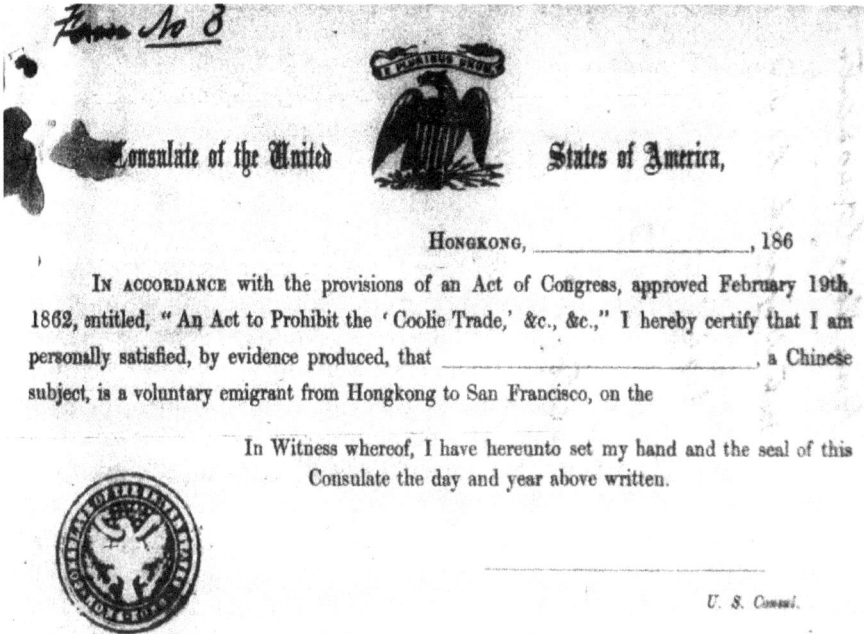

Figure 15: AMCONSUL Hong Kong Immigration Certification in accordance with the 1862 Act to Prevent the Coolie Trade Courtesy U.S. National Archives (Archives II)

The original manifest for the voyage was developed by the Pacific Mail Steamship Company. This was then sent on to the American Consulate to be certified by the Consul General. An example of this certification that was examined during the State of California's inquiry into "The China Question" in early 1876 stated:

Consulate of the United States of America, at Hong Kong

I the undersigned, Consul of the United States for the Island of Hong Kong and the dependencies thereof, do hereby certify that the within named persons, being inhabitants, and subjects of China, to the number of eight hundred and seventy-six (876), are, each and all of them, free and voluntary emigrants, going hence to San Francisco, in the United States of America, on board the steamship Colorado, of New York. And that I am personally satisfied, by evidence produced, of the truth and facts herein mentioned.

Done in conformity with the provisions of the Act of Congress entitled an Act to Prohibit the Coolie trade, approved April nineteenth, eighteen hundred and sixty-two; and an Act supplemental to the Acts in relation to immigration, approved March third, eighteen hundred and seventy-five.

There was a sense of excitement and anticipation for the Chinese emigrants as the morning progressed. For the laborers, an anxious night had passed, as their future lay ahead of them. Typically, the new emigrant's departure ritual included saying prayers and burning Joss paper to ensure a prosperous voyage. With the payment of $45 in gold, a bamboo berth and three meals a day were now waiting on the ship.

Not all of the Chinese passengers assembled in Hong Kong for the *Colorado*'s July 13, 1868, departure were ordinary laborers. Some were merchants of considerable importance in Canton, as well as representatives of the traditional Canton Hongs that maintained lucrative trading relationships with American and international traders from Britain, the Netherlands, and France. They were also heading to San Francisco to expand and grow the future trade between the U.S. and China.

The July morning in Hong Kong was already oppressively hot and steamy. The British Crown Colony's government houses, colonnades, verandas and trade houses along the Praya stirred to life against the already awakened busy harbor now that the sun had escaped from behind the welcome shade of the nearby 2,000 foot Victoria Peak. A variety of harbor junks, go downs and sampans reminded the travelers and merchants that Hong Kong was a flourishing and growing seaport.

The flagship of the U.S. Asiatic fleet, the USS *Piscataqua* was a conspicuous visitor at anchor in the stream close by the *Colorado*. Alongside the Praya quay and the Hong Kong & Macao Steam Company pier area west of the Clock Tower were a number of Chinese chandler boats and go-downs recovering their stretched bamboo connectors. They were getting ready to receive their Chinese passengers for the transit out to the *Colorado*.

In small groups, the emigrants departed their Hong Kong living quarters and made their way down to the Praya quay and Hong Kong docks to board the chandler boats for the voyage across the harbor. Over the next few hours, hundreds of emigrants were ferried between the quay and pier to the *Colorado*. The first arrivals looked-up with astonishment at the "mountain" that the ship represented. They boarded their new temporary home by walking up two brows (the nautical term for the gangway) – positioned fore and aft –

from floating dock platforms alongside the ship at its anchorage. At the top of the brows, the emigrants were met by crew members who led them across the deck into their berthing area in the forward part of the ship.

Each emigrant's living quarters consisted of a couch stretched between bamboo poles where he would sleep and stow his personal gear and luggage. Thomas W. Knox, author of an 1870 article of a similar Pacific Mail voyage entitled *"The Coming Man,"* had noted that Chinese emigrants had been "accustomed to small quarters at home, and so he can be stowed away closely when afloat."[16] From these small, dark, and stuffy quarters, each emigrant laborer would play cards and dominos, be called to his daily meals, and listen to his native music during the 33-day voyage across the South China Sea and the Pacific Ocean.

THE COMING MAN.—AT SEA, BETWEEN DECKS ON A PACIFIC MAIL COMPANY'S STEAMSHIP—CHINESE PASSENGERS LISTENING TO THEIR NATIONAL MUSIC.—FROM A SKETCH BY OUR SPECIAL ARTIST.

Figure 16: The Coming Man-At sea between decks, Chinese passengers listen to music on an early 1870's Pacific Mail Steamship Voyage. Frank Leslie's Illustrated, May 7, 1870 (Author's Collection)

As the day progressed, more than 800 Chinese laborers and merchants were quartered in their berthing areas. A little past 10:00 AM in the morning, the *Colorado* was finally ready to make preparations to get underway from

Hong Kong. Down below, the furnace crew increased the amount of coal shoveled into the mouths of all four boilers.

The *Colorado*'s engine and furnace-room spaces were engineering marvels of 1860s American steamboat engineering. Thirty-six men were required to operate the engineering department. They ferried the coal from the ship's bunkers and then, by the shovel load, pitched it into the new furnaces, watching as the steam gauges rose to the necessary levels – twenty pounds of steam pressure per square inch – needed to move the *Colorado*'s enormous 105-inch, twelve-foot stroke piston that was the motive force for the sidewheel steamer.

When the 20 PSI mark was reached, the demanding routine was started that would need to be maintained for most of the voyage. The engineers would demand 45 tons of coal a day to keep the boiler pressure at that level, which meant many hands would be engaged day and night to hoist the black coal from the forward hold.

Fresh water was also needed for the passage. The *Colorado*'s distilling plant was brought on line, beginning to distill the large volume of potable drinking water needed for consumption by crew and passengers and for food preparations in the ship's galley.

As the greater quantities of coal were shoveled in, the *Colorado*'s furnace room grew hotter. The little ventilation available was superheated by the stifling external air of Hong Kong. It would get worse as they departed Hong Kong. The "snipes"– as engineers of steam vessels were known – knew that the *Colorado* would be sailing "before the wind" to take full advantage of the southwest monsoon. If all went well, the wind in the sails would shave a whole day off the entire voyage. But it would be hard to breathe as the ship traveled with the wind. In the heat of the furnace room, the hope was for a couple of days of a northeast headwind to meet the topside ventilators and cool the main spaces.

Soon, the all-wooden *Colorado* and her engineers had enough steam up to the throttle valve to answer the engine bell from the pilot house. First Officer Warsaw assumed the watch. He would soon be underway toward his American West Coast home, Perhaps he also was looking forward to the day soon to come when he would have his own command as captain of one of the new China-trade steamers just beginning their service this month. At the end of this voyage to San Francisco, he expected to see the *Great Republic*, the *Japan*, and the *China* at the pier upon arrival.

He particularly looked forward to seeing the *Japan*. The largest and newest of the steamers, her entry into service would establish the required monthly travel that the merchants, railroad planners, and business interests in New York were counting on.

At 3:00 P.M. the *Colorado*'s brows were placed aboard from the floating dock. The last of the cargoes had been delivered by the sampans and go-downs, and the carpenter's gang sealed the cargo ports with caulking, hoping to secure the 20,000 packages of tea and silk from the elements of rain and seawater.

The passengers were all aboard, "berthed, messed and made comfortable." The deck gang was up on the *Colorado*'s forward deck or forecastle, looking over at the port chain that angled down to its mooring buoy, made fast with moderate strain.

The manned and ready reports now completed, the ship's engines and the 1500-horsepower "walking beam" began to turn the 40-foot sidewheels. The *Colorado* began to ease forward taking the strain off the mooring chain. A Chinese stevedore looked up at the *Colorado*'s forecastle as the ship's bow approached the barrel buoy.

The ship's engine stopped as the slack allowed the chain to be released from the buoy, and the *Colorado* was underway. The deck crew smartly pulled the chain aboard and secured the port anchor for sea.

The ship steamed slowly out of Hong Kong harbor.

The Asiatic Fleet flagship nearby sounded a ceremonial cannon salute that echoed throughout Hong Kong as the *Colorado* steamed out of port. The saluting battery's smoke wafted through the assembled officers and crew of the USS *Piscataqua*, then the smoke cleared and the men of the U.S. Navy quickly dispersed to deal with the rest of the busy harbor's afternoon activity that awaited.

Aboard the *Colorado*, a search was made for stowaways. With the report of "none found," the ship continued at a speed of six knots out of Hong Kong, passing nine pins before entering the South China Sea. Below decks in the forward steerage area, the gentle motion of the steamship combined with quiet conversation. Then, after just an hour, the Chinese emigrants prepared to receive their first meal at sea. Each man searched for his book of tickets to present to get his boiled rice when the roll call took place.

As described by Thomas W. Knox in 1870, "immediately after their arrival on shipboard, the passengers are divided into messes, and each mess chooses a chief, who is to draw the rations from the official who serves them put. The scene on board is an animated one…A Chinese clerk keeps the record and an American one takes the tickets, as the chiefs of the messes, one by one, are let out from the crowd and pass before them. John does not use knife or fork, but works his food into his mouth with chop-sticks, which are simply a couple of rods like long pencils; grasped in the thumb and forefinger of the right hand. When his meal is finished, he reclines upon his couch stretched on bamboo poles between decks, where he smokes his long stemmed-pipe, and goes to sleep to the sound of a Chinese grival, that gives forth strange barbaric music as it is touched by feminine hands through which the blood of the Celestial Empire flows."17

Figure 17: Distributing food rations for the day's meal.
Frank Leslie's Illustrated, May 7, 1870 (Author's Collection)

The ship's routine was quickly being established. In short order, a fire drill was called. On a wooden vessel, with stokers shoveling coal into multiple red-hot furnaces around the clock, it was an essential safety precaution to get everyone into the mindset of being prepared for the most dangerous of all at-sea possibilities: a fire at sea.

To douse a fire, giant steam-fired pumps were designed to feed salt-water into the ship's full-length fire main, which was capable of providing 32 streams of water when needed. For the drill, the ships boats were manned and made ready to let go. The passengers assembling at the boats, more excited by the thrill of the journey begun than worried about the risk of fire, were a diverse lot: Asiatic Fleet officers returning home, American and Chinese merchants and businessmen, Chinese missionaries, and, the largest number by far, the 818 Chinese steerage passengers.

After the drill, the first-class passengers would return to their "large and comfortable" staterooms aft by the lifeboats. Meanwhile, the hundreds of Chinese steerage passengers would return to their quarters below decks, located well forward of the lifeboat areas, to prepare for the evening meal hour.

The *Colorado*'s dining area saloon was soon getting ready for the 6:00 PM evening meal. The menu for first evening underway had a great number of choices for the first-class passengers. The culinary options included:

- Soup: Tomato
- Fish: Salt salmon and anchovy sauce
- Boiled: Chicken, tongue, corned beef
- Roast: beef, pork, chicken
- Entries: Fricassees of mutton, beef heart and olives
- Tenderloin of beef with mushrooms
- Rice croquets with jelly, curry and rice
- Vegetables: baked beans, broiled and roasted potatoes, green peas, beet root, carrots, and tomatoes
- Puddings: English plum pudding
- Pies: Mince, apple, plum; and jelly cream puffs
- Wine, cake crackers, and cheese
- A dessert of oranges, figs, raisins, almonds, and filberts
- Coffee and tea to conclude the meal

In the pilot house, First Officer Warsaw observed the Third Officer set the watch that would take the *Colorado* up the China Coast. His instructions to the watch were to check the charts, to keep an eye out for junks and sampans, and to be prepared for pirates. Warsaw was pleased with the afternoon. It was good to finally be underway, and he was satisfied with the professionalism of the watch in the wheel-house.

The *Colorado* was picking up speed, now making nine knots, and would arrive at the area off Swatow (Shantou) by morning. The sea was dark, and the dimly lit coast of China would remain in view throughout the evening. As the walking beam powered up and down and the sidewheels churned steadily through the sea, the *Colorado* passed Cup Chi and Breaker Point and made the important turn to port for the cruise up the coast to the White Dogs of Foochow.

At 11:00 PM the word went out to "douse the glint." After the lights were extinguished, the *Colorado* sailed as a darkened ship, well-prepared for

43

a comfortable night steam. Below decks, the Chinese steerage passengers each found what private space they could in their tight, darkened quarters, forward and well below the waterline, as the *Colorado* continued its night passage along the China coast. Some of the men continued playing their domino games. Others fell asleep to the sound of music.

They were one day closer to California's Gold Mountain.

On the main deck, the new watch adjusted their eyes to the darkness. The Chinese coast was mostly dark, with just an occasional light to indicate the distant land mass off the ship's port side, passing by at a steady rate of nine knots.

In the wheel house, the Third Officer was relieved by the Second Officer, with First Officer Warsaw present to oversee the turnover. "Steer northeast by east," was the order for the watch. Warsaw then headed aft on the deck house, located behind the wheel house, to his sleeping quarters.

As First Officer, Warsaw stood no watch himself, but was on duty in a supervisory role. Four quartermasters took turns steering the *Colorado,* keeping a sharp lookout for junks, ships, shoal-water, and land. As Warsaw left the wheel house to step outside, he probably paused to listen to the cadence of the *Colorado*'s walking-beam engines, a remarkable piece of technology that drove the paddlewheels as they plowed through the waters of the South China Sea. He might have glanced skyward at the coal embers leaving the *Colorado*'s stack, moving ahead of the ship with the strong southwest monsoon wind from behind.

The *Colorado*'s bridge was located in the most forward part of the ship. It had two large windows on each side of the centerline and ship's forward mast. The watch would keep a sharp lookout across the ship's forward bow for the any shipping vessels coming south from Shanghai, as well as for local junks or fishing vessels that might be on the waters at night.

Mid-watch, entries were made into a log: the *Colorado*'s total coal consumed, sidewheel revolutions per day, coal on hand, steam pressure, and cut-off steam pressure was all recorded. The ship's navigation and seamanship observations were also noted, including the latitude and longitude off the China Coast, distance traveled from Hong Kong, air temperature, water temperature and barometric data.

The July sunrise off Swatow was orange and sultry. Another warm day welcomed the *Colorado* at dawn as the walking-beam pushed and pulled the massive single piston up and down with a steadfast conviction. Smells of fresh bread emanated from the galley where the bakers had worked through the early morning hours.

Figure 18: The Colorado underway (1870)

The waiters, all Chinese men, took their orders from the European or African-American head waiter. There were up to 32 waiters on the saloon crew available for breakfast, lunch, and evening meals. They wore black caps, long black pigtails down to their heels, and dark blue tunics with white stockings and black felt shoes.

The breakfast gong sounded at 9:00 A.M. sharp. The passengers welcomed the new day with a plentiful meal of fish, hashes and stew, bacon, eggs, warm rolls and bread, corn cakes, waffles, tea and coffee.

The meal hours in *Colorado*'s dining saloon were breakfast at half past 8, lunch at 1 PM and dinner at 6 PM. The Chinese stewards were quiet, attentive, and efficient. They awaited their direction from the head steward, who would sound the bell once the passengers were seated for breakfast. At the first bell, the Chinese "blue gown boys" advanced with the breakfast dishes. At the second bell, they placed the food on the table; at the third bell, they took the covers off for the food to be eaten. This routine took place for all of the courses during each meal.

The Chinese steerage passengers would receive most of their meals at sea on the saloon deck, open to the sea air. Their food consisted of rice, boiled pork and tea, and they were served in their eating room adjacent to the Chinese kitchen. Almost one thousand pounds of rice was cooked for them and served up in 110 messes each day. Each steerage passenger had as much rice as he wished.

Figure 19: A mid-day lunch enroute to California.
Harper's Weekly-(1876) (Author's Collection)

In the Chinese kitchen, the rice was cooked in large boilers heated by steam from the main and donkey boilers, and doled out to a messman to ferry to the serving area. After their meal, some of the steerage passengers would head topside to catch some fresh air and then return to the berthing area to begin a game of dominoes or to rest. At 11:00 a.m., they would be rousted to gather topside for the daily sanitation inspection.

As the day's morning advanced, the *Colorado* was now about 150 miles from Hong Kong and was making better than 9 knots (10 miles) an hour up the coast. The steady pace required the "snipes" (the engineers) to keep the steam pressure up at 20 PSI. The *Colorado* had an engineering department of over 30 men who were kept constantly busy moving the 45 tons of coal per day. The engineering spaces were adjacent and just aft to the Chinese berthing compartment and about 17 feet below the water line. The ship's 24 furnaces needed to be continually fed. Coal was shoveled in at a constant pace by Chinese crewmen who wore only pants bottoms. The furnace room was a dark chamber lighted only by the glare of the fires that illuminated the Chinese crewmen as they worked. The heat was tremendous. The Chinese coal-heavers worked four hours and then rested eight, the arduous labor performed in the intense heat making it necessary for them to rest at regular intervals.[18]

Adjacent to the furnace room was the engine room that received the generated boiler steam. The steam power was required for the 750-horsepower walking-beam cylinder piston to generate torque across the 79-foot shaft that moved the paddlewheels, which measured 40 foot in diameter and weighed 66 tons each.

Besides the meals and the daily inspection, another afternoon fire drill (called at the discretion of the First Officer) rounded out the day for the steerage passengers.

Over the next two days, the *Colorado* sailed along the China coastline until she reached the stepping-off point, the Dogs of Foochow. Reaching "The Dogs" was significant, as it was the "go - no go" decision point for the ship, the moment to commence the open ocean passage across the China Sea to Japan, where she would take on coal in Yokohama.

The temperature of the coal bunkers was one of the essential considerations for the passage. The *Colorado*'s bunker temperatures were measured three times daily. The purpose was to discover and control any hidden coal-bunker fires. Similarly, temperatures and checks of the furnace and engine rooms and the cargo hold were also recorded in the ship's log, along with water measurements.

The ship's passage from Hong Kong to San Francisco also required the ship's routine to be set and the duty day to be carefully followed. A watchman patrolled the decks day and night. To further ensure the safety of the *Colorado*, the Captain, the ship's doctor, and the steward were required to inspect every part of the ship daily. The inspections, conducted at 11:00 AM, looked into the passenger staterooms to check cleanliness and proper ventilation, the kitchens and pantry, the butcher shop and bakery, and the steerage area for the Chinese passengers.

Each day the Chinese steerage passengers were subjected to the fumigation of burnt red-pepper spices and inspected for their health, as they stood next to their bunks or sat on their matting on the hurricane deck in the open air, where they would play dominoes or card games.

The engineering spaces were also inspected. Afterwards, the officer of the deck would report at noon the results of all of the ship's daily inspections.

Noon was a particularly important time aboard the *Colorado*. In 1868 shipping, before the days of GPS or electronic systems, the ship's position, was determined the old-fashioned way – by dead reckoning, by readings taken along the shore, and by measuring the latitude based on the alignment of the sun at noon. The ship's chronometers were also wound at this time, to provide an accurate time comparison with Greenwich Mean Time (GMT), and the nautical almanac was consulted, using the local noon-hour angle of the sun.

After the Captain and First Officer Warsaw worked out the *Colorado*'s latitude and longitude, they calculated the number of miles made in the last 24 hours, and placed the distance traveled on a bulletin board for the passengers to read.

One of the most important events of the voyage occurred at 4:00 PM in the afternoon - the surprise fire drill.

"Fire, fire, fire...." The cry occurred to test the crew. The bells rung feverishly and the *Colorado*'s steam whistle roared. As a passenger observing a subsequent fire drill on another voyage noted:

> "...two Chinamen, grinning with excitement, got on a hose and pump and pumped hard at the stern. Meanwhile, greasy-faced cooks -black, yellow and white - and gangs of Chinese sailors and Yankee officers swarmed all over the place. The engineers opened valves, the stewards hoisted extinguishers on their backs, and in a few minutes the whole gang was spouting sea water into the sea over the starboard bow. Then an officer with a big pistol slung to his waist, trotted to the wheel house and blew a steam blast. Pails of water were replaced, hose and extinguishers were carried off at a trot, and all hands went to the boats. In ten minutes more these were off the chocks, slung to the davits ready for lowering, crews seated, with oars tossed and provisions on board. Then the officer blew another steam-blast, and all was replaced, and we went to dinner." [19]

The *Colorado* made a safe passage to Yokohama, Japan, arriving Wednesday, July 23, 1868. There, the crew was busy for three days, dealing with replenishing the coal, loading and unloading cargo, letting off and taking on new passengers, and, as this was a U.S. mail route, seeing to the transfer of mail. As they waited for the trip to resume, the Chinese steerage passengers played dominoes, ate, and watched the busy coaling and cargo activities in Yokohama in the shadow of Mount Fuji.

Then, on Saturday, July 26, 1868, at 3:00 PM, the ship got underway and steamed out of Yokohama Bay for the 23-day voyage to San Francisco. Out at sea after the 3-day visit, the *Colorado* headed southeast to join up with the 30th parallel for the trans-Pacific transit. Cooler weather and stronger headwinds thankfully cooled the main spaces, yet caused the snipes to shovel more coal to compensate for a slower speed. The ship would be lucky if she made 200 miles per day.

On Sunday mornings aboard the *Colorado* and other steamers of the Pacific Mail, the Captain (or a Protestant or Episcopalian clergyman) led shipboard services in the social hall or main-deck saloon. The services were attended by the Christians on board and an occasional Chinese crewman. As one passenger on a subsequent voyage observed, "Our missionary women sang their hymns, and the piano, acting as organ, accompanied them."[20]

The ship's routine after these Sunday's continued their regular cadence. As the days passed, with the daily consumption of coal, the *Colorado* got lighter and therefore faster. The distance run told the tale. At first 133 miles, then 150, 177, and increasing mileage per day thereafter as less coal was aboard. The weather also got better as she crossed atop the 30th latitude line across the Pacific. The log told the tale: 208, 227, 217, 228 miles a day.

Underway again, passengers could look forward to several exciting events anticipated to occur. One was the crossing the line (the 180th parallel or International Date Line). This happened two days after leaving Japan, when the *Colorado* began the first of two adjacent Wednesdays.

As Frances D. Thurber noted in "*Coffee: from Plantation to Cup*" on a subsequent voyage:

"...we were not manifestly threatened with the immediate loss of the whole of our lives, it was clear that on passing the 180th degree of longitude we should at all events be deprived of one day. As we approached the fatal spot, many jokes were tried by the old hands, such as remarking that having gone up hill so far, we should now begin to go down again, or saying the place was marked by a magnificent buoy, always illuminated at night; but at last the reality came."[21]

The ceremonial fun was also recalled by Thomas W. Hinchcliff in *Over the Sea and Far Away* as he described his experience crossing the line with the Pacific Mail.

"The occasion of crossing the line is generally signaled by some kind of ceremonies and in our case an oil barrel painted to resemble a buoy was dropped overboard, a gun fired, and the passengers of course all rushed on deck to find out which marked the 180th parallel of longitude. Of course they accepted this statement of 'gospel truth' and due note was made of it in diaries, but after the joke had been carried sufficiently far, it was duly explained by the Captain, much to the enjoyment of the few who were in on the secret, and the chagrin of those who had been taken in."[22]

Another welcome sight was the sighting and the rendezvous with the outbound San Francisco steamer. On this voyage, that, vessel encountered on the high seas would be the *Japan* on her inaugural trip. By First Officer Warsaw's calculations, the *Colorado* would rendezvous on August 10, 1868, with the outbound *Japan*. The rendezvous would occur 1,400 miles out from San Francisco.

After a month in San Francisco, the *Japan* had set sail for Yokohama and China on August 3, 1868 at 10:40 PM. Her departure represented the first time in U.S. history that a monthly line of steamships transport had ever occurred between the U.S. and China. She carried 272 passengers with 600 tons of manufactured goods, agricultural machines, carriages, furniture, flour, butter, fruit, drugs and patent medicines – merchandise valued at $90,000; mails and $878,000 in Mexican Silver Dollar treasure.

Aboard was J. Ross Browne, the new American Minister to China as a replacement for Anson Burlingame, who was now in San Francisco representing Chinese interests. Browne was bound for Peking via Shanghai and Tientsin, where he would be responsible for managing the new Burlingame Treaty between China and the U.S.

Two weeks into their eastward voyage from Hong Kong, the passengers and crew of the *Colorado* eagerly anticipated the rendezvous of the *Japan* at sea. The posting of the Captain and First Officer Warsaw on the bowsprit with their telescopes pointed to the east signaled to all that the rendezvous would occur in the near future. The meeting of two steamers at sea would be an opportunity for the passengers to pass on letters to be posted by the incoming vessel and for the outgoing vessel to bring desperately needed news of the world, passing on the latest newspapers and telegraph dates from New York. For the directors of the Pacific Mail Company, the meeting was a public-relations event. The captains of the ships, as a point of honor, prided themselves on precise navigation leading to a successful rendezvous. Amongst the crew and passengers, bets were taken on the time of rendezvous.

If it was to be a daylight meeting, a sharp lookout was required to see the ship's distant shape. A morning sunrise or evening sunset would help illuminate the hull's sidewheeler profile as it approached. An evening rendezvous was helped by the launching of hourly rockets, penetrating the dark Pacific sky or a moonless night.

Then, the *Japan* appeared on the horizon, the lights of the approaching vessel sending a lightning bolt of excitement throughout all on the *Colorado*. Many of the Chinese steerage passengers watched from the foc'sle and heard the enthusiastic cheers of the cabin passengers and crew as a cannon signal was sounded as the vessels neared each other and stopped.

MEETING OF THE STEAMERS IN MID-OCEAN.

Figure 20: Meeting of the Steamers in Mid-Ocean
from William Seward's Travels Around the World (1873)

For First Officer Warsaw, the rendezvous held special significance. He was due to become a new captain on *Japan*'s sister ship, the *China*, later in 1868. Seeing the large new steamship approach surely served as a happy reminder that his time to command was soon to come. As the *Colorado's* boat cruised toward the *Japan* with newspapers and mail, Warsaw's keen eye must have taken delight in the sun-splashed panorama of the *Japan* set against the backdrop of the cobalt-blue Pacific.

She was magnificent. Here was the world's largest side-wheel steamer, a beautiful ship with freshly painted black hull and red sidewheel. The *Japan* was 320 feet in length and over 4,300 tons. She boasted beautiful accommodations for its passengers and a third more space forward, to allow the berthing of upwards of 1,200 Chinese steerage passengers. Her new lifeboats glistened in the sun, and her American flag fluttered gently in the breeze. A monthly service, a new ship of the line and a promising future – Warsaw surely could feel the excitement on board on this particular rendezvous.

The Chinese passengers, although circumspect and observant, seemed to sense it as well. They could see some of their countrymen returning home on the *Japan* and imagine their good fortune and luck, with money belts heavy with gold from their wages earned in America. They themselves were now just one week away from their San Francisco arrival and the beginning of their own chances for prosperity.

After a salute was rendered and boats secured for sea, the walking-beam engine telegraph ordered "all ahead slow." The two ships did not linger long in each other's company. After just a brief 30-minute pause in the midst of the Pacific, the *Colorado* and the *Japan* concluded their rendezvous and continued on their way.

The evening meal was almost ready. A new line for rice and pork formed, and the very precious coal shuttle in the engine room heralded the close of another day at sea. The "Douse the flame" order came at 11:00 PM, and the mid-watch turnover represented the beginning of the end, as thoughts turned to the final week of passage.

The next morning the *Colorado*'s topsails were set by the Chinese crew in order to take advantage of southwest winds that would push the *Colorado* above nine knots as she angled on a northeast heading on the final days of steaming. The headwinds along *Colorado*'s path remained steady, yet because she was getting lighter she was making over 200 miles per day. The sea revealed porpoises, flying fish, whale pods, and a variety of sea birds. The nights were cool and clear and presented stars upon stars, from the pinnacle of heaven's dome down to the water's edge.

The morning of August 15 arrived clear and pleasant. Warsaw studied the *Colorado*'s Plan of Intended Movement (PIM), noting the ship would pass by the South Farallon Island at 0700 the next morning, Saturday August 16. The Farallon's are a group of small rocky islands that lie 22 miles from the Golden Gate. The rock outcrops are home to seabird rookeries, sea lions, and seals, as well as the best lighthouse on the Pacific coast. Beyond the Farallon's, the outline of the mountains of California could first be seen.

Warsaw looked up from the chart and indicated that he thought the *Colorado* would be on time for the Farallon's passage and would soon after make it up to "The Handle" – as the Golden Gate was called. The *Colorado* was making good speed. Her sails were set and she was higher still in the water with another 40 tons of coal consumed by her hungry boilers. The sidewheels seemed to move faster as they got closer to the Gate. At 7:30 AM on August 16, the ship passed South Farallon Island and was now two hours from the Golden Gate.

FAR ALONES.

Figure 21: The Farallon Islands (1870's)

But ahead of the *Colorado* was a massive fog bank. It was, after all, August in San Francisco. As Mark Twain had quipped of the cool surroundings of the Pacific Ocean and the peninsula's weather, "The coldest winter I ever experienced was a summer in San Francisco."

So close to arrival, the Chinese steerage passengers would have to wait until the fog cleared for a safe passage and San Francisco arrival. The *Colorado* slowed and took on a pilot, then anchored off the bar at the entrance to San Francisco Bay in dense fog at 5:00 PM. She would make a morning arrival on Sunday. Ashore in San Francisco, "Steamer Day" would have to wait.

By late Saturday afternoon, it was evident in San Francisco to the members of each of the Six Companies anticipating the ship's arrival, as well as the leading merchants, including one of the original Canton merchants, the Chy Lung Company, that the *Colorado* would be delayed until the next morning.

The Chinese quarter in San Francisco communicated the news street by street, the message exchanged from person to person in one of many Cantonese dialects. The word spread slowly along the six blocks of Chinatown north to south, along Dupont Street from California to Broadway, then east and west on Sacramento, Clay, Commercial, Washington, Jackson, and Pacific Streets to Stockton Street.

The wagons that were to carry "the Celestials," as they were picturesquely named by the press, returned from the Pacific Mail wharf on First and Brannan to get the word to the Globe Hotel. At the Globe, a number of Chinese men were seated, enjoying meals of fish, meat, and rice, as the smoke from the cooking fires wafted gently down the street. Many of the Chinese passengers were to be berthed at the Globe Hotel, which had a Joss temple and pictures of Canton Province with its valleys, rivers, cities, and famous pagoda temples.

Down at the Pacific Mail Steamship offices on the southeast corner of Sacramento Street, the long-time Pacific Mail agent Oliver Eldredge also received word of the Colorado's anchorage as it waited for the fog to clear. The pier area was cleaned up to await the dawn of tomorrow's steamer day. The covered docks and their doorways were secured for the evening. The southern pier area cleared of obstacles, and the brows stowed. In the bay, the steamer *China*'s lines grew slack as the evening flood tide pushed her 4,000 tons against the pier.

Outside the Golden Gate on the *Colorado*, the Chinese crew washed the decks of the steamship and polished the brass. The ship would be shiny and neat for her Sunday arrival.

When daylight came the next morning, "The Handle" could be clearly observed from the *Colorado*'s pilot house. First Officer Warsaw consulted with the captain and recommended that the ship make preparations for getting underway, to steam into the harbor to the wharf and a mid-day Sunday arrival. The word went out through the ship to make ready. Topside on the bridge, a signal flag was hoisted up on the halyard for the white lighthouse on the cliffs to observe and then to telegraph the news to the city. The *Colorado* would be arriving before noon at the Pacific Mail wharf.

Also watching the beginnings of the ship's preparations and signal were observers on the balcony of the Cliff House, which could only hear the banter of the sea lions with their morning chorus against the sea birds as large, roaring breakers crashed onto the jagged rocks along the shore.

When the telegraphed notification from the white lighthouse reached San Francisco's merchant exchange, a messenger from North Beach would mount his horse and begin a gallop throughout the streets of San Francisco, shouting the arrival of the steamship from Japan and China.

This communications set in motion "Steamer Day." The San Francisco streetcars also got into the act, adorning small white flags with the letters "U.S.M." In the alleys and streets of Chinatown, usually busy each day with pedestrians, the days of steamship arrivals and departures were particularly crowded. The streets and alleys literally swarmed with the people…

"…all day long, and often until late at night, the streets are crowded with Chinamen of all ages and sizes, and speaking various dialects, with shaven crown and neatly braided cue, sauntering lazily along, talking, visiting, trading, laughing, and scolding in the strangest, and, to an American, the most discordant jargon. Here and there they gather in groups, very much like Americans, mostly on the corners of the streets, and amuse themselves in trying to cipher out the meaning of some of the thousands of strange hieroglyphics of their own language that are placarded upon the walls."[23]

Down at the San Francisco Custom House, anticipating the beginning of the influx of the Chinese steerage laborers, the officials brought a few extra-large bags with them to the wharf to throw all confiscated contraband from each arriving member. The Custom officials' job at the dock would consume most of the entire afternoon. Smuggling was a big concern to the San Francisco police and Customs Officers, and they expected trickery and cleverness from the steerage-class passengers. As described Reverend Gibson's "*The Chinese in America,*" 'John', as the Chinese were called, "is an inveterate smuggler, and is a perfect adept at all kinds of tricks to further the nefarious trade. Silks and opium being of great value to their bulk"[24] which are hidden in false box bottoms and their possessions. All of their belongings had to be searched.

The residents of the Globe Hotel sensed that they would be receiving almost all of the *Colorado*'s arrivals as a "half-way" lodge, pending labor assignments in either San Francisco or the wheat fields of the Sacramento and San Joaquin valleys or for the fall work in the Sierra Nevada's cuts and trestles for the Central Pacific and other railroads throughout California. Their stay at the Globe would not be long. There was, after all, an acute labor shortage in the region, and new arrivals from the *Colorado* would be put to work right away.

The merchant class of San Francisco also anticipated the arrival of some new "accredited" representatives of the old established Canton Hongs, the greatest exporters of all in China. These merchant-class arrivals would not be staying at the Globe Hotel; they would be taken to the businesses along Portsmouth Square in the heart of San Francisco, not far from Chinatown.

The Six Company representatives dressed up for the *Colorado*'s arrival. They and other Chinese merchants expecting cargo hitched up their wagons, drags, and private carriages to begin their journey down to the docks. They joined many others of the city's merchant class, as the wave of activity grew and the melee of humanity made its collective way to the docks below Rincon Point at South Beach.

As described by an October 1868 *Overland Monthly* article entitled "The Six Companies," each company "served the purpose of the caravansary of eastern countries in olden times [an inn built around a large court for accommodating caravans.] To them the emigrants resort on landing from ships, some servant of each Ui Kun [Company District] going off to meet them and to give them the necessary instructions to those on board who have come from the districts which are represented in his particular company. In the caravansary he is furnished a room in which to spread his mat in oriental style with water and facilities for cooking. The arrangement saves him much expense, and also protects him from those who otherwise might take advantage of his ignorance of the country and its ways of doing business."[25]

As the *Colorado* neared the San Francisco harbor, after almost two weeks at sea after leaving Japan, excitement was shared by all as they passed the Golden Gate. The Golden Gate Strait is the entrance to San Francisco Bay from the Pacific. The strait is approximately three-miles long by one-mile wide, and was said to have been named "Chrysopylae," or Golden Gate, by John C. Fremont, the famous explorer and captain of a team of U.S. Army engineers, circa 1846. It reminded him, it is said, of a harbor in Istanbul named Chrysoceras or Golden Horn.

For the Chinese steerage passengers, this moment meant an imminent arrival in the land of their new Gold Mountain. When the final approach to San Francisco was underway, they took the opportunity to change into a fresh set of clothes for arrival.

The momentous culminating event of the trans-Pacific voyage from Hong Kong was the pierside arrival in San Francisco at the Pacific Mail pier at Brennan Street. The *Colorado* was welcomed by throngs of townsfolk, city officials, businessmen, newspaper reporters, family members of passengers, ordinary citizens, representatives of the Six Companies, and many members of the Chinese merchant class of San Francisco, all gathered at the pier to welcome the paddlewheel steamship to the city.

Aboard the *Colorado*, the harbor pilot watched with the captain through the pilot-house windows as the anchor was secured and the order given to the engine room "half speed ahead." The walking-beam engine began its predictable motion and the sidewheels dug into the cold waters of the entrance to the Golden Gate and San Francisco Bay. The 37-star American flag was closed up on the stern, the yellow dragon flag of China and the Pacific Mail and ship colors spread out and became unfurled against a light wind. The brass fittings glistened and the ship's black hull reflected the early morning sun.

The *Colorado* passed through the Golden Gate and turned right onto the inbound leg abeam the fort. The city of San Francisco opened up to the ship. The tall black cross in the cemetery on "Lone Mountain" was clearly visible. So was Telegraph Hill, the ship's turning point to slow and approach the quarantine anchorage. The inner bay was crowded with merchant ships from around the world and the wharves were quiet this Sunday morning north of the Rincon.

The *Colorado* stopped her engines as she approached her anchorage and backed her engines one half to stop the ship and let go the anchor with a little sternway. When the vessel was anchored, the Health Officer boarded the ship and proceeded to the foc'sle to begin the required passenger check and clearance. His job was to ensure that no more than the lawful number of emigrants were aboard and that they were all in satisfactory health.

Writing of the arrival of Chinese emigrants from a Pacific Mail steamship in *An Old World Seen Through Young Eyes*, Ellen H. Walworth noted that:

> "a sailor stood at one side of the narrow hatchway, and at the other one of the mates, who counted out in a loud voice, as the Chinamen came pouring up the steep ladder: 'One, two, three, four, five, six, seven, eight, nine, ten-tally! One, two, three, etc." and each time he said 'Tally" the doctor would make a mark in his book. This they were counted in tens…They were all dressed for the occasion of landing, in fresh green, yellow, red and brown clothes, their pigtails newly braided, and their faces, which had been besmeared with dirt during the voyage, were shining yellower and more heathenish than ever."[26]

The Chinese steerage passengers were then ushered to the other end of the ship to a holding area for their arrival at the dock. Down at the mail pier, the covered area identified the "New York via Panama" dock where the *Colorado* would berth "port-side to." Looking out from the *Colorado*'s wheel house, Warsaw could see that the *China* was berthed "starboard side to" alongside the pier and covered deck area, which was now open to the crowd and advertised on the external frontage: "PMSSC China via Japan."

Outside the gates, a group of police officers held back the vast crowd of San Franciscan Americans, Europeans, and Chinese gathered in anticipation of the ship's arrival. Many had arrived with wagons to transport goods or humans to intended destinations in the city. The Customs House officers and an entire watch of San Francisco police, dressed in gray uniforms and armed with clubs and revolvers, were allowed to pass through inside the covered docks.

Next to be allowed in were the leading Chinese merchant members, Six Company representatives, and cargo consigners. They were directed to general waiting areas outside the Custom official cordons on each side of where the ship's brow would be placed.

Out on the *Colorado*, First Officer Warsaw could hear the growing excitement on the pier. The health check for the *Colorado* had been completed and she was now underway for the wharf. A half-engine bell was ordered from the wheel house, and the snipes in the engine room answered. "Over the line" came the order as the *Colorado*'s bow came abeam of the pier. The line was handled responsively by the handlers and immediately placed on a bollard to take the strain.

The line held, and the *Colorado* began to spring as the quartermaster held the ship's head steady. The *Colorado*'s bow mooring hawser was then tended, and she made her mark, moored in San Francisco at last! The ships walking-beam engine and side wheels were placed in full reverse to stop any forward motion. The *Colorado* had arrived in San Francisco 33 days after leaving Hong Kong and was stable in position to receive the two large gangways, forward and aft, to begin off-loading her human cargo and freight.

The colorful Chinese arrivals looked along the wharf and along the Rincon at San Francisco for the first time from their observation area on the foc'sle. The first individual to depart the *Colorado* was the Health Officer, who smiled and signaled to the Customs Officers as they began to board. The detectives and policemen stationed themselves at each of the two brows.

The ship was now ready to disembark its passengers. The forward brow was used for the exclusive disembarkation of the Chinese. The word "all ready" was given. A stream of the Chinese steerage passengers began to walk down the brow bearing long bamboo poles across their shoulders, from which were suspended packages of bedding, matting, and clothing. Most appeared to be twenty-five years of age, a few under fifteen, and none over forty. As they walked out on the wharf, they separated into groups of ten, twenty or thirty and were assigned places by agents of the Six Companies.

As colorfully described by in an Atlantic Monthly article by Albert S. Evans entitled *From the Orient Direct*, "they were all dressed in coarse but clean and new blue cotton blouses and loose baggy breeches, blue cotton cloth stockings, which reached up to the knee, and slippers or shoes with heavy wooden soles. Most of them carried broad-brimmed hats of split bamboo, and huge palm leaf fans, to shield them from the burning sun in the mountains or the valleys of California or the fertile fields of the south, toward which many of them would eventually direct their steps."[27]

Figure 22: Arrival at the Pacific Mail Steamship Dock at First and Brannon. Leslies Illustrated Newspaper May 1870. (Author's Collection)

On the wharf, the Customs agents searched each person and his luggage as thoroughly as possible. Once clear from inspection, the steerage passengers' luggage received a chalk mark with the private symbol of the inspector. With the mark, the Chinese passenger was able to pass through the gate to the assembly area for his Six Company representatives. With their help, each passenger would then be shuttled out the gates to the express wagons and foot patrols to begin the journey to the Globe Hotel and the first night in San Francisco.

Figure 23: Chinese Immigrants at the Customs House, San Francisco

Special consideration was taken with 30 women Chinese passengers. They were held aboard under the suspicion that they had been sent for purposes of prostitution. The press was there to report their presence, and the *Daily Alta* reported that the "importers of Jackson and Pacific Streets and the adjoining alleys were on hand to receive their chatters."[28] After some discussion, the police eventually escorted the Chinese women to St. Mary's Hospital, a shelter for women in San Francisco. The Chinese companies involved would be forced to resort to a *habeas corpus* procedure to free the women.

By nightfall, the *Colorado* had offloaded more than 800 steerage passengers, 80 cabin passengers, and 20,000 packages of tea, silk and general cargo.

As Warsaw left, he passed the *China*. His thoughts must have been cast ahead to beginning his own command of that ship with her next voyage in the fall. For now, after the weeks at sea, he headed to his home at the Occidental Hotel to finally get some rest.

The paths of the Chinese steerage passengers and Edward Warsaw would cross several times over the next six years. Six years hence, 1874, would prove to be a fateful year for both.

Chapter 5

John Chinaman and Chinatown 1868-1874

The Chinese labor question is destined within the next ten years – five years, perhaps– to become what the slavery question was a few years since, to break down, revolutionize and reorganize parties, completely change the industrial system of many of our States and territories and modify the destination of our country for generations to come...
"From The Orient Direct,"
Atlantic Monthly, **November 1869**

The Chinese emigrants' home on arrival was San Francisco's Chinese quarter. The district ran north to south on Dupont Street from California to Broadway streets and from east to west on Sacramento, Clay, Commercial, Washington, Jackson, Pacific and Broadway streets from Kearney Street to Stockton crossing Dupont street.

Over the six years from 1868 to 1874 about 150,000 Chinese from the Guangdong provinces travelled to San Francisco for work that was secured by the agents by the Six Companies. The Six Company representatives had coordinated their labor assignments from their company houses. Of the six, the Sap Yup Company was the most powerful regionally and the Ning Yeung most powerful within San Francisco.

Year	Arrived	Departed
1867	*4,200*	*4,475*
1868	*11,081*	*4,210*
1869	*14,990*	*4,895*
1870	*10,870*	*4,230*
1871	*5,540*	*3,260*
1872	*9,770*	*4,890*
1873	*17,065*	*6,805*
1874	*16,085*	*7,710*
1875	*18,021*	*6,305*
1876 (first quarter)	*5,065*	*625*

Figure 24: Chinese immigration (1867-1876). Compiled from San Francisco Customs House and Six Companies records

Overall, upwards of 90,000 Chinese steerage passengers arrived and 28,000 departed aboard the sidewheel steamers during the 1868-1874 period. A census completed on April 1, 1876, by Reverend O. Gibson, *"The Chinese in America,"* provided important insight into the Six Company districts in Guangdong. The company representation and their approximate geographical locations in China and office location in San Francisco were:

The Sam Yup Company took care of emigrants from three districts: Namhoi, Punyu, and Shantak areas that embrace Canton and the country surrounding the city. Their San Francisco population was approximately 11,000 and their company house was located on Clay Street above Powell Street.

The Ning Yeung Company was the largest. Its members from the populous Guangdong district west of Macao bordering on the sea coast and stretching inland. Their San Francisco population was approximately 75,000. Their company house was located on Broadway Street between Kearney and Dupont Streets.

The Hop Wo Company represented the Chinese from three districts southwest of Canton (and north of the district represented by the Ning Yeung). Their San Francisco population was approximately 34,000 and their company house was located on Commercial Street.

Kong Chau Company took care of members from three districts southwest of Canton. Their approximate population was 15,000.

The Yeung Wo Company represented the emigrants of the districts from Macao to the Namhoi and Shantak counties. Their San Francisco population was approximately 12,000 and their company house was located on Sacramento Street.

The sixth company, the Yan Wo Company, had a different membership. Instead of a specific district, it took care of people known as "Hakkah" (foreigners from the north) who entered the southwest of China for business. Their San Francisco population was approximately 4,300 and their house was located on Dupont Street between Washington and Jackson Street.

The final and smallest company, Hip Kat, represented the "Hakkah" people -foreigners from the north who had entered the southwest of China.

During their time in San Francisco, the Six Company steerage passengers were employed in a variety of work that contributed to the growth of San Francisco and commerce in California. The primary occupations were as merchants, sewing-machine operators, house servants and laundry men; as well as more skilled boot, slipper and shoe and cigar makers.

Outside of San Francisco, the Six Companies spread their countrymen into the wheat, vegetable and fruit enterprises of northern and central California and as right of way teams for the Central, Union and Southern

Pacific railroads. Corinne Hoexter in her book, *From Canton to California*, described Chinese contributions to California agriculture in the "the feudal seventies" when the large ranches were still developing out of the haciendas of the Mexican era. "Most of the California grain was plowed, planted, harvested and bound in sheaves by the Chinese. Two-thirds of all vegetables cultivated by them. In the wine country of Napa and Sonoma...memorials of the Chinese role in the early development of California wine making survive...California fruit growers were almost totally dependent on Chinese workers."[29]

The Chinese population during this period, illustrated on the 1872 Census map, aligns with these observations, with an affinity to reside by rivers and near the growing railroad network.

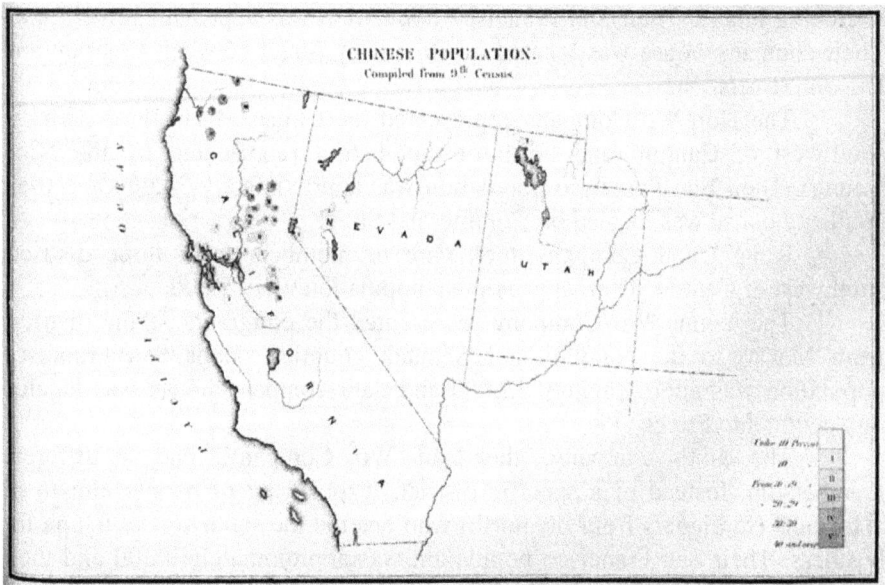

Figure 25: Chinese Population in California (1872)
Courtesy Perry-Castañeda Library Map Collection-University of Texas

The pejorative word identifying the Chinese emigrant - in San Francisco, California, and the country at large - was "John Chinaman." The six years of "John Chinaman's" existence between 1868 and 1874 involved providing needed labor to a variety of trades throughout the region. Their numbers, estimated in the 100,000 to 150,000 range, were made possible by the monthly transport provided by the Pacific Mail steamship steamers.

With the increasing visibility of each steamer arrival, a festering political movement against the Chinese, their emigration to San Francisco and

64

the Pacific Mail Steamship Company began in the early 1870s and culminated in severe and increasingly violent labor rallies and agitation against the Chinese. The productivity and visibility of the Chinese over this period spurred the most visible resentment from the San Francisco working classes, mainly the "red-haired" Irish. The greater the number of Chinese emigrant arrivals between 1868 and 1874, the greater the level of the political, economic, and racial resentment against the "Heathen Chinee" newcomer, "John Chinaman."

Attitudes varied somewhat depending on the economic situation. There were two distinct California boom-and-bust cycles between 1868 and 1874. The Six Companies and the Chinese steerage passenger emigrants found themselves needed during the boom – and reviled during the bust. The first boom period lasted roughly from 1868 to 1870, as "John Chinaman" came and built the Central Pacific Railroad through the Sierra Nevada mountains and beyond into Nevada. Four out of five Central Railroad workers were Chinese, and their labor services were much respected and appreciated by those familiar with the quality of their work.

In the winter of 1869-70, however, after the Union Pacific Railroad and the Central Pacific Railroad were joined at Promontory Point, Utah, in the famous "Golden Spike" ceremony, the railroad economy experienced a severe downturn throughout California. As described by Stephen Powers in a November 1871 *Atlantic Monthly* article titled "California Saved."

"In many a mountain mining town, which once resounded with the blast of the powder, the click of the pistol, the doors were shut in the streets, and the sound of grinding was low. Silver mines were dry, the gold ran thin in the sluices, in many places the harvest had been shortened…the mortgages on real estate in San Francisco crept up to the alarming figure of $30,000,000. The immigrants did not arrive in the multitudinous the hosts expected.[30]

The popular prejudice and anti-Chinese sentiment grew with the increasing number of emigrants that arrived at the Pacific Mail docks in the 1870s. The belief that the Chinese displaced the new immigrants and the red haired Irish, was strong during the first boom period and intensified during the bust. Sensing the growing cultural conflict and immigrant unrest, the Six Companies stepped in and telegraphed home manifestoes at a rate of one every two years, causing the temporary suspension of emigration on the Pacific Mail steamers because of the anti-Chinese feeling. As an example, a later dispatch (March 26, 1876) signed by the Six Companies and sent to Hong Kong is representative of their awareness of the popular prejudice and growing anti Chinese sentiment in San Francisco. Fearing a political, social, and legal backlash, the companies wanted to decrease the numbers of emigrants wishing to make the trip to California.

"Yung Wah Hospital, Hong Kong: Laws passed and measures being taken to discourage Chinese emigration. Inform the Chinese that they must not come. Danger to life and property if they do."[31]

Such warnings worked, and the numbers of Chinese emigrants coming in dropped to 4,964 in 1871 and 9,377 in 1872, down from 10,311 in 1870.

The second boom period lasted roughly between 1873 and mid-1874, and was more diverse and short lived. The silver bonanza and the sale of Nevada Comstock lode mining shares contributed to a new financial boom in San Francisco. Coincident to the silver boom and its speculative enterprises in San Francisco, the building of the Southern Pacific railway to Los Angeles, a growing Central Valley agricultural labor demand, and the growing Chinatown merchant trade, with continued expansion of trade with China, caused the Six Companies to urge a renewed transport of Guangdong Province laborers.

During this second boom period, over 17,000 men and women came to San Francisco. The second boom lasted until March 1874, at which point the anti-Chinese feeling intensified, compelling the agents of the Six Companies to send another of their telegraphic dispatches to China, calling for the temporary suspension of immigration.

Stephen Powers writing in the *Atlantic Monthly* in 1871 also described the financial and labor sector attitudes that prevailed during 1870 and 1871. Financially, "the Chinaman performs as tidy scrubbing and cooking for $20 or $25 a month as Irish girls do for $30 or $35. He is tractable, patient and obedient."

The view in the community of American laborers differed considerably in their views on the matter.

"He [the Chinese worker] buys the least possible of home produce and manufactures on which he can keep body and soul together, bringing even his wretched clothing and his rice from China; therefore he starves the butchers, grocers, bakers, etc...He carries away all of his earnings to China, makes no improvements, except the vilest huts, which were better burned; and will not even enrich the soul with his miserable body, but gathers up two car loads of bones all along the Central Pacific and ships them home. He has carried away millions which ought to have gone to encourage our artisans and grocers."[32]

Financiers were torn. In any event, their view on the benefits of Chinese labor would be drowned out by San Francisco's labor and political voices. Nonetheless, many were aware of the value of the contributions of the Chinese emigrant workers to the West Coast economy. As Powers noted:

"...the improvements for which we are indebted to his cheap and supple utility! But for the Chinese, the Union Pacific with its easier grades and swarms of Irishmen would have outstripped the Central Pacific, forced the point of junction far westward and so have thrown the vast trade of Utah, Idaho and Montana into the hands of Chicago. The Chinese rescued the commercial future of San Francisco [italics added]"[33]

Their intense business spirit in Chinatown and hard-work ethic grading the railway pathways and in the fields of California challenged labor and politically became "The Chinese Question" - was it coolie or free labor?

Adding fuel to the anti-Chinese movement was the arrival of Chinese women. Some were coming to Chinatown and San Francisco to rejoin their husbands or find a husband to marry. However, there was a parallel trade of importing women to serve as comfort women and prostitutes within Chinatown and the extended labor areas. The most noteworthy merchant affiliated with the trade of Chinese prostitutes was the Chy Lung Company. The women were recruited from the same counties in Guangdong Province, however, and some were sold into the nefarious trade for shipment.

The growing numbers of Chinese women tallied about 2,600. They were described as "enslaved prostitutes" by the San Francisco customs house. Their presence so enflamed the political and moral passions in San Francisco and California that the local and state governments began to take action beginning in 1874 to compel the U.S. Consul in Hong Kong to screen and certify every female passenger coming to San Francisco. That screening required a photo and complete documentation that concluded with the women emigrants attesting to their purpose of emigration and their occupation.

The question of the Chinese prostitutes remained supercharged with the importation of unmarried "Chinese Maiden" women into San Francisco by the Chy Lung Company in August 1874. The incident, initially involving the Pacific Mail Steamship Company, evolved into a complex case dealing with the power of the state to regulate emigration, and the Fourteenth Amendment to the Constitution involving the Right of Aliens to Equal Protection of the Law. The Chy Lung/Chinese Maiden case and its implications for the "Chinese Question" quickly wended its legal path from the piers of the Pacific Mail to a greater stage. It would go all the way to the Supreme Court, playing out in the landmark "*Chy Lung vs. Freeman*" Supreme Court case of October 1875.[34] The decision established equal protection, the right of the Chinese to freely emigrate under the Burlingame Treaty, and reversed the authority of California to regulate Chinese emigration. The issue of Chinese emigration and whether it should be limited began its slow boil in the Congress and the Grant Administration, which would eventually address "the Chinese Question." The country was on the road to the passage of the Chinese Exclusion Act of 1882.

Chapter 6

1874 – A Turning Tide

I call attention of Congress "to a generally conceded fact—that the great proportion of the Chinese immigrants who come to our shores do not come voluntarily, to make their homes with us and their labor productive of general prosperity, but come under contracts with headmen, who own them almost absolutely. In a worse form does this apply to Chinese women. Hardly a perceptible percentage of them perform any honorable labor, but they are brought for shameful purposes, to the disgrace of the communities where settled and to the great demoralization of the youth of those localities. If this evil practice can be legislated against, it will be my pleasure as well as duty to enforce any regulation to secure so desirable an end."
President Ulysses S. Grant, Annual Message to Congress, December 7, 1874

By the summer of 1874, the changing luck of the Chinese steerage passengers continued to be shaped by a number of forces. These included new technologies, a growing U.S. financial crisis in the wake of the "Panic of 1873", and growing fears of San Francisco natives and the State Government in Sacramento that caused a markedly less welcoming environment.

Figure 26: President Ulysses S. Grant, (1869-1877)

The Six Companies officially noted the anti-Chinese sentiment, and they would eventually petition President Ulysses S. Grant directly for his involvement and relief. However, within a one-year period from late 1873 through 1874, a perfect storm of political forces took hold in the United States that increased the political momentum leading to the first federal regulation against Chinese immigration.

All of the anti-immigration laws against the Chinese emigrants originated from the piers of the Pacific Mail Steamship Company. In December 1873, the Pacific Mail Steamship Company was under enormous political and oversight pressure, as it attempted to convince Congress to renew its one million dollar annual mail subsidy. The pressure led to charges (later proven true) that it bribed members of Congress to secure the subsidy.

The tense political environment was further exacerbated by the legislative efforts of Representative Horace F. Page of Placerville, El Dorado

County. In December 1873, Page had offered a bill to prohibit the importation of Chinese "coolies" (laborers) and Chinese women who were allegedly being used for immoral purposes. One year later on November 13, 1874, Representative Page met with President Grant on the issue, securing a commitment from the President to include the matter in his annual address to Congress.

The Chinese Six Companies of course had a different view. It was a source of great pride in 1874 that so many of the Guangdong Chinese emigrants had played such a major role in building America's trans-continental railroad. When the railroad had been completed in May 1869 (and the commerce began to flow east and north from California), the workers had made themselves available to fill new roles as farm workers 35 in California's Central Valley, helping to produce two-thirds of the vegetables grown and helping California to become the wheat capital of the United States.

The Chinese had done a good deal of work that the native California men would not do. Recall the inability of the Central Railroad to recruit American workers, despite several years of attempts at the beginning of the railroad construction phase. In addition, Chinese work crews had helped to clear the mucky, mosquito-infested Sacramento and San Joaquin River deltas and had been involved in building a network of irrigation canals critical to California's agricultural industry.

During the boom years, Chinatown had grown quite large. The city's growth had expanded in general because of its location along the bay and due to the considerable financial and business wealth being created by the banking, mining, shipping, trade and merchant industries. However, San Francisco's business and general economy were not immune from the bust years.

In particular, the city and regional economy was hit hard by the effects of what was originally considered a "Wall Street Affair" –the Panic of 1873. This was a financial panic caused by the overexpansion of the American economy during the Civil War, based on the issuance of a large quantity of paper currency that was not backed by gold or silver specie. The Grant Administration would attempt to correct this problem in the American economy by moving it away from inflationary "greenback" policies toward the traditional gold and silver-backed currency.

The effect of this tight money policy, however, caused job shortages, as the American economy tightened. In turn, this exacerbated an already racially charged climate in San Francisco. The native inhabitants consistently felt that they couldn't compete with the presence of cheap labor, characterized by writers such as Herbert Asbury, who in "*The Barbary Coast*" described the "poverty-stricken, meek and cheap 'coolie,'" now know by many as "John Chinaman." [36]

Although the Chinese had experienced acceptance, tolerance, and even a welcoming atmosphere on their arrival, considerable anti-Chinese feeling had developed. This was most strongly felt among American-born laborers and other members of California's lower social orders and it increased in intensity, leading to a movement to convince Congress to pass exclusion laws.[37] These passions came to a head at the "gigantic" anti-Chinese mass meeting on April 5, 1874. There, city and state officials, through their harangues, caused the attendees to adopt several resolutions that demanded the ejection of the Chinese from California and made charges against the Chinese as a race.

Copies of the resolutions and also of the speeches were sent to Congress and President Grant by a special committee. The accusations made by the anti-Chinese factions included:

- That not one virtuous Chinawoman had been brought to America, and that the Chinese living here had no wives and children.
- That the Chinese had purchased no real estate.
- That the Chinese ate rice, fish, and vegetables, and that otherwise their diet differed from that of white men.
- That the Chinese were of no benefit to the country
- That the Six Companies had secretly established judicial tribunals, jails, and prisons and secretly exercised judicial authority over the Chinese.
- That all Chinese laboring men were slaves
- That the Chinese brought no benefits to American bankers and importers.[38]

By the summer of 1874, the focus and the promise of a future life for the Chinese in San Francisco and Gold Mountain had changed. It felt like a good time to return home – later in the year, perhaps, after the growing season and harvest were in and the work was done in Chinatown.

Time was needed to work with the agents of the Six Companies to clear the debts owed to them and to provide them with a list of items that would need to be transported back to China. For some families, these items including the bones of those departed and recently deceased, whose remains had been preserved in Chinatown, embalmed in caskets, which were to be laid sent home to rest along the terraces of the Pearl River valley around Canton.

Many of the Chinese began by acquiring money belts for the voyage home. It was a protective device intended to secure the life savings of gold and silver a worker had earned in the United States. Cargo chests were also purchased to transport the savings and important items of value back to Guangdong. Some laborers had already left earlier in the year. Having been released from their labor obligations and cleared to leave San Francisco, they settled up with the Six Companies and got their tickets for passage home, making their voyage across on one of the older Pacific Mail Steamship side-wheelers that they had originally come across on.

These enormous, grand ships, the crowing glories of the age of the paddlewheel steamship – the *Great Republic*, the *China*, and the *Japan* – were still in service. However, technical advances had created demands for more efficient freight service. A change in Congressional support that meant a possible loss of the annual Congressional subsidy for the Pacific Mail. Suddenly, the future was uncertain future for the shipping community along the San Francisco waterfront.

As tensions ran high against the Chinese community, intensifying the desire of many to return home, a historic event occurred that would impact both the Chinese and the Pacific Mail Steamship line: the August 1874 *habeas corpus* trial of the so-called Chinese Maidens.

In addition to its business with the Six Companies, the Pacific Mail Steamship Company also had an important business relationship with the Chy Lung Company, recognized as one of San Francisco's most established and respected trading houses with its agents in Hong Kong, Shanghai, Yokohama, and San Francisco. The agency was named after Mr. Chy Lung, a native of Guangzhou (Canton), China, who came to San Francisco in 1850. Chy Lung in English meant "the beneficent dragon," and having a relationship with the Chy Lung Company was seen as good business in trade for the Pacific Mail Company. In fact, Mr. Sing Mun of the Chy Lung Company served as a passenger agent for the Pacific Mail Steamship Company and provided special treatment to the Chinese merchant passengers travelling on the line.

At the end of the summer of 1874, under the command of Captain John H. Freeman, the *Japan* had arrived back home to San Francisco on August 24 after a smooth 30-day voyage with 9 European passengers and 588 Chinese steerage passengers. Of those steerage passengers, eighty-nine were women ranging in age "from nine to ninety."

As with all China steamer arrivals at the Pacific Mail Steamship wharf, there had been significant excitement on the pier during "Steamer Day." The arrival of teas, silks, exotic cargo, family, and laborers for the Chinese community and the businesses of San Francisco were always highly anticipated as were the clandestine import of smuggled goods, including opium, and prostitutes.

The customs and immigrations officials were prepared and waiting inside the Pacific Mail's enclosed dock area. In the contingent of enforcement personnel assembled on the dock was the Commissioner of Immigration, Mr. E.B. Vreeland. As the Chinese women departed the *Japan*, and stepped off the brow into the enclosed area, Commissioner Vreeland arrested twenty-two of them on the grounds that "they were brought here for immoral purposes." The women were detained, then sent back onto the ship, and the *Japan*'s captain, John H. Freeman, was ordered by the Commissioner to not allow the women to leave the steamer. The women would have to remain aboard the *Japan* overnight.

The next morning, they were escorted from the ship to a North Beach jail.

The following week, the sensational front-page coverage for the *Daily Alta California* of the saucy court testimony that ensued not only titillated readers in San Francisco but quickly became news in New York, Washington, and Hong Kong. As described in the *Daily Alta*, the case combined elements of intrigue, sex, and issues of freedom and individual liberty. "A Chinaman named Ah Lung, who traffics in this kind of business, learned of their arrest, and immediately applied to the Supreme Court for a writ of habeas corpus, alleging that the women were illegally restrained of their liberty."39 After the writ was issued by the Judge Morrison in the Fourth Circuit court, a great crowd of "Celestials" appeared. The stage was now set for the weeklong drama that saw the women removed from the *Japan*, forced into a prison ambulance for transport to jail. They were all frightened by rumors of their pending execution and City Hall trial.

During his testimony, Captain Freeman stated that the women were first examined in Hong Kong before they received their tickets to board the *Japan*. Freeman explained the process: "They first go to the Consul's office and if that officer satisfies himself of their good character, he stamps their arms and sends them to the Harbor Master. This officer also examines them, and if the examination is satisfactory he also stamps their arms. They then procure their tickets and are allowed to go aboard the vessel."

The weeklong trial, with interpreters, produced some extraordinary personalities from the Chinese Maiden group including 22-year-old Quong Ling and 19-year-old Ah Bin, both from the Sum Yup District in China. Quong Ling testified that she had come to California when she was ten, had returned to China, and then returned to California when she was seventeen to get married "as she was engaged." Quong Ling lived with her mother on Jackson Street.

Ah Bin was a married woman. She was poor and came to meet her husband Ah Kee who had come to California earlier that year in February, 1874; his residence was on Jackson Street.

Ah Fook was another of the Chinese Maidens interviews. She was 20 years of age and married before she had come to California the first time, before returning to China. Ah Fook was described as "very obstinate and saucy." She insisted that she had returned to California with good intentions, yet she became more difficult when asked to answer questions. The courtroom drama splashed across the front page of the *Daily Alta*.

"At this point a woman jumped to her feet and let out an earthly yell. Immediately the whole lot were jabbering and screaming at the top of their voices, and it was found impossible to quiet them until they were hustled from the courtroom upstairs to the Grand Jury room."[40]

In Chinatown, the Jackson Street area in particular was known locally for the "immoral tendencies" exhibited by the women who lived there. During the trial, an American reverend with missionary experience in China testified that "there was a distinguishing mark about the courtesans in China by which they could be recognized. The distinguishing marks were the wearing of handkerchiefs around their heads and their garments embroidered with silk. They could be told very easily and could be distinguished as readily as the courtesans in this city can be from respectable women. From my observations I believe that at least one-half of those present belong to the class spoken of."[41]

The trial concluded after three sensational and highly personal days of testimony. The twenty-two Chinese Maidens were denied entry to this country, based on what was deemed to be "undeniable evidence of their immoral tendencies."[42]

On the morning of August 29th, with the *Japan* was due to depart for its subsequent voyage back to China, the judge remanded the Chinese Maidens to the custody of the captain of the *Japan*. After the decision was rendered, the women were conveyed to the Pacific Mail Steamship Company's wharf and put aboard the *Japan* and entrusted to its new captain, Edward R. Warsaw.

Chapter 7

Warsaw Returns to the Pacific Mail

"Captain E.R. Warsaw, who has been six years in command of a Pacific Mail Company's steamer between this port and China, after a year's rest on shore, has taken his old position in the line. Captain Warsaw will take charge of the steamer "China" on her arrival from Panama, and probably go to Yokohama and Hong Kong. The Captain has been going to sea for thirty-four years, boy and man, and twenty years a Captain. The company may be congratulated on the return to active work of one of their most competent officers."[43]
Daily Alta California-August 1874

Since bringing the first Chinese steerage passengers to San Francisco as first officer of the *Colorado* in 1868, Warsaw had been appointed as the captain of the steamer *China*. As such, he had completed over a dozen round-trip voyages to and from China.

In December 1869, he was recognized by General R.B. Valkenburg – the U.S. minister to Japan – and the passengers of the *China* for his ability as a seaman, urbanity as a gentleman, and kindness as a commander. He had been presented an engraved silver pitcher.

Figure 27: Pitcher presented to "Captain Warsaw, PM Ship China from his passengers on Christmas, 1869." Courtesy James Brewster, Great-great, great grandson of Captain Warsaw (1869)

He made history in November 1872, having been placed in command of the *Colorado,* when he'd transported travel pioneer Thomas Cook and a party of tourists in the sidewheel steamship across the Pacific as part of the company's inaugural "Tour Round the World" journey. An English-born promoter, Cook offered his grand tour at a cost of 200 guineas, for which Cook arranged travel in a steamship across the Atlantic, in a stagecoach across America, in the *Colorado* to Japan and concluding with an overland journey across China and India. The whole event lasted 222 days, and established Cook's reputation as the father of the tourist industry. It also inspired Jules Verne to craft his fanciful novel of a global race, *Around the World in 80 Days.*

Thomas Cook was one of those impressed by Warsaw's exemplary conduct. In two of his eighteen *"Letters from the Sea"*[44] from that historic cruise, Cook wrote about Captain Warsaw, noting his "humanity combined with stern discipline…inspecting every part of the ship with the keenest eye for dust or irregularity."

Upon Captain Warsaw's January 1873 return to San Francisco in the *Colorado,* diverse forces of change were converging that would alter the maritime landscape of San Francisco, its role in the China trade, and the Pacific Mail Steamship Company's future. Economically, the Pacific Mail Steamship Company was losing money. It was under increasing pressure to get cargoes of silk and tea to the eastern seaboard faster, and it was at risk of losing its annual subsidy from Congress. At the same time, the wooden-hull sidewheel steamer design used until the 1860s was being replaced as quickly as possible in the Pacific Mail's fleet by a newer design of iron-hulled, propeller-driven steamers, needed to compete with the PMSC's British steamship competitor, the Peninsula and Oriental (P&O) Line.

To cap it all off, the demand for Chinese labor had been significantly reduced after the completion of the trans-continental railroad. In the years that followed, the Pacific Mail's Chinese labor trade was inconsistent at best in delivering profits. Furthermore, the trade placed the company squarely in the middle of a growing political debate in California and across the country questioning the benefits of the immigration of the "heathen Chinese" to the United States.

With the concerns about the levels of Chinese immigration came pitfalls for business interests and ship captains alike. After his triumphant voyage transporting Cook's famous tour, Warsaw made less distinguished history in command of the *Colorado.* Entering the port of San Francisco on April 13, 1873, the *Colorado* returned with 1,258 Chinese steerage passengers. This was 430 more than was authorized under the "Excess in Passengers Act" of March 24, 1855. The act was being enforced more rigorously than it had in the years when Chinese laborers were welcomed with open arms. According to the *Daily Alta,* Warsaw was arrested by the U.S. Marshall and charged by the Inspector of the Customs House three weeks later on May 7, 1873. Warsaw was allowed to make one more round-trip transit on the *Colorado,* then returned to San Francisco on July 14, 1873, to stand trial.[45]

The preliminary trial before the U.S. District Court, "U.S. vs. E.R Warsaw," was tried on July 5, 1873. Warsaw was not alone. His colleague, Captain John H. Freeman was also charged for a similar violation of the Passenger Act; he had delivered 451 passengers, in excess of the maximum 828 by the art, in the *Japan*'s steerage area.

On September 8, 1873, the court found Warsaw guilty and ordered him to pay $30,458 dollars, a considerable sum. An appeal of his penalty to Judge Hoffman resulted in a judgment of carrying a "revised excess" and a reduction of his fine to $14,500[46] on November 5, 1873. Captain Freeman would also be fined, but returned to command the *Japan* for her next four voyages.

The Pacific Mail Steamship Company paid his fine. It wasn't the first time they had done this. Warsaw had also been arrested on May 2, 1873 and had a $21,000 bond posted by the Pacific Mail so he could command another voyage of the *Colorado.*

For the next year, Warsaw would take a leave of absence. Not one to sit on his hands, he spent the months in the mining business. A bonanza strike had occurred in 1873 on the Comstock Lode of Nevada, a site made famous by its vast quantities of silver and gold ore.

Warsaw was accepted onto the Board of Directors of the Humboldt Mining Company. This company operated a mine on the Gold Hill mining district near Virginia City, Nevada. On February 7, 1874, using his connections developed during his Pacific Mail contact with the president of the Bank of California, William C. Ralston, Warsaw was elected as a trustee of the Crown Point Extension Mine. Throughout the 1870s, Warsaw as a Pacific Mail captain had been entrusted by Ralston, through his banking and trade associates overseas, to deliver items ranging from Japanese figurines and rattan furniture for Ralston's personal residence and saloon.

Located on the lucrative Comstock Lode, the Crown Point mine was a significant venture for the Bank of California. In 1873, Congress passed a coinage act that officially made gold the U.S. monetary standard, switching away from a silver base. However, the act also created a "trade-dollar," a special silver dollar coin to be used in international trade. China was still on the silver standard, and the new trade dollar was intended for use for the Chinese trade. The 1873 Coinage Act authorized the minting of the new coin, and it would be the currency of commerce among bankers, merchants, and traders, and accordingly, a major part of cargo shipments in steamships plying between San Francisco and Hong Kong.

When the trade dollars arrived in Hong Kong via a Pacific Mail steamer and were delivered to the appropriate recipient, they often were stamped with "chop marks" – Chinese characters that a Guangdong merchant house or Hong trader would hammer onto the obverse (back side) of a silver U.S trade dollar. In this process, the coins typically were first weighed on a scale against a one-ounce (one "tael") piece of silver. Once the weight was determined to be equal to one tael, the merchant would affix (chop) their mark on the coin. This meant the coins were accepted, and the merchandise being bought would change hands to the agent for transfer to the Pacific Mail agent, to go into the cargo hold for the return shipment to California.

With the discovery of the Comstock silver, the establishment of a U.S. Mint in Carson City to convert the silver to specie, and the approval of the new trade dollar, the Bank of California moved in to exert considerable control over the Virginia City mining operations, buying up smaller banks and taking over mines and mills. The bank needed reliable men to oversee the diverse businesses they were acquiring, and they used their connections to recruit solid men like Captain Warsaw.

Warsaw's stint in mining and out of the steamer rotation was not a long one. In early August 1874, he was recertified and his assignment to what he understood to be the *China*. The "Chinese Maiden" legal action caused the Pacific Mail to get him back as the appearance of Captain Freeman as a witness was required. He would now be reassignment to the *Japan*. The Pacific Mail had their old China-line veteran back, as he returned to the familiar office and dock area where he had started in 1868, now ready to begin his second round of service with the line.

The Pacific Mail dock area was busy with cargo handlers when Warsaw arrived at the corner of First and Brannan Streets and passed through the gathered citizens of San Francisco, a large group of Chinese businessmen, and a gathering of officialdom. He had read the sensational headlines about the "Chinese Maidens" all week long since the *Japan*'s return that previous Monday. He looked forward to another week off but there was work to be done and the famous "Chinese Maidens" were now scheduled to return to China under his command.

Warsaw passed through the assembled throngs and walked up the *Japan*'s gangway, crossed the main deck, and then climbed the internal stairway, the shortest route to the captain's cabin and pilothouse. He needed to get underway at noon on the tide and made his plans against the backdrop of wailing Chinese women and the unsavory crowd.

Outside the pilothouse, the final coal cars rolled toward the pier bunker to deliver the last of the 1,500 tons of coal that the *Japan* would need to complete her trans-Pacific voyage of 7,000 miles to Japan and China.

About an hour before the ship's departure, the San Francisco coroner, accompanied by the counsel for the women, arrived and served a new writ, issued by Chief Justice Wallace of the California Supreme Court, upon Captain Warsaw, directing the sheriff to take the women from the custody of whoever had them in charge. Captain Warsaw "was only too glad to get rid of his unwelcome passengers, and they were rushed ashore as quick as possible. The women were then conveyed to the County Jail, where they will await the action of the Supreme Court."[47]

The plight of the Chinese maidens remained front-page news and would end up as the landmark Supreme Court case on the federal authority on immigration matters and Chinese immigrants (Ah Fook (Chy Lung vs. Freeman et al.)[48]

The November 1874 voyage of the *Japan*, that imposing vessel Samuel Clemens had once called a "Perfect Palace of a Ship," was about to turn out to be even more shocking.

Chapter 8

The Final Voyage – Preparations

The Pacific Mail Steamship Company's steamer "Japan"
4351 33-100 tons, E.R. Warsaw, Commander, left San
Francisco on Saturday, November 14, 1874 at noon, with 24
Cabin passengers, 6 European steerage, 8 Japanese, 422
Chinese, 975 tons of cargo, 168 boxes treasure value
$368,608, and 21 packages mail
From "The Japan" Daily Alta California signed by
Captain Warsaw

The mid-November weather in San Francisco in the year 1874 was inviting for the returning Chinese steerage passengers. But the pull of home after what for many of them had been four to six years of labor was much stronger. Down at the Pacific Mail docks, the cargo loaders and crew of the *Japan* had been getting the ship ready to steam westward again. She had been in port for three weeks since her October 21 return from Yokohama. Each steerage passenger on the outbound voyage ahead had met at the Six Company offices to clear his debts. Each had gather his belongings, and, as many were returning with a good deal of wealth, at least for a laborer, had taken special pains to buy a money belt, a place to carry his $20 dollar gold pieces and silver coins with security.

Figure 28: Pacific Mail Steamship Company steamer "Japan" at the foot of Brannan Street with coal chute and brow extended (Circa 1873)

The San Francisco departure ritual for returning Chinese workers had been described in the *Overland Monthly* in an October 1868 article entitled "The Six Chinese Companies."

"A person proposing to return to China has been required, a certain number of days previous to sailing, to report his name to the company to which he belongs, whereupon the books are searched to see whether all dues are paid: also to see whether a person bearing his name has been reported to the company as indebted to other parties. Once satisfactory arrangements have been made with the creditors, he can leave the country."[49]

Once their debts were cleared, the Six Company office issued them a check or ticket to use toward their purchase of the Pacific Mail steamship company ticket. The check was the final hurdle needed to leave Chinatown and return home. The Pacific Mail refused to sell a ticket for steerage passage without it.

Since their arrival in 1868, steerage passengers with names like Ah Sin or Ah Wan had become John Chinaman. In 1874, once they returned home, they would again be known only as Ah Sin or Ah Wan, but to a more prosperous Ah Sin or Ah Wan. They would also leave behind the merchants –

men known in the Chinese community as Hop Sing, Fat Wau, Bing Yon, Ah Ching, Lee Yon, Ah Quing, Chiang Wong Kee and Ah Sing - to prosper.

Were they making the right decision to return home? Would they –or any other new arrivals prosper?

The *Japan* was moored on the south side of Pacific Mail dock at the First and Brennan pier area to begin loading its coal, cargo, and steerage passengers.

On the day before its Saturday departure, Captain Warsaw walked down First Street and through the entryway portico adorned with "PMSS Co: New York and Panama", through the covered wharf and onto the pier adjacent to the *Japan*. He passed by his old ship, the *China*, which had arrived from her voyage from Yokohama the week before.

Captain Warsaw would now prepare for the *Japan's* 25th voyage and second crossing of the Pacific since his return to the Pacific Mail. He knew the challenges in taking these ships across the northern Pacific and the China Sea as the winter approached and the northeast monsoons prevailed.

Boarding the ship via the forward gangway, he proceeded up through the main deck forward steerage area up the stairway to the upper deck emerging on the starboard side hurricane deck to enter his captain's quarters behind the pilot house.

Captain Warsaw's quarters were handsome and well-appointed with walnut woodwork. He had a bed and an exit door onto the starboard deck and a door forward that allowed him to enter the pilot house to be with the watch officers and quartermasters. Behind his cabin were the quarters for First Officer F.W. Hart, Second Officer H.H. Andrews, and Third Officer J.P. Gallagher.

Always a meticulous planner, Captain Warsaw called together his three officers in the pilot house to discuss the upcoming voyage. He was well aware of the dangers of transiting the northern Pacific in the near-winter and the South China Sea during the northeast monsoon season. As captain, his responsibilities included ensuring that the cargo was secured and that fire-fighting and life-saving boats and equipment were in working order.

The weather news provided from the return voyage of the *Great Republic* and *China* in the previous week from Yokohama and Hong Kong confirmed his instinct and sense of the need for preparation. The 34-day voyage would occur in two parts. First the 26-day journey from San Francisco to Yokohama with a two-day stopover at anchor there for passenger and cargo transfer and for new coal. Then underway from Yokohama for the six day run through the South China Sea to Hong Kong.

The log from the *Japan's* 22nd voyage in May 1874, by Captain Freeman reported that the ship was using up to 55 tons of coal a day for her trans-Pacific runs, was heavier and needed a new copper bottom in order to improve her fuel and coal usage efficiency. On this final winter voyage, the *Japan's* boilers were expected to consume more coal per day – 55 tons a day instead of 45 tons. Her coal bunkers, located amidships on the orlop deck on either side of the engine room, needed to be fully loaded to the design maximum of 1,500 tons. This quantity would be sufficient for a safe passage from San Francisco to Yokohama, but with the increased usage, an increased amount of coal in Yokohama would be required.

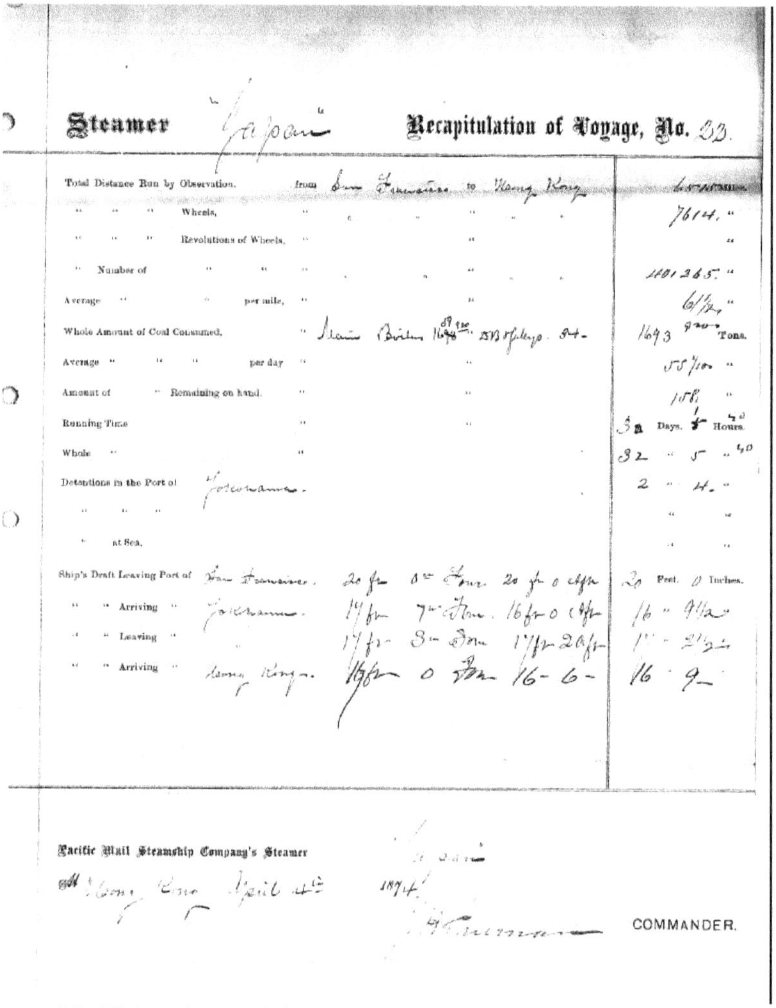
Steamer Japan — Recapitulation of Voyage, No. 23.

Total Distance Run by Observation, from San Francisco to Hong Kong		Miles.
" " " Wheels,		7614 "
" " " Revolutions of Wheels,		"
" Number of " "		1101265 "
Average " " per mile,		6½ "
Whole Amount of Coal Consumed,	Main Boiler 1693 ...	1693 Tons.
Average " " " per day		55 "
Amount of " Remaining on hand,		158 "
Running Time		32 Days. 5 Hours. 40
Whole "		32 " 5 " 40
Detentions in the Port of Yokohama		2 " 4 "
" " "		" "
" at Sea,		" "
Ship's Draft Leaving Port of San Francisco	20 ft 0 in Fore, 20 ft 0 Aft	20 Feet. 0 Inches.
" " Arriving " Yokohama	14 ft 7 in Fore, 16 ft 0 Aft	16 " 9½
" " Leaving "	17 ft 3 in Fore, 17 ft 2 Aft	17 " 2½
" " Arriving " Hong Kong	16 ft 0 Fore, 16-6	16 " 9

Pacific Mail Steamship Company's Steamer Japan
at Hong Kong April 4th 1874
COMMANDER.

Figure 29: This sole surviving log of the Japan from a May 1874 voyage, Captain John H. Freeman, Commanding
Courtesy, San Francisco Public Library

There was little margin for error, therefore, for this voyage. The coal would be loaded in a forward and lower hold and the engineers below would have to put their backs into it on the orlop deck to manage the distribution of the coal below decks.

A full cargo of valuable California flour in barrels and bags would also be stowed adjacent to the forward coal bunkers. There were also two bulkheads on *Japan* that separated the coal from the cargo and from the engine and firerooms.

Kathryn Hulme in her book on her grandfather, Warsaw's Pacific Mail colleague Captain John Cavarly, wrote in *Annie's Captain* that "on every crossing, Captain's wrote something about the coal. It was like a special passenger to him, a black temperamental presence aboard, liable at any time to flame in spontaneous combustion, given often to brooding heats which required frequent shoveling over to keep it dry."[50]

The weather on the Pacific and the South China Sea would be very rough this transit. Captain Warsaw was aware of the treachery of the winter weather in both of these areas of water that he was being called upon to safely sail almost 800 passengers through to their destinations. He had been in these conditions before and was now the Pacific Mail Steamship company's senior captain and Master mariner.

Captain Warsaw left the *Japan* for the evening. She would depart the next day at noon with 537 souls on board including 128 crew, two cabin passengers, two white passengers, and 423 Chinese steerage passengers.

"They came here because they have good wages, and after serving two or three years, they gain a competence, and away they go. In the autumn a great many go home, so as to be there during the Chinese New Year, and have a great blowout." [51]

The *Japan*'s most distinguished passenger on this voyage would be Dr. Robert M. Tindall, a Mississippian nominated by President U.S. Grant to serve as U.S. Consul in Canton, China. Tindall was slated to relieve a fellow Mississippian, Judge R.G.W. Jewell in the post. He was heading to Canton to help further U.S.-China trade, improve revenue accountability for the Treasury department, and to understand Chinese immigration to America from the surrounding six counties of Guangdong Province.

Tindall was a 1858 graduate of the Memphis School of medicine, a Mississippi State representative in Jackson in 1862 and 1865, an Assistant Surgeon in the Provincial Confederate Army and a member of the U.S. Military Academy Board of Visitors in 1866. President Andrew Johnson nominated him in 1868 to be Assessor of Internal Revenue in Okolona, Mississippi where he also served as a Mississippi delegate to the Republican conventions in 1868, 1872, and 1876. He was recommended by the entire

Republican delegation for Consulate in Canton and confirmed by the Senate in late 1873.

Dr. Tindall would likely have been highly interested in the *Japan*'s Chinese steerage returnees and their lives in America and in particular the motivating factors that had brought them from their homes in the surrounding areas of Guangdong province. He undoubtedly was aware of Congressman Horace Page's November 13th meeting with President Grant and his opposition to the coolie trade and the importation of women for alleged immoral purposes. It had been on the front page of the *Daily Alta California* newspaper that morning.

As an Internal Revenue assessor in post-Civil War America when President Grant put in place a tight money policy that switched the country from silver to the gold standard, while introducing the silver trade dollar, Tindall was also aware that *Japan* had on board a full load of the new trade dollars. The shiny new dollars were in their second year of production and had become more acceptable to the textile, tea, and silk traders in Southern China and the Guangdong Province. He looked forward to being installed in Canton as Consul and becoming an important source of policy intelligence that would help address the "China Question" for the President.

Dr. Tindall was making the crossing in his own cabin - a four-foot-wide living space conveniently located to the upper deck adjacent to the Purser's office, Surgeon's Office, Social Hall, and Dining Saloon. He would be able to observe the returning Chinese steerage passengers first hand throughout the voyage, and would be assisted in his stateroom by one of the *Japan*'s renowned "Celestial" servants.

Francis Thurber in *Coffee: Plantation to Cup* described her experience when boarding a Pacific Mail steamer preparing for a trans-Pacific journey to China. "One of the first things that strike a passenger on the ships of the Pacific Mail Steamship Company is the omnipresent Chinaman – Chinese waiters, Chinese cooks, Chinese firemen, Chinese sailors and Chinese steerage passengers are everywhere to be seen. Indeed the only white men on board the ship are the officers and cabin passengers."[52]

A cabin description from a voyage on *Japan*'s sister-ship *Great Republic* by J.F Campbell in a piece entitled *My Circular Notes* provides a sense of what Dr. Tindall's cabin probably felt like. "My cabin is a little room with a two-foot square window opening on the deck and looking over the south sea. I awake to look at the long-winged birds who have followed every Saturday, and are back to follow us to Japan."[53]

Dr. Tindall would also need to know a little "Pidgin" English to communicate with his Chinese servant. An observation recorded by the New

York Times on an August 1874 trans-Pacific voyage of the Pacific Mail steamship *Colima* captured a passenger-Chinese servant exchange. "As servants they are much preferable to any other. A traveler needs to pick up a little 'Pidgin English' to make himself understood. For instance he would say to the waiter, 'Ah, Chung, catcher me plate licce chop, chop' which means 'bring a plate of rice quickly.' This pidgin English so-called is the regular medium of communication between foreigners in China and the natives... 'Pidgin' (not pigeon) is the Chinese pronunciation of 'business' and so the name has been given to the patois used in transacting business, and is ordinary household affairs." [54]

Before the *Japan's* departure, Mr. Tindall completed a quick letter for the mails to Secretary of State Hamilton Fish.

San Francisco Cal Nov 14 1874
Hon Hamilton Fish
Secry of State Washington, D.C.

Sir:

I have the honor to inform you that I will set sail this day for Canton, China on the PMSS. Cos Steamer "Japan" direct for Hong Kong. On my arrival there I shall proceed to my post of duty without delay, and will notify the Department of my arrival.

I have the honor to be
Very respectfully,
Your Obt Servt
R.M. Tindall,
U.S. Consul to Canton, China

The *Japan*'s crew and shore stevedores loaded a cargo of over 970 tons of freight, consisting of thousands of quarter sacks and barrels of California flour, tons of borax, sacks of beans, boxes of tinned abalone, and barrels of beef and pork.

Hundreds of packages were loaded. It seemed that half the population of Chinatown was involved in loading the ship's cargo and steerage passenger packages, which were stowed in the 'tween decks near the area of the Chinese steerage passenger accommodations. From an earlier voyage involving the *Japan*'s sister ship, the *America*, Harold Williams in his essay *The Burning of the America* observed that:

87

"It was said that somewhere in those packages was a king's ransom in the form of silver dollars and $20 dollar gold pieces representing the savings of a lifetime that some of the Chinese were taking back to China on which to retire...many who had been working in the California Gold fields were carrying nuggets of gold too. Nobody but the owners knew what was in each package." [55]

The food service would be exceptional, and would include a glorious bounty of fresh vegetables from the California valley, still being harvested after a golden Indian summer. Lettuce, rice, tomatoes, turnips, and nuts would also be available. Livestock berthed in the *Japan*'s two large cattle pens would provide the saloon passengers and officers and crew freshly dressed beef "on the hoof" and chicken for the entire voyage.

On the morning of the ship's departure, the crew and the Purser loaded 168 boxes of trade dollars' worth $368,000 in an iron treasure tank that was located in the forward hold of the *Japan*. According to Captain John P. Roberts, writing in 1876, "The tank was about twenty-eight feet long, five feet deep, wide at one end and pointed at the other, and very much the shape of a flatiron." The key to the treasure tank would be securely stored in the combination safe under the watchful eye of the purser. The source of the specie was the Bank of California, various Chinese merchants, and representatives from the Six Companies who were shipping the coinage to be used in their expanding business interests in Hong Kong, Shanghai, and Guangdong Province.

Based on similar shipments recorded on other ship voyages to Hong Kong, approximately 60% of the trade-dollar or bullion treasure were likely owned by U.S. and English bankers, specie being sent to their agents in China for purchases made or to be made. Chinese merchants owned about 30% of the treasure cargo; they also used the trade dollars and bullion for commercial exchange to pay for tea, rice, and imports. The savings of the Chinese steerage passengers represented the final 10%. According to the records of a voyage of a sister ship, *Colima*, this represented about $300–$400 per person being shipped as part of the treasure cargo. [56]

The active commerce was good news for the new U.S. silver trade dollar coin as it entered competition with the silver Mexican dollar for trade in China. The American trade dollar coin, minted primarily at the Carson City and San Francisco mints, had become more popular in late 1874, its first anniversary of use in China's treaty ports, and the coin was in greater demand from the San Francisco banks and Chinese traders who were beginning to take a competitive position in Canton, Hong Kong, and the coastal treaty ports of Foochow and Swatow. The *Japan*'s December delivery of trade dollars would help ensure that the banks and tea hongs would have enough silver on hand for the January and February tea trade, when the best teas were harvested and packed into containers and cargo boxes for the return trip to San Francisco. The 168 boxes of trade dollars was consistent in value when compared to other recent voyages and was necessary for the burgeoning tea, silk and textile trade that the *Japan* would help facilitate for the Pacific Mail Company and the railroads.

Protection of the treasure from the South China Sea pirates and from pierside robbery was also part of the planning. The *Japan*'s armory consisted of small arms, cutlasses, and the deck mounted howitzers available for protection.

A number of coffins, containing with the embalmed remains of the Chinese being returned to their ancestral homes, also had to be loaded. They were stowed in the lower hold. For most of the morning before a Pacific Mail steamer's departure, the coffins were placed forlornly alongside the ship waiting to be loaded and stowed away. The coffins were usually the last items to be loaded after other cargo had been loaded, so they could be stowed on top in the holds where they would not be crushed. When the time came, the coffins were hauled up in slings and stowed on top of the cargo in the mouth of the hatch.

The carrying of the coffins back to China represented a lucrative trade and provided useful employment to the Six Companies. A Sam Yup Company bone-shipper made $720 annually, an assistant bone-shipper $480. A *Scribner's Magazine* article on the embalming process, in the article "John Chinaman in San Francisco," described the different services offered for the wealthy or ordinary preparation of bodies and bones.

> "If the late lamented was wealthy, he is embalmed and taken to China by the next steamer, being technically known as a green body. If John when alive enjoyed but an ordinary amount of this world's blessing he is buried in a very moderate state and his bones are left under the sod and the dew until they (literally) are bare, when they are gathered into bundles and sent home to their sorrowing relatives. The bones of as many as six adults are frequently tied up in a compact little package that a boy could carry down to the steamer."[57]

The expected navigation track for the voyage was approved, per the directions of the Pacific Mail agent in San Francisco. The *Japan* would clear the Golden Gate and leave the Farallon Islands to starboard and then proceed southwesterly from the 37-degree north latitude line to the 30-degree north latitude line. Once on the 30th parallel, the ship would then proceed westerly from there, navigating by sun line and by Polaris, the North Star.

Crossing the Pacific along the 30-degree latitude line in the days before electronic navigation by Loran, Omega, and GPS would allow the *Japan* to cross the Pacific below the more significant weather patterns along the great circle route through the higher latitudes and also allow the meeting of other vessels of the Pacific Mail along the route.

There would also be routine preparations for an emergency at sea. The *Japan* would be conducting a fire drill on the afternoon after departure and throughout the voyage. Her 13 lifeboats, with a capacity of 150 passengers each, were readied with a chart, compass, and provisions for 12 days.

Before getting underway the sails, the ventilation systems for the passengers and crew and the ship's steam whistle were tested. Chief Engineer, John Hargrove, was responsible for providing Captain Warsaw with a report of readiness after the onloading of the coal, and testing of the firefighting gear (which would provide 24 streams of steam pump-driven pump water within minutes of a fire).

The concerns about a fire on sidewheel steamers were very acute in the aftermath of the loss of *Japan*'s sister-ship *America* in August 1872 by fire in Yokohama harbor. Since that tragedy, the Pacific Mail Company had placed extra emphasis on fire prevention by posting new procedures that demanded an emphasis on safety and required each Pacific mail vessel to conduct drills. Ever diligent, Captain Warsaw would ensure that the drills were conducted on this voyage.

The ship's routine would include washing the decks every morning, polishing the brass, establishing the food service routine for the first-class passengers and steerage passengers, and conducting the daily shipwide inspection for cleanliness and fire hazards.

Two women would also board as passengers for the *Japan*'s voyage. Miss Mary Stott was a saloon-cabin passenger, heading to Hong Kong to become a school teacher. Miss Stott was likely berthed in the third-deck ladies saloon, located in one of the designated staterooms, aft of the *Japan*'s paddlewheels.

Miss Nelly Noble was part of ship's company and would be Mary Stott's voyage stewardess. She also served as the ship's barber in the *Japan*'s barbershop, which was located on the port side, forward of the sidewheel on the main deck.

There was no mention of Chinese women returnees on this final voyage. If aboard, they would have been berthed on the third deck women's steerage, forward of the paddlewheels.

"Commences with clear weather. Received on board two Europeans and made them comfortable. Carpenters gang employed caulking ports. Getting ship ready for sea. Examined cargo and side lights. Found them tight and well secured. Coal on board, 1400 tins. At 12:05 cast off from the Company's dock as San Francisco and proceeded to sea. Passengers berthed, messed and made comfortable. Crew variously employed."
–**San Francisco log entry for the pre-departure period, from PMSS *America* Log, 1869**

The November 14 San Francisco weather for the *Japan*'s departure was delightful. It was finally time to get back to sea. Warsaw walked through the gates of the Pacific Mail Company and checked in at the agents' office to get a sense of the cargo and paid and steerage passenger numbers.

All told, 973 tons of freight, including the Chinese steerage-passenger packages and coffins, $375,000 in treasure consisting of new trade dollars and bullion, and 424 Chinese passengers (with some amount of their accumulated wealth carried on with their personal effects) were aboard as he walked down the pier. Captain Warsaw received confirmation from the purser that he had placed the treasure-tank keys in the purser's safe with a smaller quantity of bank drafts, bullion, and coins.

The passengers embarking the *Japan* for this voyage were subject to some important regulations:

"Pacific Mail Steamship Company Cabin regulations:
1. All lights will be extinguished by 11PM. None will be allowed after that hour, except in the case of sickness, when permission must be obtained from the Captain or Surgeon.
2. No smoking allowed in Cabins or Saloons.
3. No dogs, animals, or birds of any kind will be allowed in the cabins or state rooms. All such must be shipped as freight and will be charged accordingly.
4. Gambling is strictly prohibited, and no card playing will be allowed after 11 o'clock PM.
5. Meal tickets will be issued to each passenger soon after leaving the wharf or anchorage, and each one is required to occupy the seat called for by the ticket.
6. Passengers wishing wines or ice with their meals will please order them before the bell rings, as the servants will not be

allowed to leave the table until all are served. Particular attention is required to this rule.

7. Passengers are not allowed in the paddle boxes or outside the rails on the promenade deck and are requested not to converse with the officer of the deck.

8. No firing of guns or pistols from any part of the ship without permission.

9. In event of accident, passengers are assured that every exertion will be made by the Captain and officers of the ship to protect life and property and that any unnecessary excitement or confusion among themselves will only serve to increase the danger.

10. Books from the library may be obtained upon application to the Purser.

11. Any inspections of the cabins and staterooms by the officers of the ship will take place at 11 o'clock AM.

12. No interference with the officers or crew in the performance of their duty will be tolerated. But passengers are requested to hold themselves in readiness to render any assistance.

–From Lucius A. Waterman *Journal*, Library of Congress (1869)[58]

Crowds gathered at the Pacific Mail wharf for the send-off. The officers and crew of the *Japan* was "manned and ready" to sail with the following official manifest of ship's officers, PMSS employees, and passengers:

Captain: E.R. Warsaw
First Officer: F.W. Hart
Second Officer: H.H. Andrews
Third Officer: J.P. Gallagher
Chief Engineer: John Cosgrove
Purser: John Rooney
Surgeon: V.B. Gates, MD
Freight Clerk: C.C. Gorham
Storekeeper: W.B. Horn
Steward: O.N. Clark
Second Steward: William Ray
First Assistant Engineer: W. Bennett
Second Assistant Engineer: James Hoery

Quartermaster Harris
Quartermaster Sutton
Cook: Martin Gassick
Passengers
F.W. Crocker
R.M. Tindell
Mary Stott
424 Chinese passengers

The Pacific Mail agent was happy. The Chinese steerage passengers had paid $50 per head and Dr. Tindall and Mary Stott had paid $250 apiece. The seven bags and 21 packages of mail would garner an additional $2,000, and cargo carried would bring a total payment of approximately $27,000 for the voyage.

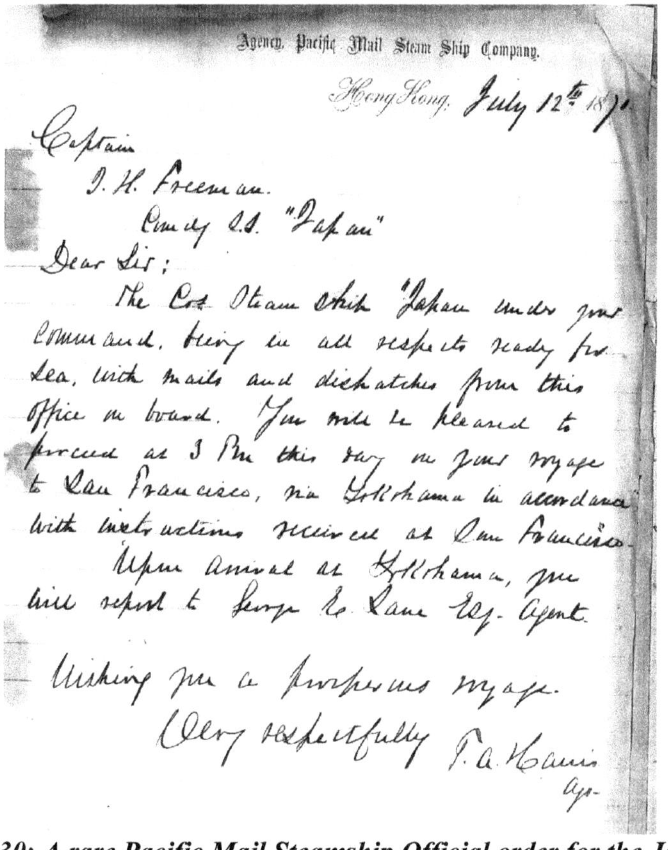

Agency. Pacific Mail Steam Ship Company.

Hong Kong. July 12th 1871

Captain
J. H. Freeman.
Comdg S.S. "Japan"

Dear Sir;

The Co's Steam Ship "Japan" under your command, being in all respects ready for sea, with mails and dispatches from this Office on board. You will be pleased to proceed at 3 PM this day on your voyage to San Francisco, via Yokohama in accordance with instructions received at San Francisco.

Upon arrival at Yokohama, you will report to George E. Lane Esq. Agent.

Wishing you a prosperous voyage.

Very respectfully
T. A. Harris
Agt.

Figure 30: A rare Pacific Mail Steamship Official order for the Japan to proceed to sea (1871). Courtesy San Francisco Public Library

Captain Warsaw stood atop the paddle-box and waved his hand to signal for the quarter line to be dropped. Many of the Chinese steerage passengers were up on deck scattering pieces of paper on the waters of San Francisco Bay as an offering to their Joss God of the Sea, a ceremony described by James Brooks in *A Seven Months' Run* that was intended "to bribe him [the sea-god] to give us a prosperous voyage."[59]

At noon on Saturday, November 14th, the bow line of the *Japan* was let go and the ship's head maneuvered into the stream of San Francisco Bay. The walking beam began to sway up and down and the red paddlewheels pulled through the waters of the bay. The *Japan* fired three guns, as customary to announce her departure, which was answered by four guns from the wharf. Heading though the bay, the ship was "fare welled" by the assembled vessels as she stood out for the Golden Gate and passed Fort Point. By 1:00 P.M., the *Japan* passed through the entrance of the Golden Gate Straits. Against the clear November sky, the passengers looking back could spy the tall black cross in the cemetery on "Lone Mountain."

Captain Warsaw directed the watch officer to come to a southwesterly heading to leave the Farallon islands on the *Japan*'s right hand, then follow a southwesterly course for about 23 miles from the California coast, coming due west into the sun. The distant barking of the sea lions of the Cliff House was concealed by the sounds of water passing down along the side of the *Japan* and the rhythm of the her sidewheels against the sea.

Looking out of the pilot-house window, Warsaw could just make out the craggy outline of the Farallon Islands to the southwest. Glancing at the charts, he then stepped out on the port side bridge wing, glanced aft and said farewell to the "Handle."

Chapter 9

The Final Voyage – Crossing the Pacific

The shortest route to Yokohama from San Francisco was known as the Great Circle Route. However, to avoid the rougher waters of the North Pacific approaching December, the steamships took a more direct course from port-to-port. In making the westward trips, the *Japan* would run about two degrees south of the eastbound Pacific Mail steamers going east, making 9 knots and about 200 miles per day (250 on an exceptional day.)

The Chinese crew – waiters, cooks, firemen, and sailors – as well as the more than 400 Chinese steerage passengers provided Captain Warsaw with the feel of China, and he liked that. He regarded the Chinese as dependable and professional. J.F. Campbell in *My Cultural Notes* observed this directly during a subsequent Pacific Mail voyage. "They are steady, quiet, cleanly people active and busy, and all the officers are loud in their praises. They never get drunk or give trouble, and they never shirk work."[60]

> *"At 4 exercised ship's company at Fire Quarters, playing six streams and our hand pump. Hose and pumps in good order. Crew employed by hoisting coal out of fore hold. Crew employed by hoisting coal out of lower hold."*
> **Representative voyage entry from the PMSS *America* Log, 1869**

As part of the precautions taken after *Japan's* sister-ship, *America*, had been lost by a coal fire at Yokohama in August 1872, notices had been put up in every Pacific Mail steamer stateroom forbidding smoking in the cabins or in the staterooms.

The company fire rules were very specific, as described in a front-page *New York Times* article on September 4, 1872 after the loss by fire of the *America*.

"In prominent parts of the ship, a fire bill is posted which reads in substance as follows: Fire alarm signal - continued ringing of the large ship's bell. The officer in charge will, when fire is discovered, stop the ship, lower all wind-sails, and turn the ventilators from the wind. The first officer, with the port watch, will immediately report to the place of fire. The second officer, with the starboard watch, in charge of a quartermaster, will repair to the promenade decks and take charge of the boats. The third officer will take his station in the pilot house. The cadet officer will join the second officer, and the boatswain will join the chief officer; also the carpenter. The quartermaster on watch will remain in the pilot house.

The quartermasters off watch will act as messengers to the Captain. The purser, surgeon, and baggage handler are detailed to mingle amongst the passengers to ally excitement and prevent confusion. The freight clerk and storekeeper will remove all inflammable materials in their charge from the vicinity of the fire, and prepare to throw the same overboard when ordered to do so.

The chief engineer's station is in the engine room, with the assistant engineer on watch remaining with his men at their duties as under ordinary circumstances; the senior engineer off watch with his men at the steam pumps; the junior engineer off watch with his men at the forward steam pumps; the chief steward in charge of the saloon department, with one half of his men on each after guard; the porters and butchers to repair to the dispatch house with the axes from the hurricane deck, and there receive their orders; the steerage steward with his men, to remain in the steerage, the saloon watchmen to close at once all the port and deck lights; those in the steerage do the same.

The saloon cooks with their assistant's man their buckets on the starboard side, and the steerage cooks on the port side. The deck boys on the force pumps on the after guards. The deck storekeeper is in charge of the storeroom and the magazine. The senior porter is stationed at the ax rack on the hurricane deck. The barber and the captain's servants are assistant messengers.

As soon as all hands are stationed, the heads of departments report to the Captain at the pilot house. Officers of each department must arm themselves that they may be prepared for any emergency. Immediately upon the alarm of fire, the hose in each department must be stretched out. The stop valves to be opened only by the first officer. Passengers are particularly requested to remain as quiet as possible in order that these regulations may be strictly carried out and the cause of alarm be removed as quickly as possible." [61]

The ship's bell tolled, signaling the fire drill, and the steam whistle commenced a long blast. Responding to the bell and whistle, members of *Japan*'s Chinaman crew got out the hoses and started the pump, and within four minutes the hoses were unfolded and run aft outside the stern. Soon, six streams of water generated by the *Japan*'s engineroom steam pumps were providing streams of water over the side.

Meanwhile greasy-faced Chinese, African-American, and Anglo cooks, along with gangs of sailors and officers, swarmed all over the ship. The engineers opened valves, the stewards hoisted extinguishers on their backs, and in a few minutes a whole gang was spouting sea-water back into the sea over the starboard bow.

The crew also performed a boat drill in order to perfect the management of the boats and their lowering to the water's edge. This drill sequence was initiated by the watch officers using the steam-whistle blast from the pilot house. The hoses and extinguishers were carried off and all hands on board went to the lifeboats. In a little over ten minutes, all thirteen of the 50-person capacity life boats were off of their "chucks" and slung by the davits ready for lowering with the crews seated and oars tossed and provisions on board. With the sound of another steam whistle blast, the boat drill secured all the boats for sea. The fire drill concluded, the *Japan* prepared for her first night at sea and everyone on board prepared for dinner.

On another day, the life raft – a large India-rubber float – was got out, put in perfect order, and made ready for launch.

The *Japan*, like her sister ships, served excellent food that was fresh and of wide variety. Benjamin Robbins Curtis writing in *Dottings Round the Circle* described his food service experience. "On board all the boats of the P.M.S.S co. it is the custom to carry live cattle and poultry, which are killed when needed; and the consequence is that the most varied chorus comes from 'between decks' at all hours of the day and night, - the lowing of cows mingling with the bleating of sheep, the quacking of ducks, and the cackling of hens."[62]

A black saloon steward led the efforts of *Japan's* more than 30 Chinese waiters to prepare the saloon for the meal. Baron von Huber writing in his *Rambling Around the World* noted that:

"although short, they look well enough with their black caps, their equally black pig-tails, which go down to their heels, their dark blue tunics, their large wide trousers, their gaiters or white stockings, and their black felt shoes with strong white soles. They form themselves into symmetrical groups, and do everything with method. Fancy a huge cabin with twenty-two guests, with all these little Chinamen fluttering round them and serving them in the most respectful fashion, without making any noise." [63]

Figure 31: The dining saloon of the steam America-sister ship of the Japan Courtesy Mariners Museum, Hampton Roads, VA.

For the night steam, all open lights in any part of the ship were required to be extinguished. The saloon lights were extinguished at 10:30 in the evening, the stateroom's by 11:00 P.M.

Each morning during the transit, European and English passengers would bathe in the paddle box. The decks were washed and brass polished, as the ship was brought to a state of shining neatness by the Chinese crew. Passengers also enjoyed an uninterrupted promenade, seven hundred feet in circuit, on the upper deck. The gentlemen amused themselves with gymnastic games; the ladies with music and books.

The *Japan* was now one day out beyond the Farallons and steering westward along the 30th parallel. As with the 24 voyages before her heading west, the routine aboard the ship was a critically important thing to establish for the crew and the passengers. The striking of the bell every half hour kept the time on board - eight bells struck at 4, 8, and 12 o'clock each day.

Figure 32: Representative Pacific Mail Officers in uniform

First Officer Hart, on duty at all hours, stood no regular watch. Second Officer H.H. Andrews and Third Officer J.P. Gallagher rotated the watches in increments of four or six hours at a time (known affectionately as the "port and starboard watch.")

Quartermasters Harris, Sutton, William Blanchard, and Edward Murdoch served as helmsmen. They had no radar and had to rely on dead-reckoning along the navigational track. Noon sun lines, taken by Captain Warsaw and First Officer Hart, ensured that the *Japan* stayed on the 30th parallel and made progress by longitude along the Plan of Intended Movement (PIM.) After determining *Japan*'s latitude and longitude, Captain Warsaw and First Officer Hart placed the result, with the number of miles travelled in the previous 24 hours, on a bulletin board for the passengers.

Looking out at the clear night skies to the north, the North Star also provided an assuring reminder when sighted with the ship's sextant at its 30 degrees of altitude above the horizon that the *Japan* was indeed along the proper latitude.

The ship's routine also governed the meal hours aboard the ship. The food for the Pacific Mail Steamship voyages was described as luxurious by many of the passengers. Salmon and other foods were kept fresh on ice for the greater part of the voyages. Strawberries were also served fresh during the first few days.

Thomas Woodbine Hinchcliff in *Over the Sea and Far Away* on a similar Pacific Mail voyage stated that:

"The Chinese waiters were admirable drilled, and did their spiriting gently; there is a kind of delicacy and lightness in these China boys which make them go about their work more in the manner of a 'neat-handed Phyllis' than in that of the sterner sex. They are very clean and painstaking, and their white dresses and long black pigtails look exceedingly picturesque. One day, when a heavy northwest wind was rolling the ship a good deal and damaging the crockery, I saw a nice young pigtail struggling with a pile of about twenty plates, and having to resolve upon either dropping the plates or falling forward on the passengers at dinner: he preferred property to politeness, stuck to his plates with all his might, and saved them by throwing himself forward between the heads of two stout gentlemen, whose shoulders saved him from falling with his nose in a dish of stewed chicken."[64]

Colonel J.P. Sanford in his *Letters of Travel from Different Lands* on an earlier voyage on the *Japan* noted that:

"at half past 7 in the morning a gong is sounded to awaken the passengers in time for them to prepare for breakfast, which is served at half-past 8. At 12 o'clock lunch is on the table; 6 o'clock finds the principal meal of the day, which is dinner all ready for us. An hour and a half is usually spent at this meal. At half-past 8, tea is served to all who wish. Aside from these meals, coffee, tea, and bread are all on the table at 6 o'clock in the morning for early risers. Passengers may retire when they please, but all lights in state rooms are extinguished at 11 o'clock."[65]

In their free time, some passengers played draw poker for beans. The *Japan*'s large upper deck also had a clear promenade nearly 400 feet long and a snug library within the social hall. The large social hall had luxurious lounges, armchairs and a piano. It was essentially an elegant saloon cabin, a place for first-class passenger relaxation, be it socializing, reading, or piano playing. The panels were elaborately decorated walnut and white oak wood.

Down below decks and on deck during their fresh air periods, the steerage passengers played Tan - a simple banking game that consisted of rapidly dividing buttons into three or four heaps and betting on whether the heap contained an odd or even number.

"No sooner do the celestials get their eyes open in the morning than they collect in groups on the deck, sitting cross-legged on mats, and commence playing games and dominoes and cards, etc. Once started the game is kept up until nightfall only interrupted by the serving of boiled rice, beets, turnips, and fish oil which the Chinese eat vociferously using their chopsticks."[66]

The *Japan*'s Chinese in steerage "pay less than half price, and are fed with the simple fare of their country. In the middle of their cabin they have made, with canvas, a dark room for opium-smoking. When on deck, they appear neatly clad, and amuse themselves with unintelligible games of chance." [67]

One of Captain Warsaw's most important duties was the daily inspection for fire hazards, cleanliness, and seaworthiness. His inspections took him through the *Japan*'s food service areas in the saloons, and into the berthing areas, which included the Chinese steerage area.

The captain was accompanied on the inspections with the ship's surgeon and chief medical officer, Dr. V.B. Gates. Gates inspected the steamer with Captain Warsaw at 11:00 AM daily to check the passengers' and crew's physical welfare, ensure that cleanliness standards were maintained. His other duties included embalming the Chinese who died at sea so that they could be sent back to China - a necessary condition for their getting to heaven. In fact, there were Chinese who came aboard ill - came aboard knowing they would die - but intent on being carried home to China and there burned. "Every coolie makes a contract that he is to be carried home dead or alive."[68]

The Chinese berthing areas were particularly dense, and it was important to ensure that they stayed as clean as possible in order to avoid the risk of diseases like smallpox. Rats were also seen on board the *Japan*.

On an 1871 Pacific Mail voyage, Baron de Huber recorded a captain's morning inspection in *A Ramble Around the World*. "The captain does not fancy himself an admiral or commodore. After having given his instructions to his chief officer, he is not above visiting himself three or four times a day (according to his instructions) the machinery, the kitchens, the cabins of the passengers, everything, in fact, down to the hold."[69]

Once the Chinese steerage passengers were out on deck, Captain Warsaw (with Dr. Gates) began the steerage area inspection, opening the large port-holes to allow the ocean air to enter and burning red pepper.

One of the steerage passengers was a rich merchant whose chest contained $3,000.

A *Putnam* magazine article from an earlier voyage on the Great Republic described the living conditions in the Chinese steerage area. "To-day I went with the surgeon to inspect the steerage, and it was frightful to see creatures in human form stowed away as these Chinamen are. Three decks are devoted to them, each of which was filled with bunks four deep, and so close together that it is impossible to pass between them without turning sideways. The upper deck is comparatively light, but the lower two are pitch dark, and what will seem almost incredible, that they seem to be perfectly satisfied to remain here; indeed, the only way in which officers can get them on the hurricane deck, is by burning red pepper, the odor of which they have a strong dislike to. Just think of it: Here are creatures, supposed to be men, who are willing and contented to lie in the dark, packed like herrings four weeks without moving. These are the Celestials. The surgeon says that it is one continued fight against disease."[70]

Captain Warsaw would also look into the covered area that served as an opium-den for the Chinese to use as a smoking room. There were no open fires allowed, and he made sure that the space was secured prior to climbing up the stairwell to the main deck.

At eight o'clock each evening, Captain Warsaw inspected one department in particular: food service. He went through the bakery, the pantry, and the kitchen, where the cooks and waiters were on hand, with every drawer open for inspection, all the dishes and cooking utensils shining on the shelves, a model of perfection of neatness and order. The butcher's quarters was then visited, where the various noises of a farmyard were heard; there were cows, chickens, sheep, and pigs, whose late companions, killed and quartered, were suspended from the ceiling nearby. He also passed through a small dining room, with a table set for those officers who were on watch during the night took their meals at different times. The hatchway into the forecastle where sailors sleep was also checked on by Captain Warsaw.

In the Chinese kitchen and eating-room, he observed the bill of fare for the next day-rice, with variation required each of the Chinese steerage passenger to present a meal ticket for their food.

John Cosgrove was the *Japan*'s Chief Engineer. Captain Warsaw would occasionally have Mr. Cosgrove take him through the *Japan*'s engine and furnace room spaces. Her sidewheels were driven by a vertical beam engine with a cylinder 105 inches in diameter and a 12 foot stroke. The enormous side wheels were attached to a shaft weighing 30 tons. Each sidewheel cost approximately $20,000, weighed 74 tons, and was 120 feet in circumference. The furnace room was also 17 feet below the water line and operated 24 furnaces.

The ship's propulsion system produced 20 PSI steam pressure from its boilers, 24 furnaces and donkey boiler steam pumps. Keeping the *Japan* underway required the full labor of John Cosgrove's engineering department of approximately 36 personnel. The men of the furnace room were required to load between 45 and 55 tons of coal daily just to keep the fires burning. The heat in the main spaces was tremendous.

Into the furnace mouths, half-naked Chinese crewmen worked four hours a watch shoveling coal before they got 8 hours off. A balcony on the upper level surrounded the engine room and the dark chamber of the engine room received its only light from the glow of the furnace fires, which were snuffed out by the occasional passage of one of the Chinese furnace handlers shoveling another load of coal into the fire pit.

The ships distilling plant took water from the Pacific and distilled it for drinking water and boiler feed water.

As he exited the berthing area on deck and observed the Chinese steerage passengers sitting around in groups during an enthusiastic dominos game, the captain was reassured of their contentment and happiness, and glad that he could return them to their homeland.

Warsaw was likely nostalgic about the sidewheelers which were gradually being removed from commission and replaced by the iron-wheel steamers. The passage of this group of Chinese steerage felt like a throwback to his first years of service. As Charles Coffin described this choice in his *Our New Way Around the World*, "the action of the Pacific Mail Company in adopting side-wheel vessels, when all Europeans companies are building screws, has been much criticized; but the company, looking to the transportation of Chinese emigrants as the chief source of revenue, chose a model which would give room for a large number of steerage passengers."[71]

Captain Warsaw's intimate inspection of the *Japan's* berthing spaces likely made him think back over earlier voyages to China and the stories he remembered- stories that help us recall the voices of their lives and their experiences:

On prosperity: "One little chap, eighteen years old, who is in steerage as a passenger told me he had been earning $50 per month and board as a cook in San Francisco."[72]

On love: "In the steerage are one hundred sixty Chinese, mostly men, but also including a few women and children, returning to their homes in China. Some of them speak English quite well. "Said one of them to me, in answer to an inquiry as to why he was going back to China: 'Go China to gettee wife, then go back to Californee.' I asked him if he had one picked out and he said 'No, I but one' I asked him how much she would cost, and he said: 'Ninety dollar buy nice one with small footee'"[73]

On food: "Even the wealthy Chinese prefer the steerage, where they have been cooking according to their national taste."[74]

On music and entertainment: "Chinese musicians in steerage, with the Captain's permission, were invited aft into the saloon to provide musical entertainment. There were three Chinese instrumentals - a sort of banjo, a kind of violin, chiefly on one note, another Chinaman did the vocal part-chiefly on one note and this through his nose....They played for fun, not money."[75]

On being a Chinese sailor: "Every morning the decks are washed and the brass is polished and the ship is brought to a state of shining neatness by the Chinese crew. When a sail is to be set or changed it seems to be done with the engine. One night all the sails were furled at once while we were smoking in the room or on deck. Not a sound was heard. There was no swearing or whistling or stamping of feet, or 'Yo-Ho.' A lot of silent Chinamen quietly furled and stowed all the sails without our knowledge."[76]

Lat: 38.48	*Rev: 10301=62*
Long: 130.00	*Steam: 18*
Course: 270W	*Cut Off=3*
Dist: 166	*Dist by wheel: 220*
Wind	*Coal Consumed: 30*
Bar: 30.15	*Coal on Hand: 2001*
Air: 58	
Water: 55	

Made all sail at 0930 AM. Stopped engine for five minutes. At 0830 AM took in square sails. At 4 exercised as Fire Quarters and inflated life raft. Found all working well and in good order. Crew employed by hoisting coal out of fore hold. Crew employed hoisting coal out of lower hold.
Representative log entry from PMSS America Log (1869)

Dr. Robert M. Tindall was finally on his way to his new posting in Canton. He looked forward to be briefed on the details on the trade and revenue responsibilities from his predecessor, fellow-Mississippian R.G.J. Jewell. Tindall was an impressive cross-section of talent - a surgeon, Internal

Revenue Assessor, and U.S. Consul to Canton, China-the center of Chinese immigration to the United States. His interest and relationships with Captain Warsaw, the ship's Surgeon, Dr. Gates, his observations of the Chinese emigrants returning home to Guangdong Province, and the direct observation of a Pacific Mail Steamship in action would help inform his service and decisions as Consul.

His main deck cabin was close to one of the busiest areas on the ship: *Japan*'s central stairway, which was used by passengers and crew to come topside or head below for meals in the dining saloon. Dr. V.B. Gates, *Japan*'s surgeon, had his quarters one deck above Dr. Tindall on the spar deck with a view of one of Japan's lifeboats, the rocking arm motion of the engine, the two sidewheels, and in hearing distance of the piano playing in the social hall, the voices of the passengers taking their one mile walks on the top deck, and the Chinese crew going about its topside business with the masts.

Around the corner from Dr. Tindall's room was the purser's office and the ship's safe. Inside the safe were the keys to the *Japan*'s treasure tank, located forward below the cargo hatch between the cargo and orlap decks and the coal bunkers, carrying the almost $400,000 in silver trade-dollar treasure to Hong Kong.

The purser held "the purse strings" and secured passengers' valuables in the ship's safe for safe keeping and the treasure tank in the forward hold as well. The tank was twenty-eight feet long, five feet deep, wide at one end and pointed at the other along the athwartship area below the after cargo hatch on the *Japan*'s forecastle.

The purser also was responsible for the ship's safe, which contained on this voyage about $8,300.00[77] in a mixture of gold and silver coinage. This supply was typically used for onboard transactions, logistical expenses that needed to be covered in Yokohama and Hong Kong, and for transport of Pacific Mail working capital.

A week into the voyage, the *Japan* experienced steady weather and the beginnings of a southwest swell that grew over the coming days along the 30th parallel. There is no record of any ships meeting the *Japan* at sea on her final voyage. The *Great Republic*'s December 18, 1874 voyage report does note, however, encountering heavy southwest gales for four days, then variable south and east winds thereafter. The south and east wind weather period coincides with the most plausible rendezvous period that the two ships could have experienced.

The *Colorado* was two weeks ahead of the *Japan* and Captain Warsaw likely knew that he would possibly encounter her while he was on the downhill run to Hong Kong as the *Colorado* headed northeast toward

Yokohama. The *Colorado*'s outbound report indicates that she had a very rough sea with "unceasing up and down motions."

The evenings across the great Pacific often evoked a sense of wonder and beauty especially during the presence of the moon. The sentiment provided by Benjamin Robbins Curtis in *Dottings Round the World* is representative. "The moonlight nights, at present, are delightfully picturesque. The full moon shines clearly over the waters. Our steamer glides smoothly along through the glimmering belt, leaving behind a long dark trail of smoke, while multitudes of stars of unusual brilliancy shine out from every part of the heavens above us."[78]

There were five Sundays during this voyage and on the 3rd Sunday the *Japan* crossed the International Date Line. This must have pleased Captain Warsaw, who had mixed feelings about Sunday services, according to American Consul Charles O. Shepherd, who noted on an earlier voyage with the Captain:

Figure 33: Sunday Service on Board a Pacific Mail Steamship
(Author's Collection)

"Warsaw was not a pious man. Nor was he fond of missionaries, of whom there were six or eight on the ship. They began to "bother" the Captain, so he said, for opportunities to preach on the four Sunday's of the voyage. He rather impatiently told them to settle it among themselves and he would agree. The first and second Sundays went by all right enough but when the third Sunday came it was different. The appointed missionary and his wife appeared in the saloon a little before 11 o'clock, Bible in hand. They found the usual weekday bustle going on and no preparation for the service. Half an hour went by and no preparation and no audience...The captain was found and questioned, 'Services!' said he, 'we have services only on Sunday.' 'Well, this is Sunday' said the parson. 'Not much, 'replied the Captain, 'this is Monday.' The missionary was dumbfounded. He had discovered the hard way that when the ships cross the 180th Meridian, a day is dropped if the ship is headed west but has to be added, i.e. repeated, going east. It is said that the Captain tried never to repeat a Sunday." [79]

Colonel J.P Stanford captured the sentiment of those travelling on the *Japan* on a previous voyage. "Let us, by the way of illustration, take twenty four hours in the history of a great steamer like the "Japan," upon which so many of us for weeks have found a home. Thousands of miles in safety, this noble vessel has borne us along toward the land of the Celestials; day and night the great wheels turn and we hear the ceaseless pulsations of her mighty engines."[80]

A few days from Yokohama and the steerage passengers headed to the main deck, to spend another day sitting cross-legged on mats to play endless games of dominos. At noon, the First Officer and the Captain worked out the *Japan*'s latitude and longitude and placed the ship's position with the number of miles made in the last twenty four hours on a passenger bulletin board. As they continued west toward Japan, the passengers looked for a seldom - sailing vessel and more often than not stared out on a dreary expanse of water. They also told stories, walked the deck, dozed away the hours, watched the sparkling foam at night and threw crumbs to the seagulls.

Yokohama
Arrival in Yokohama-December 10, 1874
From Captain Warsaw:
Had pleasant weather with variable winds during passage to
Yokohama.
Arrived December 10 at 10:10 4 M
Yokohama landed 22 cabin passengers
4 European steerage

8 Japanese
400 tons cargo
10 packages of mail
Received on board
1 European steerage
3 Chinese steerage
46 tons cargo
600 tons coal
1 bag mail
Stores, etc.
From "The Japan" Daily Alta California

"Land off the port bow . . . Fujiyama's in sight." Everyone on board knew that snow-crested, conical top of Mount Fuji would be the first land they would spy. At daybreak on December 10, the passengers were on deck trying to get their first glimpses of land since San Francisco 25 days hence. Mount Fuji could be seen clearly in the early morning sunlight.

Captain Warsaw and the officer of the deck steered the *Japan* into the bay, passing a variety of Japanese boats and watercraft including junks, fishing boats, and the revenue cutter that would note *Japan*'s American colors. The deck gang was up on the ship's forecastle preparing both anchors for letting go. At the Pacific Mail's agency along the waterfront of Yokohama, a two-gun salute heralded the arrival of the ship as soon as she was sighted in the bay. Passing the boats and fishing towns along the bay, the ship slowed to approach her anchorage amongst the warships and support craft.

At 10:10 AM on December 10th, 1874, the *Japan* anchored in 7 fathoms of water and veered her chain to 30 fathoms in Yokohama Bay. She fired a saluting battery round and ran the Japanese colors up on the foremast to join the American flag on the stern flagstaff. The dynamics of taking passengers ashore and loading coal was just beginning.

Boats from the Yokohama waterfront made their way toward the Japan to take the passengers ashore. As they approached the ship, there was a great deal of maneuvering and boisterous clamoring to get adjacent to the *Japan*'s ladder.

A steam tug approached the anchorage to collect the mails. Once alongside, Japanese attendants climbed the ship's ladder to retrieve the mail while others distributed advertisements for businesses in Yokohama. The *Japan*'s passengers enjoyed the scene before them - a mixed population of unpainted boats attended by boatmen looking up at them to make eye contact and persuade them to ride ashore with them to the passenger wharf.

The departing passengers bid Dr. Tindall, Mary Stott, Captain Warsaw and the officers of the *Japan* farewell. Then they followed the Japanese baggage attenders down the ladder and boarded the boats for the ride ashore, little aware that they were leaving a ship that would not arrive safely at its next intended port, Hong Kong.

As the boats headed toward shore, the passengers looked back at the *Japan* to see her at full length at anchor for the first time since leaving San Francisco. She had just brought them safely across the Pacific at wintertime. Chandler boats were already alongside and the discharging of 400 tons of cargo had begun.

It had taken the *Japan* 26 days to get from San Francisco to Yokohama, during which she had consumed about 28 tons of coal a day – about 1400 tons of coal in total. Somewhere at mid-voyage, the steamer crews had transitioned from hoisting coal from the forward holds to the lower holds, which increased with frequency in the morning and afternoon. From the mid-point on, the crews would hoist coal from the lower holds. The forward hold would have to be replenished at Yokohama.

The slow-moving Yokohama coal barges were loaded down with 140 tons of Sydney coal and 480 tons of Japanese tako coal. Overall, the *Japan* took on 620 total tons of coal for the round-trip voyage from Yokohama-Hong Kong and back. A check of the coal bunkers by the engineer confirmed that they were almost depleted from the passage. According to the *Japan*'s Engineer John Hargrove, no coal remained in the forward bunker and only five or six tons in total remained from the trans-Pacific voyage.

She would need over 600 tons of coal to make it to Hong Kong and the return voyage to Yokohama at the beginning of January 1875.

Captain Warsaw and the *Japan* had also returned to the approximate location where America had burned two years before in August 1872, from a coal bunker fire that killed 52 people. During this fire many Chinese passengers went over the side with their bodies laden with silver and gold coin

BURNING OF THE PACIFIC MAIL COMPANY'S SHIP AMERICA, AT YOKOHAMA.

Figure 34: The burning of the Japan's sister ship, the Pacific Mail Steamship America, Yokohama, August 1872 Illustrated London Tribune, p453, Author's collection.

Once a transit had been completed between ports, ships of the Pacific Mail completed a recapitulation of the voyage.

Recapitulation	
Total list by Observation	*7158*
Coal Consumed	*1104*
Total List by Wheels	*9843*
Average per day:	*28 345/2240*
Number of revolutions	*4582 of 3*
Coal on hand on Arrival	*1056*
Draft leaving NY	*20.7*
Engine Stopped on Voyage	*55*
Draft Arrival Simons Bay	*17.4*

Sample PMSS America Log, Tuesday July 6, 1869

Now loaded, the 620 tons of fresh coal in her forward coal bunker would need to last until the *Japan* returned to Yokohama a week later. The ship's Chief Engineer, John H. Cosgrove, responsible for *Japan*'s coal onload, reported that the coal barges brought 140 tons of Sydney coal and 480 tons of Tako coal.

The Tako coal was loaded dry in the aft bunker and the Sydney coal in the empty forward bunker and the after bunker. That afternoon, the weather turned wet, and a violent rainstorm ensued, leaving the stored coal in a damp and wet condition.

On a hill overlooking Yokohama Bay, members of the Transit of Venus delegation were waiting to receive mail and send their reports on their progress home.

The next morning, December 11, 1874, the departure of the *Japan* from port was recorded for the final time by the one of the Transit of Venus delegations on the Hill.

THE TREE GOD — Page 176

Figure 35: The Guangdong Province Chinese emigrants making offerings to their Joss on a tree before departure.
Praying for safe passage to America.
From "How and Why The Chinese Emigrate." (1871)

THE COOLIE'S HOME. — Page 131.

Figure 36: A representative home in the surrounding hills of Guangdong Province. From "How and Why The Chinese Emigrate." (1871)

112

SOLD FOR DEBT. — Page 274

Figure 37: A handsome girl of 16 will command a price from twenty five to fifty dollars. In this case they are bought by Europeans.
From "How and Why The Chinese Emigrate." (1871)

DEPARTURE OF THE EMIGRANTS — Page 211.

Figure 38: The Guangdong Province Chinese emigrants were screened at Canton and then boarded the twice-daily Pearl River down-river steamer to Hong Kong-the stepping off point for passage to America aboard the new Pacific Mail Steamship trans-Pacific sidewheel steamers. From "How and Why The Chinese Emigrate." (1871)

Figure 39: The Pacific Mail Steam Ship Japan in port Hong Kong after completing her maiden voyage (1868)
Courtesy Bancroft Library, University of California

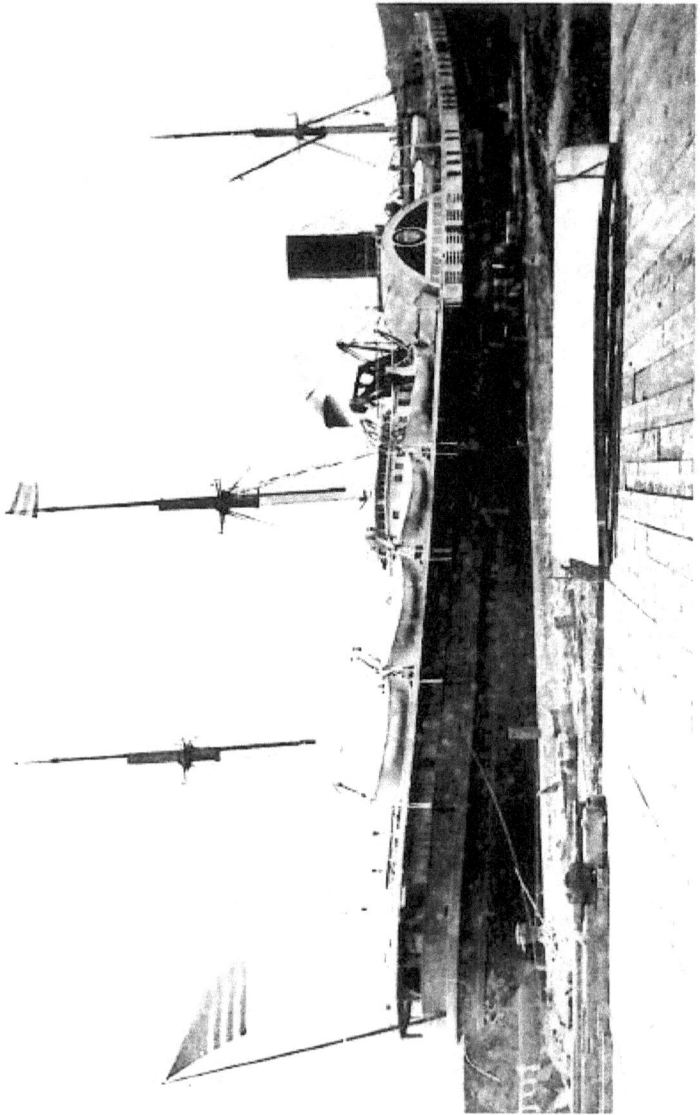

Figure 40: Pacific Mail Steamship Japan. (1870's) A rare starboard-side aspect of the ship illustrating the side free of fire and the lifeboat deck where the survivors assembled and went over the side. The fire had cut off the Chinese on the forecastle from the lifeboats. Captain Warsaw went over the side aft of the starboard sidewheel- just after midnight on December 18, 1874. Courtesy of Belvedere-Tiburon Landmarks Society, Tiburon, CA

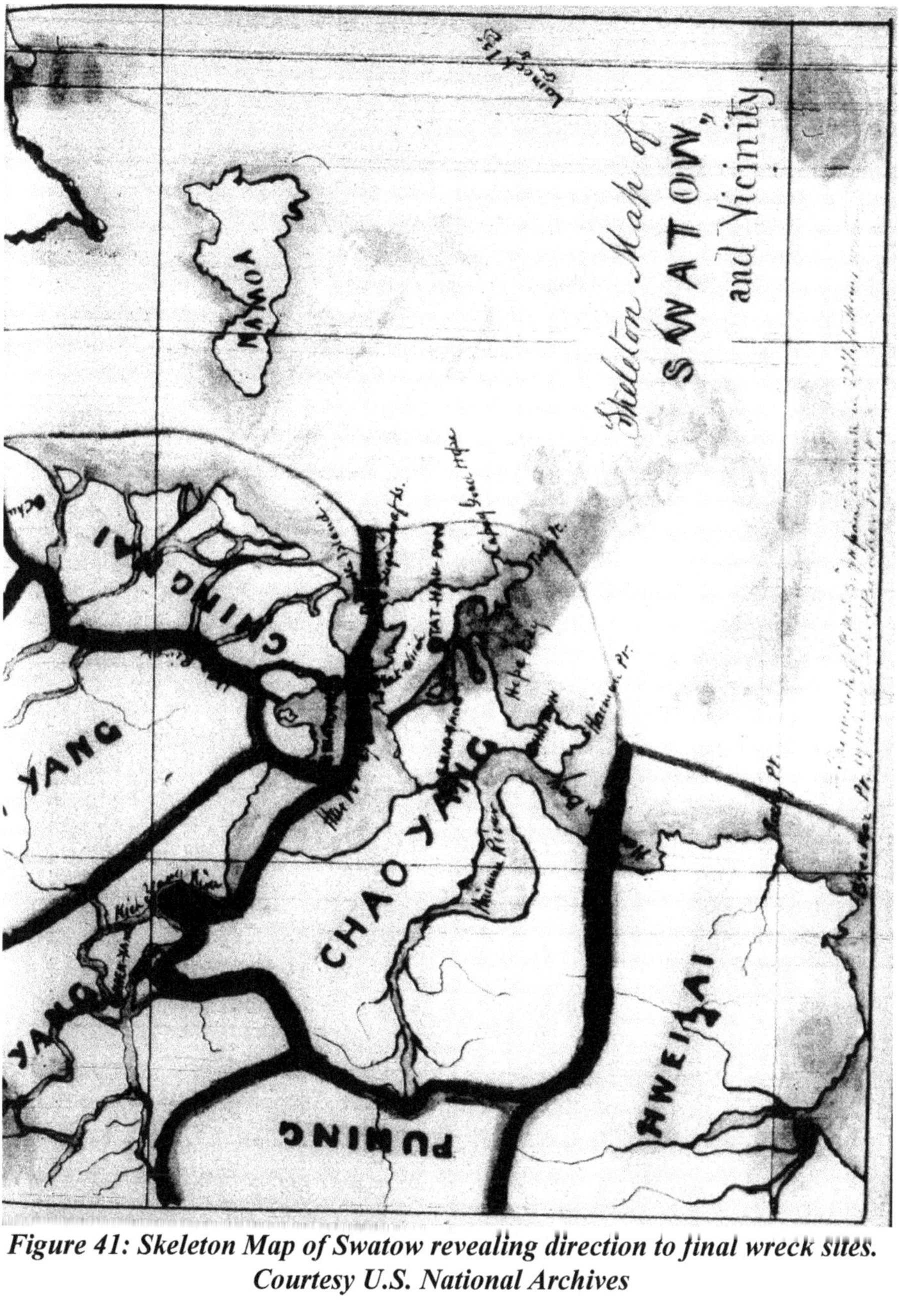

Figure 41: Skeleton Map of Swatow revealing direction to final wreck sites.
Courtesy U.S. National Archives

Chapter 10

The Final Voyage – Into the South China Sea

Departure from Yokohama

Yokohama sailed with captain and crew 128 men
2 Cabin passengers
2 European steerage
426 Chinese
667 total souls on board
Yokohama sailed with captain and crew 128 men
2 Cabin passengers
2 European steerage
426 Chinese
667 total souls on board
-Captain E.R. Warsaw, Japan, December 28, 1874

It was raining in Yokohama. After 24 hours of work, the 140 tons of Sydney coal and 480 tons of Japanese Tako coal was finally loaded. In the early afternoon, the carpenters began to seal the cargo holds and caulk the cargo ports. The crew of the *Japan* was getting her ready for sea. Dr. Tindall remained on board as one of two cabin passengers for the 6-day, 1,500-mile transit to Hong Kong.

Captain Warsaw and Second Officer Henry Harrison Andrews reviewed the navigation track. The route would take the ship out of Yeddo Bay to the southwest along Honshu Island, passing Mikomoto (Rock Island) at the mouth of the Bay of Yeddo, south of Kyushu. With a final sighting of the "Ingersoll Rocks" on the morning of December 14th, the *Japan* would head across the East China Sea. They should sight China off the cliffs and "Dogs of Foochow" on the morning of December 17th, and a midnight sighting of Breaker Point off Swatow. If all went well, they would arrive at Hong Kong on the morning of December 18, 1874.

The rainy Yokohama weather had changed into a cold and clear transit day. The *Japan*'s engineering department reported "manned and

118

ready," with 20 PSI of steam pressure available for the paddlewheels. Just before 4:00 PM, Captain Warsaw began to heave around and haul in the *Japan*'s anchor. Once clear, the anchor was hooked up, and the ship proceeded smartly down the bay.

Looking down from their Yokohama vantage point as a member of the Transit of Venus delegation, Mr. J.F. Campbell witnessed the paddlewheel's final departure for Hong Kong. He recorded in his Circular Notes that his duties that day consisted of temperature recordings with diagrams, writing letters home, and sending off some boxes of curios. On Friday, December 11, 1874, he wrote "some of these letters never got home at all. The steamer was in the bay going south."

The departure voyage from Yokohama to Hong Kong was Captain Warsaw's first since he'd taken a year off from the line. By 6:00 PM on December 11th, the *Japan* passed Kawasake Light and into Yeddo bay heading southwesterly by sunset. She steamed heavily into the Pacific and passed south of Honshu Island at midnight. The watch received the report that the cargo tracts and side lights had been examined and found to be "all secure."

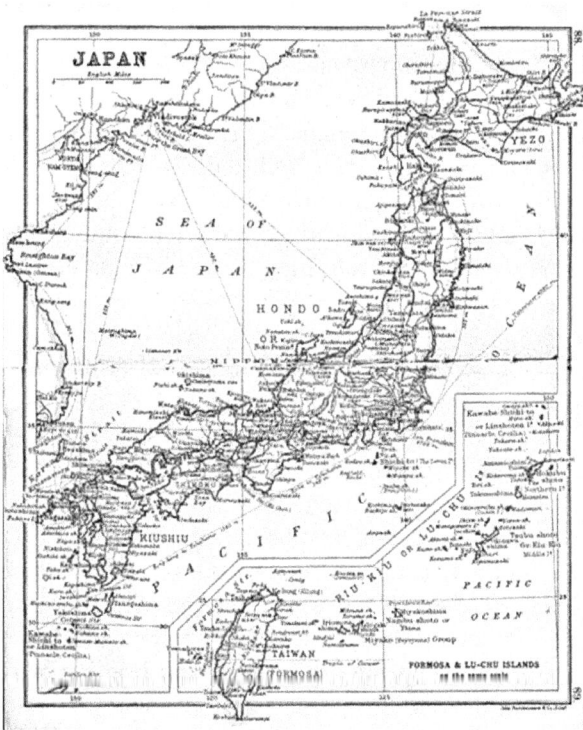

Figure 42: Map of Japan (1871)

119

Three days later on December 14th, the *Japan* sailed south of Kyushu at sunset and by midnight entered the East China Sea China south of Ingersoll Rocks (Kusaki Sima) for the 2-3 day transit across the East China Sea and the first expected sighting of the Dogs of Foochow and the China Coast. Warsaw prepared to sail the *Japan* into the East and South China Sea and with the winds of the northeast monsoon.

The "White Dogs of Foo Chow" is a mariner's term describing the White Dog Islands off Foochow, China. Their observation represented a "go-no-go" point of departure from the China Coast and a point of concern and trepidation during the northeast monsoon season for ships completing the voyage across the Pacific and the East China Sea. After sighting of the White Dogs, Captain Warsaw glanced southward to "Turnabout Island" and made the go-no-go decision. The safe anchorages and shelter from the northeast monsoon winds along the China coast would lie inward toward the White Dogs and Foochow and could be used if he decided not to proceed on to Hong Kong.[81]

The White Dog Islands consisted of two large and one small islets and were named the Middle Dog, South Dog, and Tong-sha Island. Since the East China Sea weather had been pleasant and the stronger winds of the northeast monsoon had not made their appearance, Captain Warsaw decided to press ahead and take the ship toward her destination.

It was December 15, 1874, and the *Japan* was just three days out from Hong Kong. As the early telltale signs of dawn along the China coast emerged, the watch on the *Japan* and the Chinese steerage passengers prepared to get their first view of the White Dog islands off the Foochow coast. Russell H Connell writing in *Why and How* witnessed the reaction of the Chinese steerage passengers returning home to China on an earlier Pacific Mail voyage.

"...[L]ooking with little anxiety for the bluffs of the China coast near Foochow, which the Captain had said we were nearing, a large company of Coolies came up from steerage for the purpose of getting the first sight of land. It was to be the first glimpse of their native shore after a long absence in California....And several smiled when, in answer to their inquiry, I said, 'It is China.' Cold, stoical, undemonstrative, the others sat themselves down by the wheel-house and indulged in a quiet chat. Nearer and nearer came the great cliffs, clearer became the atmosphere and brighter the light of dawning day, but the same careless look was on their faces and the same unconcerned air about their movements.

"Even when the junks in the bays and the cultivated spots on shore were near enough to see the Chinamen at work in them, these returnees did not show in their faces any desire but that of idle curiosity.

"Fortunately, I found two that were communicative, and to them I put the following questions with the following replies in substance:

Q: How long have you been in California?
A: Nearly eight years.

Q: Are you coming home to see your families now, or on business?
A: We come to see our families. But we do not know where we will find them. When we left them they were in a village near Canton, but we have not heard from them since we saw a man who emigrated from there five years ago.

Q: Do you expect to see them all alive?
A: We hope so. We have not heard of any raids or famines, and they were generally healthy. The police do not know that we are out of the country and will not treat them harshly on our account."[82]

A bustling China coast of steam merchant and passenger vessels plying the waters of the Taiwan Strait was before the ship as the breakfast meal was served the next morning. The Captain and Surgeon conducted another shipwide inspection at 1100. Captain Warsaw and First Officer Andrews took a sun line and compared the ship's position using dead-reckoning or a running fix with the coastal landmarks of China. The *Japan* was now almost clear of the Taiwan Strait and prepared to enter the South China Sea off Amoy on the noon watch.

By noon on the 17th, the wind had freshened to a strong northeast breeze that welcomed the crew and passengers as they began the noon meal. In the pilot house, the officer of the deck reviewed the navigation plan. The *Japan* would pass near Lammock Island, past Swatow to Breaker Point on the mid watch, and travel along the Cup Chi coast after changing course to Hong Kong. The northeast winds were favorable for making a few more knots on a little less coal. Hong Kong would be reached the next morning. The crew set her topsails fore and aft. She would night steam with the sails set.

121

Just before sunset, the watch and steerage passengers began to feel the effects of a heavy swell as it set in against the *Japan*'s starboard quarter. As the sun disappeared over the Chinese mainland and coastal mountains, Engineer Hargrove inspected the engineering spaces during his eight o'clock inspection.

The *Japan* was using about 45 tons of coal a day (about 200 total tons) during the first 5.5 days of the transit. The engineers were now hauling the remainder of the Japanese Takoshima – the Tako coal – mined from around Nagasaki and now being used from the side bunkers. The reserved Sydney coal remained in the forward bunker.

Chapter 11

Fire on the Mid Watch

"The fire broke out at 11:25 P.M.; I first heard a muffled sound among my passengers on the main deck, which intimated to me that something was wrong and a minute afterward there was a cry of 'fire'."
Captain Edward Warsaw

The northeast monsoon winds continued to strengthen and the *Japan* began to rock gently on the quarter sea off Amoy. She would be home tomorrow.

Chief Engineer John Cosgrove looked forward to arriving in Hong Kong. He had been with the Pacific Mail Steamship Company since 1856 and was a seven-year veteran of its ships. He was just settling in his cabin after touring the main spaces and reported "all engineering equipment was in working order" to the officer of the watch. His stateroom was on the promenade deck aft of *Japan*'s rocking arm. The door to his room opened on to the deck and he could hear the rotation of the starboard wheel. He could feel the *Japan* rolling against a changing sea.

It was dark along the China coast and flashes of wind swept water could be seen through the glass windows of the pilot house as the starboard watch turnover began. Second Officer H.H. Andrews assumed the watch. The turnover briefed that the winds were expected to stay steady from the northeast and that the Lammock Island navigation light should be sighted in advance of the *Japan*'s course past Breaker Point. The fore-topsail, main topsail, and foresail were to stay set in order to make good speed through the night, and maybe get to Hong Kong early.

Second Officer H.H. Andrews settled in for his watch in the pilot house. Then Captain Warsaw bolted through the pilot house door which connected his cabin, with a call of danger that would send chills into any steamship officer.

"A cry of fire was heard on deck!"

Andrews then called out "fire" as Captain Warsaw moved swiftly outside of the pilot house to ring the *Japan*'s gong. The fire alarm blasted throughout the ship. As if on cue from the alarm, thick black smoke was observed coming from the engine room and ventilators.

The smoke was inky in its blackness and suffocating to the passengers. Suddenly awakened, the European and Chinese passengers pressed against each other, climbing from their berthing areas and up the stairways to the upper deck, as the *Japan* came to a rest into the wind against a rolling and growing sea.

The Europeans all assembled on the after part of the ship. Hundreds of panicked Chinese arrived on the forward part of the ship, where they huddled together, separated from the other passengers by the smoke, the emerging flames, and the motions of the fire party, who were pulling out fire hoses with their streams as the initial attempts to save the ship were underway.

In the pilot house, Captain Warsaw ordered all ventilators turned away from the wind and to let loose the topsail halyards in order to help the ship settle into the wind and get the smoke from the fire tending away from the ship.

Andrews ascertained, in the soft light of the pilot house, that the *Japan* was about 26 miles off Breaker Point and the Breaker Point light bore West 1/8 South.

Chief Engineer Cosgrove was also jolted into action. He had heard the fire alarm and the engine gong as the throttle valve was closed and the sidewheel shafts were unhooked from the ship's engine. He bolted from his stateroom and ran down the after stairwell into the engine room to investigate the problem.

Fire and smoke were coming from the vicinity of the amidship engine-room pumps – pumps that were needed to supply fire-fighting water. Cosgrove asked the third and first assistant engineers if the pumps had been started. When he discovered that they had not been, he ran to the forward fire pumps and got two to three streams of water started and sent the water back across to the amidship pumps in a little over two minutes. The engine room was now enveloped by smoke and all of the lights were out except one. Fire was now blazing through the forward bulkhead that divided the engine room from the freight deck. The smoke was getting heavier, the fire more aggressive. It was moving quickly. Cosgrove saw flames coming through another door near the engine room. The fire rapidly progressed throughout the engine room until it was entirely on fire with the flames coming up both fire-room skylights.

He looked across the engine room, and every man was at his post and working his best. The weather as the midnight hour approached was dark and cloudy with a strong northeast monsoon with a rough cross-sea running.

Andrews continued ringing the *Japan*'s Bell. In the pilot house, Quartermaster Harris arrived to relive Second Officer Andrews (as required by procedure). Andrews then quickly headed aft to alert Chief Officer Hart and Third Officer Gallagher before continuing aft to the promenade decks to take charge of the life boats.

Down on the *Japan*'s main deck, forward of the smokestack and over the fireroom, large quantities of smoke were coming from the ash-shoot. Engineer Cosgrove's success in getting the firepumps started allowed three streams of water to be aimed at the fireroom and engineroom. Through his efforts, up to 24 hoses providing 20 water streams were soon brought to bear in the fireroom, engineroom and storage area.

But the water streams were not enough to quench the blaze. The fire continued to rage, and new efforts to determine its location became the focus of the effort to control it. Holes were cut in the steerage deck on the port side abreast of the engine and fire rooms.

The smoke became more intense.

Captain Warsaw observed the first line directly. It was coming from the ventilator over the forward fire room. The after part of the *Japan*, around the after steerage hatch and the freight deck, had smoke but no fire.

Streams of water continued to be applied as the fire.

The smoke increased in intensity.

"Finding it impossible to subdue the fire, abandoned the ship with the last boat at 1 o'clock A.M., December 18th, the ship then being enveloped in flames amidships, directly in the engine rooms and fire rooms, all communications being cut off between the forward and aft part of the steamer."
Captain E. R. Warsaw

Figure 43: An artist's conception of the Japan fire. (Dec. 17, 1874)
Courtesy Sea Classics-Challenge Publications

They were losing in their battle to fight the fire's intensity. Captain Warsaw made preparations to save lives and abandon the *Japan*. He directed Quartermaster Sutton to "tell the chief officer to detail men to swing out and clear all boats ready for lowering!"

Warsaw then went below to the steerage area that was forward abreast of the foremast and cut a hole in the deck. He saw fire, applied a hose to it, and then ran to another telltale location above the ash chute where a hole had been cut. There he saw fire where there had not been fire just a few short minutes earlier.

The fire continued to rage and began to cut the ship in half.

Panic and fear were gripping the hundreds of Chinese steerage passengers who gathered in the forward part of the *Japan*. They clustered on the bow, many in a state of utter panic, realizing that their situation was dire. There was no place to go. The fire amidships had cut them off from access to the ship's lifeboats. They were in desperate peril, penned in. Frantically, some began running around in circles trying to escape the flames.

As the fire raged and consumed more of the wooden vessel, the Chinese passengers, one by one, came to the terrible awareness that they were trapped and that no help would be able to reach them from the other parts of the ship. They could not move aft, and they could not stay where they were for much longer.

126

Some had been able to grab life preservers, and they began to jump overboard into the cold waters. Others had no such protective devices, but likewise had to climb over the railing and make the plunge.

In the waters, the scene was equally terrible, the midnight darkness broken by the raging fire that illuminated the dancing waves. Some of the Chinese managed to find pieces of the ship, as it was consumed and began to break into pieces. In an increasingly rough sea, they lucky few clung to pieces of the wreck, all the while screaming for assistance from others around the ship.

For many, though, they had little ability to tread water or swim until a lifeboat appeared. They had risen with the fire alarm wearing their money belts or had quickly grabbed them and put them around their waist. As the water soaked into their clothes, the weight of their money belts, filled with the silver dollars earned from years of hard labor, pulled them down into the waves, choking and struggling. While some may have managed to jettison the belts in time, others were dragged below the surface and drowned.

On board, panic and chaos reigned at the lifeboat stations as well. At one point, too many people attempt to board an already full lifeboat as it was being lowered, causing the davit to give way, causing the boat to careen down suddenly and ejecting all into the waters.

The only women on the *Japan*, cabin passenger Mary Stott and stewardess Nelly Noble, were caught up in the suddenness of the emergency as the flames came through their berthing area. Rising at once, they escaped from their berths and arrived on the after spar deck aft in their nightclothes waiting to board a lifeboat.

Lives became further endangered as lifeboats were swamped by the sea swells and wind-driven waves. The worsening sea conditions rendered the boats difficult to control or maneuver, and they were unable to move in the direction they wanted to pick up the Chinese passengers who had jumped overboard with and without life preservers.

On the hurricane deck, Third Officer Gallagher and a gang of the *Japan*'s crew and passengers were swinging the forward lifeboats while Second Officer Andrews was tending and swinging the after lifeboats clear of the *Japan*'s deck making them ready to ease down by the davits to the water.

The fire was getting worse and Captain Warsaw was intent on saving life. He approached Dr. Tindal and told him to ready himself for leaving the ship, and placed the women passengers, Mary Stott and stewardess Nelly Noble, in his charge.

Warsaw pointed to Miss Stott and said, "You stay with Dr. Tindall!" Assured that his officers were making every effort to extinguish the fire, the captain returned to the forward part of the ship to take part in the efforts to save his ship and lives aboard.

Dr. Tindall's overloaded lifeboat was lowered into the weather and the sea with Miss Stott and unhooked from the davit. It drifted away from the burning ship, now increasingly engulfed in flames. Shortly after, Chief Engineer Hargrove's boat approached Dr. Tindall's overloaded boat and managed the transfer of Miss Stott to his boat with seven Chinese and another passenger.

On the ship, people were running aft away from flames that were reaching for the sky, rocking the Captain's authority in a moment of crisis. Still, he exerted his command, making every effort to make the situation from turning into full panic. "At this time a man ran by me, named Denham, an oiler, crying out 'every man for himself.'" Captain Warsaw later recalled, "I caught him and asked who gave him that order. 'The Chief Engineer,' he replied. I told him that if he repeated it I'd blow his brains out, and ordered him to work with the rest."

The fire raged on as midnight passed. The Chinese passengers were fully cut off and continued to leap into the sea. Their cries and moans pierced through the roar of the fire and wind. Others remained below against their will, overcome by smoke and fire only.

Back aft on the boat decks, people were being loaded onto the remaining lifeboats. Stewardess Nelly Noble fell from the boat deck into a lifeboat just as it was entering the water. She was badly injured and bruised in the fall, but alive, as the boat backed away from the *Japan*. From her new vantage point, she was able to look up and observed Captain Warsaw on deck. The structure was enveloped in flames.

After fifteen minutes passed, Warsaw determined that the fire was rapidly gaining on everyone and that the water and fire-fighting measures were not working. The raging fire was out of control. Warsaw knew that it was impossible for any man to enter the center portion of the ship and began to turn his efforts to saving lives.

Warsaw said that he "went aft as far as the engine-room door on the port side, when the flames cut me off." He then looked down the *Japan*'s starboard side (now the "weather side," the side the northeast wind and sea was blowing and pounding against) and saw that all of the boats had been lowered away.

He then completed a similar survey of the ship's port side from the stern area and saw two remaining boats hanging by their davits abaft the social hall. Captain Warsaw then endeavored to get the remaining passengers into one of the last boats and helped lower it down off the davit to the sea.

One boat remained. Second Officer Andrews tended its lines, awaiting the captain. All of the Europeans and Chinese passengers remaining aft of the fire were in this last boat. The flames were now breaking through the spar deck along the promenade into the sky amidships. Captain Warsaw assisted Second Officer Andrews in lowering this final boat.

Once down in the water, Warsaw yelled down to Andrews to remain alongside the ship, while he made a final search of the vessel before going over the side. He then returned to the weather side of *Japan*'s quarterdeck and surveyed all of the areas that he could get to opening doors and calling down to see if any other passengers or crew remained.

There were no replies.

He looked alongside the *Japan*'s boat deck rack, noting that all of the boats, his captain's gig, and the rubber boats were all gone.

One Chinese crewman in a boat on the sea looked up at the burning *Japan*. He could clearly observe Captain Warsaw against the amidships fire on the *Japan* as he was moving to "the last boat which left the side of the ship." Flames were now shooting through the hurricane deck as high as the walking beam....Shortly after they pushed off from the vessel an explosion took place."[83]

Captain Warsaw went over the side at 12:45 on the morning of December 18th, 1874, climbing into the final lifeboat with Second Officer Andrews. The *Japan* was now abandoned. Warsaw joined the remnants of his crew and surviving passengers, all struggling to stay afloat, whether in a boat or being tossed on the wave, with the flaming backdrop of the wreckage of the doomed ship on the South China Sea.

Once clear of the ship, Captain Warsaw's boat came around under her stern. With all the efforts they could muster, they spent the remainder of the night windward of the wreck saving lives, picking up the Chinese who wore life preservers or were clinging to pieces of wreck that floated away from the flaming wreck. A reporter from the *Daily Alta* aboard for the transit said that "at the time the *Japan* was abandoned, the sea was very high, and a strong current was running, so much so that numbers of the people in the water drifted by the boats with such rapidity that all attempts to rescue them were useless."[84]

Eight boats with about 150 souls were all that was left of the *Japan* and her passengers. During the night, cries were heard from all around the lifeboats. After the boats were lowered away, it was very difficult to keep them from being thrust up against the ship's side on account of an increasing sea and wind. The boats remained in the vicinity of the wreck until daylight.

Cries for assistance were heard throughout the night from the Chinese steerage passengers, from all around the hulk of the *Japan* yet the unfortunate souls eventually gave in to the elements as the lifeboats remained challenged by the heavy seas. The small lifeboats needed to be kept headed directly into the oncoming waves in order to prevent further loss of life or the likelihood of a boat being swamped when survivors tried to board.

The lifeboats remained close to the wreck of the *Japan* all night as the fire burned the ship to the waterline. Captain Warsaw's leadership never wavered as he continued to save life throughout the night and into a miserable, most tragic dawn the next morning.

Chapter 12

Misery at Dawn

The dawn light of December 18th ushered in misery and the quest for survival for those still alive. In the vicinity of the wreck site, large numbers of the *Japan*'s Chinese passengers were seen floating in the water, drowned, with their life-preservers on. A small number of the steerage passengers had survived. Those still alive that had not yet been picked up by a lifeboat during the night were now discovered floating on chairs, many were on coffins. In total, more than 400 Chinese steerage passengers had died in the fire and wreck of the wooden steamship *Japan*. These poor souls had found no lifeboat and have succumbed to the wind and waves.

The wreckage was vast and disturbing. Amongst the charred timbers were barrels of flour, part of the hurricane deck, ships stores, furniture, chairs, a chest with $3,000 in it, and a religious monstrance parcel that was being shipped to a Christian mission in China that was snatched up by one of the *Japan*'s officers.

On the wreck itself, the area around the coal bunkers and forward cargo hold eased below the water, quenching the red-hot treasure tank with a rush of sea water. The ship's signature rocking-arm was now a mass of iron work, and the ship's hull, still intact aft of the sidewheels at the waterline, was becoming one with the ocean surface. The top of the proud eagle on the ship's stern was just below the still discernable name of the *Japan* as it, when last seen this dismal morning, shifted with the wind away from the lifeboats.

The wind continued to blow from the northeast and the swell of the oncoming sea continued to roll into the debris. A number of approaching local Chinese junks observed the hulk of the *Japan* still floating and smoldering. Seven lifeboats with survivors remained in the vicinity of the wreck.

In one lifeboat was Chief Engineer John Cosgrove, Miss Mary Stott, one passenger, and seven Chinese.

In the second lifeboat were 3rd Officer Gallagher and four Europeans, 61 Chinese, and a baby.

In the third lifeboat were 2nd Assistant Engineer James Hoery and eight Europeans, and four Chinese.

In the fourth lifeboat were several Chinese, Mr. F.W. Crocker, a saloon passenger, and the ship's storekeeper W.B. Horn.

In the fifth lifeboat were Purser John Rooney, nine Europeans, and ten Chinese.

In the sixth boat were another storekeeper, two Europeans, and seven Chinese.

In the seventh boat were the ship's baker, the injured Nelly Noble, and six Chinese. A junk would approach them and then transport them to Hong Kong.

In the eighth and final boat that escaped the *Japan* was Captain Warsaw, Captain Andrews, the 2nd Officer, a chief officer, one Chinese crewman, seven Europeans, and seven Chinese.

A reporter from the *Daily Alta California* described the scene. "As daylight appeared, several Chinese fishing junks were seen, the sight of which gave courage to all. One of them sailed close by the ship, and after palavering around for some time and prospecting on the number of dollars they were to receive, commencing in the moderate sum of $10,000, they concluded to let the few officers come on board (the time being about 8 a.m.) Another one of the junks sailed around on of the boats for some time, before taking the people on board, then searching them and taking their effects, clothes, etc., and ordering them below, out of the way, before they would allow another boat to come alongside, nearly all being used in like manner."[85]

TRADING-JUNK.

Figure 44: Chinese Trading Junk from William H. Seward's "Travels Around the World" (1873)

Captain Warsaw engaged a junk to assist in saving lives from the boats and the surrounding waters. He "cruised in the vicinity of the wreck, and succeeded in saving 117 souls from boats and water."[86]

Two waves of lifeboat survivors from the wreck of the *Japan* would eventually arrive in Hong Kong and Swatow over the next 48 hours. The first wave consisted of a lifeboat that made it on its own to Hong Kong, plus with the inhabitants of another lifeboat that hitched a ride to Hong Kong with a passing junk. These first small groups of survivors set in motion a flow of information that would first generate disbelief and incredulity, quickly followed by a push to render urgent assistance with a naval search-and-rescue effort.

The main group of survivors, under the leadership of Captain Warsaw, would not show up for another day; they were picked up the morning after the wreck by a Chinese junk, but were taken in another direction, farther away from Hong Kong, where they had to wait before catching a ride south to their intended destination.

The first of the survivors to make its way to Hong Kong was the Chief Engineer's Chinese open lifeboat. With Mary Stott and seven Chinese, it managed a voyage of 100 miles, arriving in Hong Kong mid-morning on December 18th.

Three hours behind the engineer's open boat was a Chinese junk that had picked up the survivors in the lifeboat under the direction of the ship's baker. This small group included the injured Nelly Noble, and six Chinese. The baker had paid the junk captain $800 for the passage to Hong Kong. These first two tiny contingents would be the first to arrive in the port of Hong Kong with the dreadful news of the *Japan* disaster.

The *Japan* had been due to arrive at 8:00 AM on the morning of December 18. The vessel should have passed Captain Roberts and his crews busy securing the ten pontoons that would lift the still-grounded *Alaska* off the rocks at Aberdeen, part of the aftermath of the disaster and devastation of the typhoon that had struck the Hong Kong area on September 24.

A delay by a Pacific Mail steamship, however, was not unusual, especially considering the guidelines that the company continued to operate under in 1874 (less coal for lighter weight, and slower speeds to stay economical), plus the fickle winter weather of the northeast monsoon season. The Pacific Mail agent would have known, however, that the *Japan* had departed Yokohama on time and should have had a favorable light weight and wind-aided run to Hong Kong. A *Japan* arrival on the 19th would certainly come to pass.

At the time of the *Japan*'s loss, U.S. Consul David Bailey was away in the United States. In his absence, the consulate was under the direction of

Vice Consul H. Sheldon Loring. Loring was well experienced with matters involving U.S. maritime commerce at Hong Kong and had official relationships with the Pacific Mail Steamship Company crews. "Consuls inspected the cargoes of ships bound for the United States, established official estimates of their tonnage and collected the appropriate import duties. In addition, they supervised the operations of homes for destitute sailors, arbitrated disputes concerning goods or personal property damaged on American ships, and served as executors for the estates of Americans who died under their jurisdiction."[87]

Before Sheldon Loring became the Vice Consul for the U.S. in Hong Kong in 1873, he had served as a Union Colonel in the Inspector General's Department during the Civil War. Since the beginning of the Pacific Mail Steamship service and the first visit of the PMSS Colorado in 1867, the U.S. Consul acted as the largest commercial representative of the U.S. in Hong Kong.

In late 1874, the U.S. Consulate in Hong was beginning its fourth decade of consular service in one of Great Britain's 1842 Treaty of Nanking Ports. The five treaty Ports were Canton, Shanghai, Amoy, Ningpo, and Hong Kong.

The consul lived at his own residence in Hong Kong and operated from a consular office down on the waterfront Praya west of the steamship piers. Its location afforded the consul, vice consul, and their staff to complete their duties as U.S. representatives, which consisted of inspecting the cargoes of goods, collecting duties, and working with the British harbor master and Hong Kong medical facilities to screen immigrants before they boarded the outbound Pacific Mail Steamers.

In an 1871 Treasury Department report on the condition of U.S. consulates in the Far East, Agent B. Randolph Keim found that the Hong Kong Consulate occupied "a convenient locality. The books and archives are secured in suitable cases, like the furniture, the property of the consular officer, he having purchased the same from his predecessor. I found a safe, a rare specimen of antique design and workmanship, which had been the property of the Government for at least a quarter of a century."[88]

In short, although consuls were not U.S. Ambassadors, they had the pulse of commercial and diplomatic activity going on in the Crown Colony and with other Chinese and international officials and businessmen.

"Consuls inspected the cargoes of ships bound for the United States, established official estimates of their tonnage, and collected the appropriate import duties. In addition, they supervised the operation of homes for destitute sailors, arbitrated disputes concerning goods or personal property damaged on

American ships, and served as executors for the estates of Americans who died in the areas under their jurisdiction.

They performed no regular diplomatic duties but were often used in that capacity because of their convenience to foreign governments and acquaintance with local authorities. Officially, they represented the State Department, but they also submitted quarterly commerce reports to the Department of the Treasury.

Not far from the U.S. Consul's office was the Pacific Mail Steamship Company wharf with its go-downs that ferried the Chinese emigrants to the waiting ships and transported the incoming and outgoing cargo.

The U.S. Navy's Asiatic Squadron also called in Hong Kong and was commanded by Rear Admiral A.M. Pennock. Ships in the squadron in the 1870s included the USS *Saco*, USS *Ashelot*, USS *Yantic*, and USS *Monocacy*. Two of the squadron ships were in port in Hong Kong on December 19, 1874, as news of the *Japan*'s fate began to emerge during the pre-dawn hours.

Early in the morning of December 19, around 4:00 A.M., the first survivors arrived in Hong Kong in an open boat. In a little more than 24 hours since the *Japan* had sunk, Chief Engineer John Hargrove, seven Chinese and passenger Mary Stott's lifeboat had made their way to the port. Consul Loring reported that "the first news was brought by an open boat, which arrived at four a.m., containing the chief engineer, passenger Miss Stott and seven Chinese. Later in the morning, at about nine o'clock, the second boat arrived, containing the baker, stewardess, and six Chinese. This boat was picked up by a fishing junk; which took it on board and brought it, together with the inmates, to Hong Kong."[89]

The *Daily Alta* reported that the "stewardess was only saved, as it were, be a miracle. She fell from the deck into a boat just as it had been lowered from the falls. She is so badly bruised that she has to keep to her bed, and so hysterical that she can bear no allusion to the catastrophe. She is being kindly cared for at Messrs Lammert, Atkinson, and Company's Praya House."[90]

Pacific Mail Agent Amory now knew the general fact of the disaster. The public found out in the *Daily Alta* that the "Japan was burned at midnight December 17th forty miles this side of Swatow and twelve miles off the land. The other boats made for land."[91]

After receiving the tragic news of the *Japan* disaster from Chief Engineer John Hargrove and the *Japan*'s baker, Loring immediately communicated with the U.S. Navy's Asiatic Squadron. By noon, Rear Admiral Pennock dispatched two ships: the *Yantic* (3 guns) and *Saco* (3 guns) to cruise from Hong Kong to search for the wreck of the *Japan*. Commander R.F. R. Lewis, the senior naval officer in port and captain of the *Yantic*, had steam brought up in *Yantic* and directed Captain Charles McDougall of the *Saco* to accompany the *Yantic* to the spot of the wreck. At 12:15 on December 19, 1874, the *Yantic* and *Saco* steamed out of Hong Kong harbor to search for other survivors of the *Japan*.

Figure 45: USS YANTIC, Courtesy U.S. Navy

Figure 46: USS SACO, Courtesy U.S. Navy

A Navy search-and-rescue mission was now underway.

The largest group of survivors was under the direction of Captain Warsaw. Their route to Hong Kong, however, would be more circuitous.

First, Warsaw had convinced a junk to pick up 117 survivors. Then, Captain Warsaw talked the junk crew into continuing to sail around the wreck

136

of the *Japan* until a little after noon on the 18th, staying the longest time in the vicinity of the wreck. The junk's captain was impatient to go, motioning that it was time to give up the search and head in. Eventually, Warsaw had to agree that further efforts were fruitless. "About 2 P.M. on the 18th, seeing no more life, I stood in for land," reported Warsaw later.

The junk headed for the Chinese mainland around Cup Chi Point. A *Daily Alta* correspondent happened to be aboard the *Japan* and ended up on Captain Warsaw's lifeboat, where he was able to provide a graphic account of the next day's events. "From the Chinese sailors we soon ascertained that if we were once on shore in the vicinity of where we were heading, and in the hands of our deliverers, our chances were small to have clothes to cover us, and life to breathe. The Purser had saved some coin bags that from his room and paid the junk Captain. The Chinese fishermen had a peculiar liking for the dollars."[92]

An assistant engineer of the *Japan*, Oiler Edwin Tucker, was also aboard this junk. He noted that their joy of being rescued by the fishermen on the junk was short lived. The junk captain and crew were, in fact, pirates.

"The men were robbed of their valuables as they stepped aboard the junk. Then the captors cruised about, picking up survivors from five other boats as well as a few Chinese still clinging to debris or the wooden coffins. Through an interpreter, the pirates told the survivors they were to be taken ashore and held as hostages. The Captain (Warsaw) offered them a handsome payment if they would take them to Hong Kong but the pirates knew that, once seen in that port, their heads would roll before sundown. Then followed a discreet conference between the men and the Captain where it was decided to take the junk by force. Upon a signal from Capt. Warsaw, each man was to single out of the pirates in a free-for-all, using as weapons anything that could be picked up on deck. The minutes seemed like hours as we waited, tense and straining for the signal. Just as it was getting dark, and luckily before the signal for the attack was given, one of the men spotted a light approaching. This proved to be a steamer and a lantern was quickly found to signal the ship. The pirates, knowing the steamer would be armed, offered no resistance. The captain and two men rowed out to the vessel which proved to be the British Yottung."[93]

137

As the junk approached Cup Chi, the sun was setting behind the cliffs and coastal highlands. This high point rises 210 feet above the sea to a rugged summit, with a dilapidated fort at the south end of the feature. Approaching from the south along the coast was a light from a passing steamer, heading north. The need for Warsaw and his men to try to overcome the junk's crew was thankfully unnecessary. The pirate junk hailed the *Yottung,* which altered course to approach the loaded vessel of the *Japan* survivors.

There was one problem, which would prove deadly. After the *Yottung* came about, it informed the survivors that it did not have boats available to ferry them aboard. The junk would have to go alongside the *Yottung* to disembark the survivors.

The *Daily Alta* reporter said that, "The steamer did not have sufficient boats to take us off, and at the time there being considerable chop of a sea which made it difficult and attended with considerable danger. On getting alongside, the steamer was rolling heavily, also the junk, and in confusion and excitement to get on board, a great many were knocked overboard, including the cook Martin Cussick, who was drowned."[94]

This was tragic blow to Captain Warsaw and First Officer Andrews. The surviving passengers and *Japan*'s crew had made it aboard the *Yottung,* only to have Mr. Bennitt (the First Assistant Engineer), the two quartermasters (Harris and Satea) along with Cussick drown while being transported between the two vessels.

Captain Warsaw was exceedingly grateful, nonetheless, to have been rescued by the passing British ship, and he was impressed with the courtesy and professionalism of *Yottung*'s Captain Koch. However, the vessel was steaming away from Hong Kong. The *Japan* survivors had no choice but to go where the ship was headed. After the *Yottung* completed its night voyage along the seventy miles of the China Coast, it passed the Cape of Good Hope, Sugarloaf and Double islands, and then proceeded into the river bay to arrive at the port of Swatow on the morning of December 20. American Consul General J.C.A. Wingate would now learn the truth of the disaster.

Consul Wingate captured the shock of the moment with his official cable (186) to Assistant Secretary of State John L Cadwalader on December 21, 1874.

Sir:

It becomes my painful duty to report the total loss of the Pacific Mail Company's Steamer "Japan." Capt. Warsaw, off Breaker point, some thirty miles south of this port, on the night of the 17th instant.

The vessel was discovered to be on fire, in the fire room, at about 11 ½ o'clock P.M. and it was very soon found that it was impossible to save her.

Capt. Warsaw, with 28 of the European crew, 58 of the Chinese crew, 1 American cabin passenger, and 34 Chinese passengers, arrived here in the British steamer "Yottung" about 9:00 A.M. on the 19th, and all of these left for Hong Kong by the "Yesso" at 2:P.M. of the same day.

As the Captain was anxious to reach Hongkong as soon as possible, and his and my own time was fully taken up with other necessary work, I attempt no full report of the disaster, that duty will devolve upon the Hong Kong Consulate.

Capt. Warsaw reported that the steamer had on board 2 Cabin passengers, 2 European steerage passengers, 425 passengers steerage passengers, 36 European crew, 91 Chinese crew.

Also 620 tons cargo, 168 packages treasure, $358,508; and 7 bags mails; all of which is lost.

Boats were lowered but the night being very rough a large number of Chinese were drowned and it is feared, also, a few Europeans.

Capt. Warsaw reported that he last saw Mr. Tindall, U.S. Consul for Canton, with the Chief Engineer, and still hoped for his safety, but was fearful in regard to him. The "Douglas" from Hong Kong this morning; reports the arrival of two boats with 4 Europeans and 13 Chinese; the Chief Engineer was in one of these boats, but Mr. Tindall was not with him. I trust that dispatches from Hong Kong may assure you of his safety.

I am very respectfully,
Your obedient servant,
J.C.A. Wingate, U.S. Consul

Exhausted, yet considerate, Captain Warsaw wrote a quick note before his Swatow departure.

"I beg to convey on behalf of my officers and crew, and self, our sincere thanks to the English and American Consul's at Swatow, Captain Koch, and officers of the steamer Yottung,

and Captain Ashton and officers of the steamer Yesso, for their kindness in rendering every possible assistance." Signed E.R. Warsaw late Commander S.S. Japan.

He would later convey his admiration and gratitude for "the kind and human conduct of the Captain and officers of the British Steamer Yottung…and Captain Koch." [95]

While the survivors on Captain Warsaw's junk had been picked up by the Yottung, the missing Dr. Tindall and Dr. Gates, the *Japan's* surgeon, were making their way toward shore. They could see the shoreline of Sengmi and its adjoining sheltered bay at Tungao. By late afternoon, Dr. Gates and Dr. Tindall had reached Tonga Bay with 10 Chinese crewmen. They remained overnight at Tonga Bay until morning when they would be picked up by a junk.

Meanwhile the Navy search-and-rescue mission headed by the *Yantic* and *Saco* had arrived at the anchorage at Tongao Roads and sent two armed boats ashore to look for the survivors of the *Japan*. While at Tongao Bay, the *Saco* communicated to the *Yantic* that three Europeans had landed there but had been taken to Hong Kong in a junk.

Several Chinese corpses had also floated ashore.

While the *Saco* remained at anchor, the *Yantic* got underway and set a course for the probable debris field. After a four-hour east by east/south east by south course at a speed of 4-6 knots by the *Yantic*, by 4:00 in the afternoon of December 20 was upon the debris field. The log of the *Yantic* noted that the ship had "observed a white object floating on the water…found it to be a metallic lifeboat with the letter "J" on the bow. Sent a ships boat over to tow. Also found numerous charred timbers of wreck floating, items including barrels and bags of flour."[96]

While on the scene, the *Yantic* took on board, and brought to Hong Kong two fiberglass metallic lifeboats, which showed evidence of being tampered with by Chinese wreckers, who had removed a few brass plates.

The *Daily Alta* reported that "the Saco intercepted the Chinese junk and took aboard 3 Europeans and 10 Chinese and also learned that two other Chinese picked up by the junk had been buried."97 Those "Europeans were Dr. Gates and Dr. Tindall who now traveled on to Hong Kong with the *Japan's* lifeboats. Finding no further survivors, both vessels returned to Hong Kong arriving on December 22, 1874

Figure 47: Secretary of State Hamilton Fish

In the U.S., news of the loss of the *Japan* was electrifying and had arrived by official State department dispatch to Washington DC, which was then cabled on to New York, and finally on to the *Japan*'s homeport in San Francisco.

The tragic news arrived in a Washington, DC, atmosphere of skepticism and political scandal regarding the Pacific Mail's poor business climate and a growing scandal involving the company's possible bribery of Congress in an effort to secure the renewal of its annual subsidy. The initial news was first received as hoax, then in shock.

Figure 48: Harpers Weekly illustration of a child getting his hands burned by a Pacific Mail subsidy (1875) (Author's Collection)

In New York, the "P.M.S. Company has received a dispatch from Washington saying that the State Department has a dispatch that the *Japan* burned near Hong Kong with fearful loss of life; All the mails were lost. The *Japan* is one of the old wooden ships and is insured for $150,000 in French and English companies."

In San Francisco, the city was noted as greatly excited over the telegraphic announcement of the burning of the steamship *Japan*. From the incomplete nature of the dispatches, commercial parties are disposed to discredit them."[98]

142

The business wire and "the Merchant Exchange also received advises from New York to the effect that the Pacific Mail Steamship Japan had been burned forty miles below Swatow. On inquiry at the office of the Mail Company in this city we learn no news of the burning of the steamer has been received. The news then from New York is supposed to be a hoax. It is thought that the false telegram was gotten up for the purpose of "bearing" the stock. The Japan is insured for probably half her value."[99]

News on the *Japan* indeed had an adverse effect on the company's stock value on the New York exchange. About the time the news of the disaster was received at the office of the company Pacific Mail stock stood at 38 or thereabouts. Fully an hour elapsed before the intelligence was made public and meanwhile the stock was gradually dropping, until finally it reached 36 ¼. The *New York Times* reported that "The feeling on the street when the intelligence of the disaster became generally known, was that only by radical change in its present management can the waning fortunes of Pacific Mail be retrieved, and the company placed in a position where it will command the respect and confidence of the public."[100]

With the Navy search-and-rescue operation by the *Yantic* and *Saco* concluding, the greatest number of the *Japan* survivors prepared to return to Hong Kong from Swatow, 120 miles up the coast from the Hong Kong harbor. On the morning of December 20, U.S. Consul J.C.A. Wingate saw off the more than 100 of the *Japan* survivors at Swatow as they boarded the China coastal steamer *Yesso*.

As the *Yesso* cleared the Han River and rounded the Cape of Good Hope, she set a course to the southwest offshore to pass through the area of the *Japan*'s loss. The correspondent of the *Daily Alta* reported that "On the passage from Swatow when in the vicinity of the wreck, we spoke to several fishing junks in the hopes of getting some information on the missing boats, or in regard to the wreck; but failed to get any. We then steamed for Hong Kong, arriving at 2 P.M. on the 20th." [101]

As the *Yesso* rounded the channel into Hong Kong harbor, Captain Warsaw observed the pontoon workers working to refloat the *Alaska* from the rocks on Aberdeen point. The *Yesso* moored at 2:00 P.M. on the steamship landing, down from the Russell and Company building and the offices of the Pacific Mail Steamship Company.

The *Daily Alta* reported that on the afternoon of December 20th, "the steamship Yesso, Captain Ashton, arrived from Swatow, bringing the captain, the cabin passenger, 29 Europeans of the crew, 60 Chinese of the crew, and 34 Chinese passengers, saved from the burning of the Japan."[102]

The survivors had lost everything but their clothing they were wearing. Once moored, the survivors departed the *Yesso* and were cared for by Pacific Mail Agent Amory. Some were sent to the Sailors Home; others were sent to the steamer *Alaska* at Aberdeen. The severely injured and bruised stewardess and barber, Nelly Noble, would begin her recuperation at Lammert, Atkinson, and Company's Praya House. Passenger Miss Mary Stott would recover at the Diocean School House in Hong Kong.

Captain Warsaw thanked Captain Ashton for transporting the survivors to Hong Kong and then departed the ship to meet with the Pacific Mail Agent. He then went on to the U.S. Consulate to meet with Vice Consul Loring. There, Warsaw learned of the arrival of other *Japan* survivors, the whereabouts of Engineer John Hargrove, and the dispatch of the *Yantic* and the *Saco* to search for additional survivors along the Chinese coast and amongst the Chinese junks.

Vice Consul Loring was now responsible for chairing an official board of inquiry which he would convene quickly, less than a week later, on December 24. It was important to get the initial interviews with Captain Warsaw and the other survivors. He also needed to ensure that the survivors were cared for and were sheltered in Hong Kong. Captain Warsaw stayed close to the consulate at a nearby boarding house. Over the next three days, leading up to the Official Board of Inquiry, he was there for the return of the *Yantic* and the *Saco* from their search with surgeon Dr. Gates and Consul Tindall aboard.

He would also meet with his colleague, Captain Van Sice, on the December 23rd and congratulate him on the refloating of the *Alaska* off Aberdeen. Captain Warsaw and his fellow survivors would now have a way home to San Francisco on that vessel after the inquiry was completed.

Still at sea, however, was the wreck site of the *Japan* with the bodies of almost 400 Chinese steerage passengers. Surely Captain Warsaw was stricken with a sense of remorse at such loss of life under his command. Perhaps his nights in the Hong Kong boarding house were restless, burdened with awful dreams of fire, confusion, bodies plunging, lifeboats bobbing on dark seas.

144

Chapter 13

Inquiry

"The room was full of smoke when I got there, and all the lights were out but one. Fire was coming through the forward bulkhead, dividing the engine room from the freight deck. I do not know what freight was stowed there. I saw that all pumps and gear were in proper working order. I made an inspection in San Francisco, and found everything in proper working order and reported to the Captain. I made an inspection of everything on the night of the fire at eight o'clock and all was in proper order."
Engineer John Hargrove, PMSS Japan

Captain Warsaw awakened early from his Hong Kong boarding house bed on Tuesday morning, December 22. He was exhausted after the past 48 hours, devastated by his memories of the fire's rapid expansion and flames against the cracking wood of his ship. He had survived, but was now responsible for the greatest loss of Chinese steerage passenger life in history. In his dreams at night, did he still hear the screams of his Chinese steerage passengers as they struggled in the cold waters of a midnight ocean, lit only by the blaze of a burning ship? Did the thought of the deaths of nearly 400 of them haunt his thoughts during the day? His ship was gone and his life at sea over.

Hours later he walked down to the Praya waterfront toward the steamship landing which had brought 107 of the survivors with him on the *Yesso* two days earlier. The *Saco* and *Yantic* had just returned from their search and rescue mission after almost three days at sea and had with them the ship's surgeon, Doctor Gates and Mr. Tindall.

Doc Gates saw his captain and both men embraced each other. Warsaw then reached out to Dr. Tindall as the crews looked on. He was shaken and trying with great difficulty to maintain his composure.

Warsaw relayed to Gates that "over a hundred were saved and are here at the school and boarding house. The women are badly shaken and being cared for." Gates was greatly relieved at the news, then told the captain of his own landing on the shores of Tungao Bay.

"We made it with the crewmen and had stayed the night on the beach. The wind carried on all night and were huddled together to stay warm. The local residents were anything but kind and hospitable and stayed clear of us. By morning bodies and debris began floating ashore along the bay when, thankfully, two boats with an armed boarding party from the Saco came ashore and retrieved us for the return to Hong Kong."

Warsaw then thanked the two captains, Commander R.F. Lewis from the *Yantic* and Captain Charles McDougall from the *Saco*, who now joined them for saving Gates and Tindall. They all walked together up the steamship pier and toward the Consulate and Mr. Loring to provide their statements and the search and rescue mission report.

Warsaw also knew that within the next 48 hours he would before a formal board of inquiry, in which the men who had rescued his crew would now sit in judgment of his professional conduct and the readiness of the *Japan*.

Commander Lewis, as senior officer present would join Consul Loring and two other mariners, Benjamin Clug, the master of the American ship Malay and Lieutenant William Kilpatrick, an officer of the *Saco* to conduct the Inquiry.

Loring had been working a full day, late into the evening, receiving statements, sending short telegraphic cables to Secretary of State Fish in Washington, and laboring to pull all of the information together in order to get together the official chronology of the disaster (Appendix B, Consulate Hong Kong Cable 273).

The Court of Inquiry was convened on Thursday morning, December 24, at the U.S. Consulate and would take three days. The board was assembled in a moderately sized room in the consulate, one with a large desk. The board sat on the side facing toward the entrance. A single seat across from the board members would be used in turn by Captain Warsaw, second officer H.H. Andrews, and Chief Engineer John Hargrove to provide their testimony.

Going into the inquiry, Consul Loring had assembled an important sense of the disaster and actions of the captain and crew to fight the fire. The board was greatly concerned about the great loss of life involving the Chinese steerage passengers and the lack of organization involving evacuation of the passengers and crew into the available lifeboats. The board also evaluated the fire-fighting capability on board the *Japan* and tried to determine the location and cause of fire.

146

There were three issues for the board: to determine the cause of the fire, to evaluate the response of Captain Warsaw and his officers in fighting the fire, and to pass judgment on the overall effort to save lives.

A stoic and determined Captain Warsaw, dressed in his company's uniform of command, preceded Second Officer Andrews and Engineer Hargrove into the inquiry room. The presiding officers rose as he entered, and the assembled consular staff and a China Overland Mail reporter took in the scene. It was a little after 10:00 when Consul Loring convened the board into order.

Since he was on watch at the time of the fire's discovery at 11:30 and the "muffled sound on deck," Second Officer Andrews provided the initial testimony to the board. Andrews testified that he thought that the fire's origin was determined to be in the forward areas, under the Chinese berthing compartments somewhere between the coal bunker and the forward hold.

Consul Loring asked the first question:

Q: Where do you think that the fire originated?
A: In the fore room or bunkers.

Q: What was the nature of the cargo stowed on the freight deck over the bunkers?
A: Flour only.

Q: Was the coal taken in at Yokohama wet or dry?
A: Wet

Q: Did you suppose the fire originated in any bunker?
A: The smoke came from that direction. There was a smell of something besides wood burning.

Q: Might the fact of the coal being wet have originated it?
A: It might.

Q: So far as you have noticed was the fire apparatus in good order?
A: It was. I do not know how many streams there were.

It had been raining on the final day in Yokohama before the *Japan*'s departure, and wet Sydney coal was loaded into the forward coal bunker. When coal became wet, it decomposed and released heat and combustible gas. A heap of wet coal in this condition over a short period of time would rise in temperature and combustible gas. In the heat of a poorly ventilated bunker, this could eventually reach levels that caused it to combust spontaneously. The Sydney coal was also a richer bituminous coal with higher heating power which also generated more gas.

Chief Engineer, John Henry Hargrove was next to testify. He was questioned by Commander R.T. Lewis, the senior officer and commander of the *Yantic* for the search-and-rescue mission. Sticking to the most probable cause of the fire, Lewis then asked Hargrove:

Q: Was any fresh coal taken on board at Yokohama?
A: Yes

Q: What kind of coal?
A: One hundred and forty tons of Sydney coal and 480 tons of Tako coal.

Q: What was its condition, wet or dry when put in the bunkers?
A: The tako coal was dry. I did not see the other when it came on board.

Q: In which bunkers was the coal stowed?
A: The Sydney coal was stowed in the forward and after bunker, and the Japanese coal in the side bunker.

Q: When surplus coal happened to be in the bunkers after a voyage, was it you custom to heap the fresh coal down upon it?
A: In some cases I did do it.

Q: Was any care taken that the surplus coal should always be used first?
A: No.

Q: Was there any surplus coal in the bunkers in which coal was put at Yokohama?
A: There was none in the forward bunker, but five or six tons in the after.

Q: How often were you in the habit of taking the temperature of the coal bunkers while steaming?

148

A: We never took it at all.

Q: Where, in your opinion, did the fire originate, and from what cause?
A: I think it must have originated on the freight deck; the cause I cannot say.

Q: When you were first aware that the ship was on fire, what kind of smell pervaded the vicinity - that of coal, or gas, or wood?
A: It was the smell of burning wood.

Q: How is the freight deck, where you suppose the fire originated, situated as regards the coal bunkers?
A: It is situated immediately over the forward athwart ship bunker.

Andrews had testified that the coal was wet and that the fire had started in the forward area. Hargrove testified that the fire had started forward as well, but introduced his opinion that the fire originated in the forward hold, which contained flour.

Dignified and responsible, Captain Edward R. Warsaw was then invited to provide the concluding testimony to the board. On his firefighting efforts, Warsaw said that he had gone "below again to the steerage, cut a hole abreast the foremast, through the deck, and saw fire. I applied a hose to it, and then went aft on the port side, pulled the butt out of a hole which we had cut before, and saw fire. This was directly under the ash-shoot."

He said that all of the deck and the bulkhead between the engine room, fire-room, and wing bunkers, on the port side, were on fire. Warsaw himself inserted the a fire hose into the cut hole and returned to the hurricane deck where the third officer Gallagher and a gang of men were swinging the forward boats, while second officer Andrews and another gang were swinging the after boats.

Warsaw told the board that "during the whole of this time every effort was being made by the white men on board to extinguish the fire and told Dr. Tindall then to make ready to leave the ship, and placed the women in his charge."

He then went back to the site of the fire, where his officers and men were doing their utmost to extinguish it. He had not yet given the order to abandon ship and still depended on the effort of his firefighting crew in the main spaces to do their best. Warsaw then told the board that "at this time a

149

man ran by me named Denham, an oiler, crying out 'Every man for himself.' I caught him and asked him who gave him that order? He replied, the Chief Engineer. I told him that if he repeated it, 'I'd blow his brains out' and ordered him to work with the rest.

Warsaw then realized that the fire-fighting effort was failing. The fire was rapidly gaining in intensity and height. Fire-fighting water had been lost as the pumps lost steam power. It was now impossible for any man to enter the portion of the ship to start them up.

At that moment, Warsaw told the board, he came to the decision: "I then started with a view of saving life."

Before departing, he traversed the port side up to the flames and then down the starboard side, and then up to the hurricane deck where he surveyed the weather side of the ship and observed the final lifeboat hanging by its davit. Second Officer Andrews then assisted him while they lowered the boat.

"In the boat were all the Europeans and Chinese passengers abaft the fire, which was now right across the ship at the engine room. I gave orders to the second officer to wait alongside the ship for me, and I returned to the weather side of the quarter deck, took a general survey of the ship, saw that the Captains gig was gone, that the non-pareil raft was gone, and that all the settees on the quarterdeck had gone. I opened the engineer's room door, and called him. Receiving no response, I went aft, and lifting the sky-light called out to see if there was any more life on board aft, and, not hearing any response, concluded to leave the ship.

"I went over the ship's side at 12:45 A.M. on the 18th I shoved our boat clear of the ship, came round under the stern, and used every endeavor to save life, and picked up a number of Chinese, all of whom had life-preservers on and were on pieces of wreck, or hatches, chairs, etc. remained to windward of the wreck until daylight, when we went in search of the other boats. At about 2 P.M. on the 18th, seeing no more life, I stood in for land."[103]

On December 28, 1874, the Board of Inquiry rendered its decision (provided in U.S. Consulate Hong Kong Cable 274 in Appendix C). They fully exonerated Captain Warsaw and all of the officers – except the Chief Engineer.

The court found the cause of fire to be due to spontaneous combustion of coal in the forward coal-bunker having been taken on in a wet condition in Yokohama.

They also found that the fire-fighting equipment was in working order. However, they took exception for the lack of boat evacuation procedures and practice, which contributed to the large loss of life by the *Japan*'s Chinese passengers.

The engineer's conduct was particularly reprehensible, in the board's judgment. They deemed his "every man for himself" call as irresponsible. Although Hargrove testified that he never said that, the board still censured him.

The inquiry now concluded, Warsaw and the survivors would make arrangements for their return to San Francisco. Dr. Tindall would now be able to depart for his post in Canton and within the week had assumed his position there as U.S. Consul.

Unfortunately, Dr. Tindall's service as U.S. Consul in Canton lasted only six months. In his resignation letter, he cites the lingering after effects of his first-hand experience of tragedy of the S.S. *Japan*.

United States Consulate
Canton February, 23rd 1875
Hon John L. Cadwalader
Assistant Secretary of State
Washington, DC

Sir,
I have the honor to tender you my resignation as United States Consul at this Port to take effect on the first day of June next. My ill health compels me to adopt this course. My nervous system received such a shock from exposure on the night and day following that the Steamship "Japan" was burned as Sea, that I fear it has seriously impaired my constitution.

I have the honor to be Sir
Your Obedient Servant
R.M. Tindall
U.S. Consul

Before departing Hong Kong, an assembly of Chinese and Hong Kong merchants recognized Captain Warsaw for his leadership and life-saving conduct. The captain's return voyage home would be on the Alaska, which was finally free after three months of being driven aground by the September Hong Kong hurricane. She would begin the voyage home on January 13, 1875.

Chinese and U.S. business interests and relatives of the lost Chinese passengers would also begin pressing for the recovery of the bodies from the wreck and for the recovery of the Japan's treasure.

Chapter 14

Salvage

The art and science of shipwreck recovery and salvage in the 1860s is an interesting story, and Captain John Pratt Roberts, naval engineer, was an interesting man in the forefront of that specialized endeavor. A direct descendant of Connecticut's Pratt family, he was a seafaring officer that transported Irish immigrants from Liverpool to New York in the 1850s as the captain of the vessel *Underwriter*.

Figure 49: Captain John Pratt Roberts (1867)
Courtesy UC Santa Barbara-Davidson Library
(Bernath- Shanghai Steam Navigation Company Album)

The Civil War's disruption of Atlantic trade between the U.S. and Great Britain coincided with an opportunity presented to Captain Roberts by the Russell and Company House, the American trading agency with a base in Hong Kong, to join their effort in establishing sidewheel steamboat capability on the Yangtze River to increase the China trade to America. Captain Roberts agreed to captain the sidewheel steamer *Huquang* from New York to Hong Kong, rounding the Cape of Good Hope in South Africa on May 28, 1862. After his arrival, he joined the Russell and Company team and soon became the most well-known and established American marine engineer in China. During the late and early 1870s, Captain Roberts established the shipping concerns in Shanghai, became a co-founder of China's first navigation company, the Shanghai Steam Navigation Company (SSNC), and was directly involved in the important Anglo-American steamship rivalry with China's Treaty ports to secure market share in the rich cargo-carrying trade along the Yangtze River.

Given his considerable abilities, Captain Roberts was hired as a marine engineer by the Pacific Mail Company to refloat the company's steamer *Alaska* from the rocks. The new contract for refloating the vessel was taken by Roberts on November 28, 1874 as the SSNC Superintendent. Following his success in that project, Roberts was a natural choice to salvage the wreckage of the *Japan*.

Captain John Pratt Roberts' December 1874 Hong Kong presence was fortuitous. A knowledgeable salvor, he had been able to monitor the ongoing Court of Inquiry for the *Japan* tragedy. Once that was completed, he wasted no time in getting hired by the American trading firm of Augustine and Heard to pursue the rights to salvage the wreck of the *Japan*.

Critically important to the Chinese underwriters for the salvage effort was the attempt to recover the bodies of the Chinese steerage passengers, the poor souls who perished so close to returning home to their counties and villages throughout Guangdong. If possible, the recovery of their remains would also be included as an objective of the salvage effort. His strategy for the salvage: acquire the Magistrate's Admiralty jurisdiction, legally necessary for the salvage rights of the *Japan,* by determining the ships final South China Sea resting place.

At the Augustine Heard office, details of *Japan*'s insurance coverage were discussed"[104] *The New York Times* reported that the vessel itself was insured for $150,000 by French and English Companies. Her cargo was insured by the shippers, and the Augustine and Heard Company held a position of $47,000 of the more than $358,000 in treasure in *Japan*'s treasure tank. The remaining positions were held by the other British and Chinese traders. Together, the traders approached Augustine and Heard, Russell and

Company, and the Shanghai Steam, Shipping and Navigation Company (SSSNC) to hire Captain Roberts to organize and engineer the complex shipping challenge of recovering of the bodies and salvaging the *Japan*'s treasure.

For both the treasure and the body recovery, Captain Roberts needed to assemble the necessary equipment and personnel. He would need a recovery steamer, an on-scene schooner for the supply and business runs, a crew of divers, and naval protection of the salvage operations. The project would be conducted far from shore off Swatow and Breaker Point and would surely be under surveillance by the watchful eyes of the South China Sea pirates.

Swatow was situated on the South China Sea at the confluence of the Han and Kieh-Yang Rivers, close to the well-travelled north-south shipping route along China's coast. (The Pacific Mail steamers routinely passed 20 miles outside of Swatow.) Ships of the U.S. Asiatic Fleet would call in Swatow and visit American consul Isaac Shepard during their wreck and pirate protection service for the salvage effort during the 1875-1877 southwest monsoon period. Consul Shepard aided the operation by providing the only map, pinpointing the wreck."[105]

A schooner and a steamer were bought and equipped with the required apparatus. With little delay, under Captain Roberts' direction, the operational began the first step in January: sweeping the ocean's bed in search of the wreck.

Captain John Roberts' salvage and diving vessels arrived in Swatow with up to six vessels clearing the port in search of the wreck of the *Japan*.

Meanwhile, Captain Warsaw and the *Japan*'s crew stowed their belongings onto the *Alaska*. They were ready to go home. On January 13, 1875, the Pacific Mail agent in Hong Kong made the final manifest decisions for the *Alaska*'s return voyage to San Francisco. The ship remained anchored in Hong Kong Bay, and Captain Van Sice was thankful to get her back to sea after being aground for three months. He was now facing a dead-of-winter transit into the South China Sea's northeast monsoon, followed by the crossing of the Pacific to San Francisco.

As the *Alaska* prepared to depart, Vice Consul Loring and the American Consulate staff worked through the Milar Admiralty magistrate to clarify the "establishing authorities" for the *Japan* salvage effort. Loring also delivered the official results of the *Japan* inquiry (Cable 274) to the *Alaska* for its dispatch to the State Department. The Inquiry Report, the Hong Kong newspaper reports of the rescue operation, and an *Alta* reporter with a gripping account of the Chinese passengers, the fire, and the people in their lifeboats would all arrive simultaneously and splash across the San Francisco

155

waterfront upon Captain Warsaw and *Japan*'s crew's return to the Pacific Mail pier.

The *Alaska* got underway in the afternoon of Wednesday, January 13, for the 34-day transit to San Francisco via Yokohama, Japan. The next morning, Captain Warsaw joined Captain Van Sice in *Alaska*'s pilothouse. Off of the *Alaska*'s port quarter was the outline of Breaker Point and up Cup Chi, and up the line the coastline along Swatow and the Han River. Based on the ship's location, they were crossing over the approximate area of the *Japan*'s probable resting place. What thoughts went through the mind of Captain Warsaw, what internal doubts of inspections approved, wet coal taken on, failures of fire-fighting efforts?

The *Alaska* reached Yokohama on January 21, dropping anchor, the steamship began discharging cargo and passengers and loading coal. Underway again on January 24, the final 26-day transit to San Francisco across the Pacific had begun. It was a treacherous transit. The *Alaska* endured a sequence of dangerous Pacific storms, machinery breakdowns and a coal bunker fire. "Then, smallpox broke out among the 1,100 Chinese steerage passengers. Topping this off was a mutiny among the Chinese, quelled only by the use of steam hoses."[106]

Tuesday, February 16, 1875 was "Steamer Day" in San Francisco as Captain Warsaw and the crew of the *Japan* were finally back home again. The front-page *Daily Alta California*'s "Along the Wharves" column let the citizens of San Francisco know that "Capt Warsaw and the officers of the ill-fated 'Japan' are expected on the "Alaska" now due."

It was also a bittersweet homecoming of sorts for the *Alaska* and Captain Van Sice, after her July sailing with the "Transit of Venus" scientific and naval delegation for Yokohama, and her subsequent grounding for three months in Hong Kong after the historic September 24 typhoon. Captain Warsaw, now a passenger, watched Captain Van Sice bring the *Alaska* through the Golden Gate. After the vessel clearance and finally the arrival at the Pacific Mail dock and the lengthy customs inspection, later that afternoon, Captain Warsaw and the officers and passengers of the *Japan* departed the ship for the various hotels, homes, and boarding houses of San Francisco.

Alongside the Pacific Mail pier was the new iron-screw steamer "City of Peking." Warsaw, the line's oldest captain, left the *Alaska*, the sidewheel steamer of the past, walked by the more modern vessel, the future of the China trade, and headed to the Pacific Mail office to begin the closeout regarding the consequences of the *Japan*'s loss, the re-assignment of *Japan*'s crew and his retirement from the Pacific Mail line for good.

The morning following the *Alaska*'s return to San Francisco was horrendous for Captain Warsaw and the *Japan* survivors. All of the news arrived in San Francisco simultaneously: the Hong Kong papers, the *Alta* "special report", and the personal account of the fire, survival and rescue. He would have to steel himself and the survivors.

The *Japan* disaster would undergo a new Inquiry in San Francisco led by Captain R. Waterman, the Port Inspector of Hulls, during the last two weeks of February. This inquiry was characterized as more intense. It "launched the greatest mass of testimony" for an inquiry on the *Japan* Disaster, which suggested that the fire did not originate in the coal bunker but in the cargo hold. By the first week in March, the Inquiry was completed, but and was inconclusive in any judgment of the origin of the fire, whether in a coal bunker or in a cargo hold.

The *Sacramento Daily* noted that "the engineer, Mr. Cosgrove and Captain Warsaw, are at a variance as to what should have been done and was done when the vessel was found to be on fire...Considering that the steamer was completely equipped with boats and first class construction, this is consolatory information to the relatives of four hundred Chinamen, who lost their lives by insurmountable accident."[107]

Captain Warsaw's life at sea as a China steamer Captain was now over. He would now reside in San Francisco at 14 Oak Street and begin a new chapter of his life as a Stock Operator at the San Francisco Stock Exchange Board and eventual owner of the Vermont Consolidate Silver Mine in Virginia City, Nevada. The Pacific Mail Steamship Company would pay Captain Warsaw's $48.00 Hong Kong board (about $2.00 per day), and his name would from thereafter remain off the books and the records of the Pacific Mail Steamship Company.

Back in Hong Kong the Whelar Magistrate was taking up the salvage case for the wreck of the *Japan*. The steamer *Aden*, owned by the Shanghai Merchants Seamanship and Navigation Company, was readily available to Captain Roberts and the salvage efforts. The Inquiry report indicated that the wreck should be found in 14 fathoms (84 feet, or 28 meters) of water - a depth considered manageable for the divers Captain Roberts intended to use.

The American schooner, *Scotland*, operated by the notable Yankee trader in the western Caroline Islands of Yap, Captain Crayton Phil Holcomb, also became part of the two-vessel package that Captain Roberts' needed.

The Magistrate ruled that the privilege and jurisdiction to salvage the *Japan* belonged to the first vessel to locate the wreck and claim to be the "first salver." Augustine and Heard dispatched their intention to recover the bodies and the *Japan*'s treasure to Vice Consul Loring in Hong Kong. They designated Captain Roberts as the Engineer-in-Charge of the recovery and wrecking operations. The *Aden* would be the salvage platform, and the *Scotland* would act as a logistics vessel.

After a 15 - voyage, the *Aden* and *Scotland* arrived in the vicinity of the presumed final resting place of the *Japan*. They began their search as the northeast monsoon persisted, knowing full well that the recovery operations could not begin in full until the winds became more favorable. Their mission during this period and in these seas was to locate the wreck.

It took a week to discover the wreck's location. The following day, the divers on the *Aden* began to recover the bodies from the wreck. The *Daily Alta* reported that "many dead bodies of Chinese have been taken from the wreck of the Pacific Mail Steamship Japan, all of which were kept under water by money fastened to their persons."[108]

Only part of the vessel was discovered by the salvage operation, however. Apparently the *Japan* had broken in two. Roberts, using the Aden and Scotland, swept the ocean floor in the area surrounding the *Japan*'s last known location, but the other portion was not found in the immediate vicinity. While sweeping, they discovered the location of the *Japan*'s paddlewheel. But it was not clear which paddlewheel it was.

Captain Warsaw's testimony had noted that the flames had taken possession of the center part of the ship, thereby cutting the *Japan* in half by flame, causing the Chinese steerage passengers forward to be cut off from the *Japan*'s crew that had assembled in the aft section.

The *China Overland Mail* had reported that a Chinese crewman in the last boat to leave indicated that "flames were shooting through the hurricane deck as high as the walking beam and an explosion occurring about the time the final boat pushed away."[109]

A major fire raging across the ship at the engine room, devouring the broad part of the *Japan* between the two sidewheels, would have led to a significant structural imbalance. The damage caused by the fire's destructive power could cause the sidewheels to fall off. Furthermore, with the starboard side exposed to the northeast monsoon (weather-side) and the port side on the lee side), it would be logical to conclude that the *Japan*, lacking power to correct her course and pummeled by the high seas, would likely be listing to port.

When the explosion occurred after midnight, the ship's hull might have been breached, allowing more of the sea to pour in on the port side, If this occurred, the differential displacement in weight and weakened structure of the ship gutted by fire, the port side-wheel and surrounding steerage berthing area and purser's cabin could have broken free from the ship when its weight could no longer be supported by the *Japan*'s fire-damaged wood frame.

Indeed, a number of bodies were recovered by the *Aden* from the initial location in 14 fathoms of water. But where was the rest of the ship?

Where was the starboard sidewheel? Certainly of no less significance to the commercial interested funding the salvage operation, where was the cargo hold's treasure tank – the protective container that was twenty-eight feet long, five feet deep, wide at one end and pointed at the other – into which had been placed 168 boxes of treasure in the amount of $358,508 in newly minted 1874 Carson City and San Francisco trade dollars?

The treasure underwriters wanted results, and Captain Holcomb and the *Scotland* were losing valuable time and money on this salvage gamble. This was going to be a more challenging than expected for Captain Roberts. It would be another six weeks before Captain Roberts located the main body of the wreck eleven miles southwest of the original site. The second section of the vessel was found in considerably deeper water - 23 fathoms (138 feet. or 46 meters). The salvage operations now had to be contemplated at a depth greater than the recommended diving depth for divers of the Admiralty, and far off the coast of this busy area of the South China Sea.

The good news for Captain Roberts was that they had found a part of the *Japan* which would allow them to be recorded as 'First Salvors." English Divers would now be able to continue their work on the wreck. Encouraged, the underwriters, Augustine and Heard, and Battle and Company, then communicated through the American Consul in Swatow, their request for naval protection over the deeper part of the wreck.

As for the *Scotland*, the new reality of the deeper water and tough diving conditions weakened the resolve of Captain Holcomb. But he stayed with it during the initial deep-diving period, which began with treacherous visibility and diving conditions.

Pirates on the surface were also a threat. Pirates had recently captured a vessel in the channel leaving Canton and were particularly active along the Swatow coast. Naval protection was urgently needed. On the morning of May 10, 1875, Captain Roberts and the divers observed a welcome sight - a large naval vessel, hull down, approaching their position from the northwest and the direction of Swatow.

It was the *Yantic*, the three-masted stalwart of the Asiatic fleet. This would be the *Yantic*'s first time at piracy protection for the wrecking and salvage operations. When she sighted "the American schooner, Scotland, at anchor near the supposed wreck of PMSS Japan," the *Yantic* communicated with the *Scotland* and remained in vicinity as protection.

Over the coming months, as the unfruitful salvage operations continued in the challenging depths, the *Scotland* and the first group of divers departed for good. Two new vessels, freshly equipped, would take over for the *Scotland* and *Aden*.

Surrounding the wreck of the *Japan* for the 1875 spring and summer salvage operation were the vessels of the Peninsula and Oriental (P&O) and Chinese Maritime Steamship Navigation (CMSN) Company, the *Aden* and *Rajah*, the American schooner *Scotland*, the American tug *Little Orphan*, and the German or Danish schooner *Loitens* with its divers.

They anchored over the wreck and placed a new buoy pattern out for the diving operation which continued from the summer of 1875 until mid-September when the monsoon season reversed itself.

As the summer months dragged on, frustrations mounted. The wreck of the steamship *Japan* was in much deeper water that was thought, and the currents there were making it very difficult to get at her. The Danish left the site returned without recovering a single coin and the support schooner *Scotland* returned to Hong Kong."

"In calm weather the divers were able to see tolerably well when at the bottom, and they sent up several slats of copper and a case of canned lobster, which latter was eaten by the crew." **Captain John P. Roberts, 1876**

DIVERS IN THEIR ARMOR.

Figure 50: A deep water view from the 1874-1876 period

160

Buoys were laid out demarking the spot and a team of English divers, led by Captain Templar, prepared themselves for the deep-water salvage operation. Although the equipment description is not available, an extract from the 1875 Robert Lewis Stevenson's *The Wrecker* and R.M. Ballantine's *Diving in Deep Waters* provide likely insight into the pieces of diving equipment and a sense of an 1870s deep-water diving operation.

"Having reached the scene of the wreck...the party at once proceeded to sound and drag for it, and soon discovered its position, for it had not shifted much after slipping off the ledge....Its depth under the surface was exactly twenty-three fathoms, or 138 feet...the boat was moored over the place where the wreck lay, a short ladder was hung over the side of a smaller boat they had in tow with its pendant line and weight and pumps were set up and rigged, the dresses were put on...Thick darkness prevailed at that depth, but Denayrouze's lamp rendered the darkness visible, and sufficed to enable the divers to steer clear of bristling rods and twisted iron-bands that might otherwise have torn their dresses and endangered their lives."[110]

DIVERS AT WORK.

Figure 51: Salvage hooked up (1874-1876)

From July through September 12, 1875 the divers worked to locate the *Japan*'s treasure tank, hoping to finally begin the recovery of the 168 boxes of treasure. On September 12, 1875, the southwest monsoon had ceased and the divers were preparing to complete their work for the season. The trade dollar treasure had yet to be recovered.

In his October 31, 1877 *New York Times* report on "The Celestial Empire," author Thomas W. Knox described what happened next.

> *"On the morning of that day, Captain Roberts believed that the whole enterprise would end there, and the Japan and her treasure be allowed to rest undisturbed forevermore. But on his last plunge for the season, the Diver managed to push his hand through a hole in the tank and secured a black lump resembling a piece of coal.*

The lump on examination proved to consist of 24 American trade dollars, burned and oxidized so much that they required a great deal of scouring to reveal their true character. But they were worth much more than $24; they were valuable as an encouragement to the underwriters to continue on their work. The wreckers retired to Hong Kong for the six months of the northeast monsoon, and resumed operations the following spring."[111]

Figure 52: Picture of the 1874 U.S. Trade Dollar

The trade dollars had been packed in boxes. The shipments had been underwritten by trading agents, including the American A. Heard in Hong Kong, the Chinese Traders Association, and the Hong Kong and Shanghai Bank. Recovered from the *Japan*'s treasure tank, the coin was described by Thomas Knox as "in mostly good condition, though nearly all is black and heavily oxidized. Some near the surface of the tank was partially melted by the heat of the burning steamer, and many of the boxes are charred and broken. Some of the dollars are bright as now when brought to the surface, but they speedily turn black when exposed to the air."

Captain Roberts provided a complete account of the 1875 salvage operations on the wreck of the *Japan* in a rare letter report to the Pratt family biographer in 1876.

"I was absent from Shanghai last summer, and succeeded in finding the wreck of the Japan after a long search and much tiresome and disagreeable work in sweeping over many miles of the bottom of the sea. On the 31st of July we found the wreck, nineteen and a half miles from the nearest land, and lying in twenty-three fathoms of water, or 138 feet. The southwest monsoon was them in full force, and opportunities for diving were very rare; yet the divers were able during the following six weeks to make fourteen descents, when the northeast monsoon set in strong, and obliged us to abandon

further proceedings until spring, when there is generally fine calm weather for several weeks.

The diver found the treasure tank and brought up from it, the last time he was down, twenty-four dollars, which he got by putting his arm through a hole in the tank. The tank was about twenty-eight feet long, five feet deep, wide at one end and pointed at the other, and very much the shape of a flatiron. Through the center of it were two of the lower stanchions, about fourteen inches square, and these having burned away, left holes, through one of which, probably the diver got the dollars. The latter was in a roll, stuck together and black by heat or the action of salt water. The tank was probably red-hot when it was submerged, and collapsed by water pressure, as one would crush a paper bag in the hand.

In calm weather the divers were able to see tolerably well when at the bottom, and they sent up several slats of copper and a case of canned lobster, which latter was eaten by the crew. I expect to leave for Hong Kong about the 1st of March, and my absence from home will depend on the time required to recover the money from the wreck.

If we do succeed the feat will be the greatest ever performed in the way of submarine diving. Not one professional diver out of a hundred can work at a depth of twenty fathoms, and our work must be done at a greater depth, where the pressure is sixty-nine pounds to the square inch and the very best men and apparatus are required. Another great disadvantage is the situation out in the open ocean, where very little wind creates too much sea for work to be carried on, and where the current is most of the time too strong to allow the divers reaching the bottom, so that we need a combination of favorable circumstances-calm, fine weather, slack water, and the very best divers and appliances.

Our divers came from England, one of them a very superior man. He is to be back in March with another, as good as can be got.

Nothing is left of the Japan but the bottom and a mass of iron work. As the upper works burned away, the vessel lightened up, and when she sank all the wood work and combustible matter were destroyed down to the water's edge. "[112]

In 1876, the *Rajah* and the English submarine divers began the treasure recovery operations and by 1877 had recovered nearly $175,000 in treasure.

The English diver that Captain Roberts refers to in his Shanghai letter was likely Captain Templar. "Captain Templar and the divers employed at the wreck of the steam-ship Japan have suspended operations for the season and have returned to Hong Kong."[113]

Roberts was not so singularly occupied with treasure recovery. During the salvage effort over the wreck of the *Japan*, Roberts had time to collect and send to Shanghai museum two venomous sea-snakes that he had taken off Swatow "(Pelamis bicolor Sch. And Hydrophis caerulescens, Shaw)"[114] He also read at least a portion of Jules Verne's novel, *Around the World in Eighty Days*. When writer Thomas W. Knox encountered Captain John Roberts again in 1878 after the conclusion of the salvage effort, Knox recounted his opinion of Jules Verne's popular work.

"For a full understanding of his comments on the work, it will be necessary to explain that a powerful wind, known as the northeast monsoon, blows down the coast, from Shanghai to Hong Kong, from October to April, while an equally strong wind, the southwest monsoon, blows up the coast, from Hong Kong to Shanghai, for the other half of the year....I was talking with this ancient mariner about the book which has added so much to Jules Verne's reputation, when he suddenly elevated his nose in the air and spoke very contemptuously of the story.

> *"I came to the rescue of the author by suggesting that, in spite of its fanciful character, I had found a great deal of interest in 'Around the World in Eighty Days.' 'Interest!' the Captain exclaimed; 'I thought so, too, till I came to where he took the party on a yacht from Hong Kong to Shanghai in four days. If it had been in the summer, when the southwest monsoon is on, it would have been all right; but he had them do it in December, when the northeast monsoon is blowing a gale, and no yacht could have done it in a month. When I came to that I wouldn't read any further, but pitched the book overboard."* [115]

What do the reports of the salvage operations suggest about the fire and sinking of the *Japan* on that fateful night of December 17, 1874? The structural damage at the time of the explosion of the *Japan* probably occurred with the starboard sidewheel on the ship's weather side and airborne. In the aftermath of the explosion, the port sidewheel with the fire weakened support structure would be the most likely of the two sidewheel's to have broken off, settling to the bottom at 14 fathoms. The remaining structure of *Japan* continued to burn to the water's edge, eventually filling with water over the hours before finally sailing underwater toward the bottom landing on her port side, keel down.

The top-side promenade and hurricane decks all burned away, yet the distinctive metal works including rocking arm and engine room, boiler room, forward cargo area, and treasure tank, as well as the after passenger, cargo area, and fantail would still be accessible to divers.

The starboard sidewheel, still attached, with the flying eagle on the fantail, was accessible at an angle during the recovery operations. A second wreckage area containing the ship's port sidewheel and pursers safe, could still be located 11 miles northeast of the starboard wheel and lower hull in 14 fathoms of water.

The *Japan*'s saloon plan illustrates the location of the Chinese steerage area and forward hold on the lower deck, amidships directly below the pilot house. This is the primary area of the starboard wheel body of the wreck.

The Purser's Room, the location of the ship's safe, was located on the port side across from the port sidewheel. It was likely pulled away when the weakened port sidewheel structure gave way after the boiler explosion and increased intake of seawater just after the ship had been abandoned.

The Purser's Room appears to measure out at approximately 20X10 feet (200 square feet.) Purser John Rooney (a survivor of the disaster and returnee on the *Alaska* with Captain Warsaw) passed out some of the dollars to the Chinese rescuers on the morning from the lifeboats and to the pirates in Captain Warsaw's rescue junk. The bulk of the safe's contents remained on board and was not taken into the lifeboats as the crew escaped the fire. The ship's safe contained $8,300 and the key to the treasure tank in the forward hold. The safe is a combination lock variety.

The Treasure is still buried at sea!!

Upon departure from Yokohama, the *Japan* had one hundred sixty eight boxes of treasure valued at $358,508. The $358,508 in treasure breaks down to 2,133 trade dollars per box on average. This means that the 10-foot by 6-foot (60 square foot) treasure tank could take a row of six boxes across the bottom. The 168 boxes stacked six across would reach approximately 14 feet from the deck in the iron treasure tank.

The portion of the *Japan* with the treasure tank sank and ended up on the bottom of the South China Sea in 23 fathoms of water. As Roberts described, divers first reached the treasure tank on the final day of the southwest monsoon (September 1875) when one of them punched his hand through the treasure tank and pulled out a lump of coal-like material which turned out to be 24 trade dollars.

Upon their return the following year, beginning in March 1876, through October 31, 1877; the diving operation managed to recover approximately $175,000 of the $358,508 of the trade dollar treasure. According to reports from adventure author T.W. Knox in 1878, Captain Roberts had indicated that he had completed the salvage operation and recovered nearly $300,000.

That could leave approximately $50,000 trade dollars dated 1873-1874 unaccounted for. Reports also include no mention of the recovery of the *Japan*'s purser's safe. Arguably, valuables that remained in the Purser's safe include a number of bank drafts mentioned in correspondence from the Bank of California's President John Ralston. Knox also said that Roberts had indicated that "no attempt was made to secure anything but the coin."[116]

A physical clue which points to the location of the first of the trade dollars recovered involves their description and telltale proximity to the engine room fire. The first dollars were recovered from a hole in the tank heavily blackened and in a "black lump resembling coal." In later recoveries in the tank, many of the boxes were likewise charred and broken. Some of the dollars near the surface of the tank were partially melted by the heat of the burning steamer. The coins are mostly black, heavily oxidized and in good condition.

If $50,000 of the dollars remain unrecovered, their physical location would most likely be toward the bottom of the treasure tank, resting on a port angle.

The 168 boxes in the treasure tank were probably newly minted 1873 or 1874 trade dollars from the San Francisco and Carson City mints. The 2014 valuation of the rarity of these coins place their value in mint state condition in the $3-5,000 dollar a piece range, which would make the total valuation ranging between $60-100 million dollars with the added numismatic value associated with other sidewheel steamer salvage efforts.

After his 1877 voyage to Asia, author Thomas W. Knox in his book *Adventures of Two Youths in a Journey to Siam and Java* shed further light on the recovery of the treasure at 23 fathoms, describing the blackened trade dollars as "a surviving 1874-S coin" and noting the significance of the depth for the divers.[117]

"It is the first wrecking operation ever conducted in the open ocean at so great a depth, and the instances where divers have descended so far even in still water are comparatively few." [118]

The *Japan* was last described with its stern eagle present on a sandy bottom in the South China Sea. Using a combination of the Board of Inquiry report, Captain Warsaw's testimony, and the 1875 American Consul Swatow end-of-year report, Japan's main body location lies in 22 fathoms of water (41 meters and 128 feet). The main site is outside 12 nautical miles but inside China's EEZ between Hong Kong and Swatow. The prevailing currents in this area are 1.5 knots northeast and 1 knot easterly. In addition to the primary site, there is a secondary one with a smaller portion of the ship, located approximately eleven nautical miles northeast of the main body of the wreck.

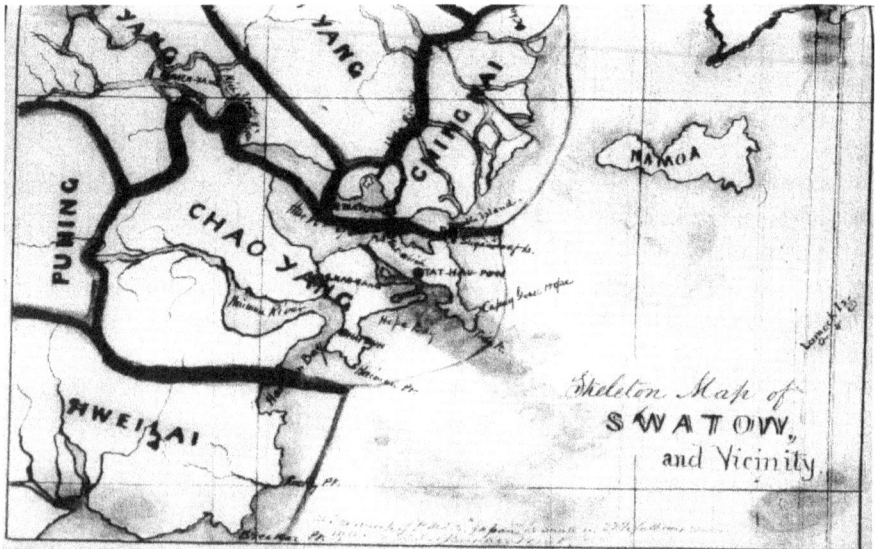

Figure 53: Final Resting Place of S.S. Japan 19nm SSE of Breaker Point

After more than 140 years since the wreck landed on the sea floor, divers on the site could expect sand-covered mounds that are typical for the local shoals or fishing grounds.

In conclusion, there is reason to believe that the divers were not totally successful in fully recovering the remaining trade dollars, the purser's safe, and possible other chests that were in the after cargo hold of the *Japan*, which could contain gold or silver hard currency.

168

It is also estimated that the forward cargo holds of the *Japan* remain un-salvaged. There is no historical record of any of the over 600 tons of cargo being recovered.

This is a treasure waiting to be found!!

Chapter 15

The Tragic Aftermath

Captain Warsaw's life at sea as a China steamer Captain ended with the loss of the *Japan*. A final Government inquiry headed by the Inspector of Hulls, Captain R. Waterman, in San Francisco after his return in late February 1875 explored the possibility that the fire had started in the ship's hold and not the coal bunker. The actions of the engineer and the Captain were also evaluated. The final determination of March 2, 1875, noted that although the ship was equipped with lifeboats of first class construction, the fire-fighting efforts when the vessel was found to be on fire were unsuccessful. The judgment was of little comfort to the relatives of the four hundred Chinamen who lost their lives.

In the eyes of most, Warsaw had done his best. He was recognized for his conduct by the Chinese community in Hong Kong and then retired from the Pacific Mail. One Pacific Mail colleague, Antonio Espantoso, presented him an engraved gold watch recognizing his historic conduct in the *Japan* disaster. His family proudly retains the watch.

Figure 54: Watch presented to Capt. Edward R. Warsaw by his friend ANTONIO ESPANTOSO as a token of regard for his heroic conduct on the occasion of the buring of the late STMT JAPAN at sea on the night of 17 December 1874. G. Falconer & Co. Hong Kong. Courtesy James Brewster, great-great grandson of Captain Edward Warsaw, NY, (2009)

With the help of his friends, Warsaw returned to mining enterprises in early 1875 as a stock broker in San Francisco and was elected a trustee of the Lower Comstock Mining Company.

There is no record of Warsaw returning to New Hampshire to be with his wife and daughter after the tragedy. There is no definitive answer as to why Warsaw's wife and daughter did not live with him in San Francisco. By this time, Captain Warsaw had been living without his wife and daughter for over 12 years. There appears to have been a mutual equilibrium in the relationship that had been reached. As a dedicated China steamship captain and trader, Warsaw lived a life of some position and prestige in San Francisco. Mrs. Anna Warsaw and their daughter Hattie, remained in their Portsmouth, New Hampshire home and lived with her sister, Nancy Weeks who was married to Warsaw's sea-captain friend, William Lester. San Francisco was certainly an expensive placed to live. All parties likely understood the cost and many wives chose to stay in their long-time family homes rather than relocated, although some captains brought their families west, as did Captain John Cavarly, of *Annie's Captain* fame who resided with his wife and children in San Francisco's well-heeled Lick Hotel.

The sole recorded time that the family was together in San Francisco occurred in March 1871, about four years after Warsaw first settled in California and several years before the *Japan* disaster, when Anna and Hattie travelled on the new trans-Continental railroad via Provo, Utah, to visit the captain in San Francisco. It was during this timeframe that the only surviving family photos were taken.

Although not conclusive, Captain Warsaw may have travelled back east to see his wife and Hattie in June 1876. He appears in records as a westbound passenger on a Sacramento-bound train from Elko, Nevada, on July 7, 1876. It was America's Centennial year, and Warsaw might have been financially secure enough as a stock operator and new mine owner to take the trip with new confidence, some 18 months after the *Japan* disaster.

The late 1870s, however, were not kind to Warsaw. He made some money in mining initially, but as the years passed, his mental and physical health began to deteriorate.

In mining, he attempted to make it rich as a stock operator involved with the mining enterprises of Nevada. Between May 1876 and August 1876, Warsaw worked at the San Francisco Safe Deposit building as a member of the San Francisco Stock and Exchange Board Mining group. In May 1876, he served as President of a Commission investigating the loss of capital investment by the Trojan Mining Company in Virginia City, Nevada, and also the Director of the Melbourne Mining Company digging for silver ore on the Comstock Lode in Virginia City, Nevada.

By late August 1876, Captain Warsaw had filed articles of incorporation in San Francisco and Nevada that established him as the President of the Vermont Consolidated silver mine on the Comstock. In that role, he endured and suffered the economic collapse of the silver market and the bankruptcy of his mine.

Captain Warsaw's Vermont Consolidated was mining Comstock Lode silver in the area that had produced the silver trade dollar treasure of the *Japan*. Many of the dollars that were minted in 1873 and 1874 at the San Francisco and Carson City mints were from the Virginia City silver ore.

It is a striking coincidence that in August 1876 Warsaw and Captain John Pratt Roberts were both recovering Comstock Lode silver at the same time-Warsaw at the source in Nevada and Roberts at the bottom of the South China Sea. Captain Roberts, aboard the wrecking steamer *Rajah*, began recovering the greater quantity of the trade dollar treasure, with the *Monocacy* offering the U.S. Navy's Asiatic Fleet protection against pirates. For comparison, the treasure recovery depth of 138 feet in the South China Sea was not too far from the 200-foot mine level of the initial dig of the Vermont Consolidated Mine.

Photo # NH 61702   USS Monocacy in Chinese waters, circa the 1890s

Figure 55: USS Monocacy in the 1890's, Courtesy U.S. Navy

Roberts would be quite successful in recovering upwards of $300,000 in treasure from the sea. The *Japan* treasure recovery effort was concluded. The underwriters and the Augustine Heard Company received their portion of the recovered treasure, and Captain Roberts returned to operating his shipyard in Shanghai, China.

Warsaw was not as fortunate. His stock capitalization of 100,000 shares for the mining effort occurred during a depressed mining industry and would end up being assessed and delinquent approximately 90,000 shares and would eventually be sold at public auction to satisfy the shareholders at Captain Warsaw's public office on Pine Street in San Francisco.

By 1880, Edward R. Warsaw was fading in vitality. His mental health began to deteriorate, and he developed heart disease. By late May 1880, he was despondent and was overheard by friends threatening to kill himself. A family far away, great financial losses, and a life on the sea as a respected captain long gone, the poor man found his mind and body was spent.

Early on June 1, 1880, at his house at 14 Oak Street in San Francisco, shortly before dawn at 5:10 A.M., Captain Warsaw retrieved a revolver, placed it against his head, and killed himself.

A Coroner's Inquest was convened afterward and the jury rendered his death a "suicide induced by severe physical suffering." The San Francisco *Morning Call* posted his obituary, requesting that New Jersey and Connecticut papers "please copy" to inform family and friends of his passing. The San Francisco *Daily Alta* and the *Sacramento Union* noted his passing and the story of his suicide with three days of press coverage, mourning his death and describing him as a gentleman, old California trader, clipper ship master, Pacific Mail commander, and master of the ill-fated *Japan*.

His funeral was at his house. Word was passed to his family in New Hampshire with Anna receiving the tragic word that she was now a widow and Hattie had lost her father. Weeks afterward, the 1880 Census would note Anna's status as a widow. Caretakers at the Shanghai Navigation Company with the photos of prominent Americans in China, would place a "d" by Captain Warsaw's picture.

Thirteen years later, within the January 1893 Jubilee edition of *Time* magazine, the San Francisco Examiner offered the story of Captain Warsaw's demise with a creatively sensational and romantic slant.

"This statement may savor of exaggeration, but there are men in San Francisco today who remember all of the facts. Warsaw was his name-Captain Warsaw, of the Pacific Mail Company. Maybe you recall the man now. He was commander of the Japan when she was burned in the eastern

173

seas about twenty years ago. Well, Captain Warsaw had wonderful whiskers, and they were dearer to him than the apple of his eye-as life itself, one might as well say when one is about it; for he shuffled off his mortal life sooner than have them shaved while he was yet in the flower of his career. The Captain met a girl one day-as captain's will-and the Captain fell in love with her. Later on he told her about his passion, and like the girl in "Bab ballads," she reciprocated it. "Will you marry me, then' said the Captain. 'Life is a blank without you.'

'I'd like to, 'answered the girl, 'but, whereas I love you, I cannot attach myself permanently to a pair of whiskers. Shave them and I am yours.'

'But I could not think of such a thing', protested the Captain.

'Well', said the maiden, with a shrug of her pretty shoulders, 'You pays your money and you takes your choice. Which is it to be? Me or the whiskers?'

'Whiskers,' murmured the mariner with a sigh, and having withdrawn to a respectable distance, he blew his brains out.

Ah those were the halcyon days when whiskers were whiskers."

Captain Warsaw's life and significance as a sea captain endures. He was one of America's pioneers of the China trade and U.S. maritime history. During the course of his 14 trans-pacific voyages on all four of the largest side-wheeler steamers in the world, he transported over 10,000 Chinese passengers from China and back. Those emigrants helped build the Central Pacific portion of the railroad at a critical time of the trans-Continental railroad construction, and offered their labors to help establish the economy of the West in many other ways.

The loss of the *Japan* was not the only ship lost to the Pacific Mail Company. After all, the Japan was the ninth vessel the firm had lost in five years, including the sidewheel steamers *Missouri* (1872), *Sacramento* (1872), *America* (1872) *Costa Rica* (1873) and the *America* (1872). However, compared to all of the Chinese steerage passenger losses on American steamships, the loss of Chinese emigrant life on the *Japan* remains the largest

Chinese emigrant disaster in U.S. history. The 391 Chinese lives lost in the burning and sinking of the *Japan* are seven times larger than those lost on the *America* in 1872 (53) or the *Golden Gate* in 1901 (58 Chinese and Japanese emigrant passengers.)

While he was captain of the ship that caught fire and sank to cause the greatest loss of life of any such disaster on the California–Hong Kong routes, Warsaw might be best remembered for his heroic conduct in saving 117 lives at sea during the midnight fire and floundering of the *S.S. Japan*. Throughout that night and throughout his career, he showed every sign of being a sea captain who was sincerely concerned about his Chinese crew and his steerage passengers. Perhaps that is why he took the loss so personally; perhaps it contributed to his eventual despair and suicide nearly six year later.

A gentleman, a maritime master and commander, Edward R. Warsaw served his country and helped transport thousands of Chinese people of Guangdong province across the Pacific to a life of potential prosperity through hard work in the land of the New Gold Mountain. For many of them, until that fateful night in December 1874, he also helped take them safely home. Perhaps his greatest legacy to those on both sides of the Pacific is how his service as a seaman and captain helped the laborers, merchants, and representatives from both countries reap the benefits of the Burlingame Treaty "Most Favored Nation" and free emigration policy, elements that survive today in modern U.S. and China relations.

At the time of her demise, the *Japan* already represented dated technology, part of the old fleet of China line vessels. The Pacific Mail was in the process of acquiring a new fleet consisting of technologically advanced and more reliable iron-screwed steamers, an improvement that was required by law and mandates from the Congress and the Postmaster General.

On the very day of the loss of the *Japan* off China on December 17, 1874, the *Daily Alta* reported that a new competitor had been established. Under the direction of Central Pacific President, Collis P. Huntington, the Central Pacific and the Union Pacific railroads would join forces with the new Occidental & Oriental iron-screwed steamers to operate from San Francisco. There was now a new player ready to enter for the China trade. Until an all-iron fleet could be acquired, the Pacific Mail would have to rely on a combination of two new iron-screw steamers with the two older sidewheel steamers.

The railroads needed a more efficient and sustained cargo carrying trade in order to deliver the mails and the trans-pacific imports of textiles, tea and silk to the eastern U.S. markets and the exports of the coveted ginseng root and California wheat to China.

For the Pacific Mail, the competition between the Occidental & Oriental and the loss of the *Japan* coincided with a more troubling political nightmare in Washington, DC: the probable loss of the Pacific Mail's annual Congressional subsidy of $1,000,000 for the China mail service. The loss of the *Japan*, while a serious blow, was far less a threat to the company than this development. During the same week in December 1874, Congressional hearings on the Pacific Mail's subsidies were happening in Washington, DC. The hearings were follow quickly by a full-blown influence-peddling scandal where agents of the Pacific Mail were discovered to have bribed Congressmen involved with the February 1875 hearings on the approval of the annual subsidy. Adding insult to injury in the Congress was the argument that the investment in sidewheel steamers was useless for any other trade and was considered an injustice to the taxpayers.

The "Chinese Question" was getting hotter and more controversial economically in the U.S. As the direct competition between the Chinese and Caucasians for jobs increased, anti-Chinese sentiment rose with each arrival of a steamer to the San Francisco docks. A *New York Times* story opined that the payments had resulted in "no better result than flooding the Pacific states with Chinese coolies."[119]

Nuisance ordnances were passed by the City of San Francisco to harass the Chinese. These included laundry ordnances with larger fees for those Chinese that did not own horse-drawn delivery carts and an ordinance that required all Chinese city jail prisoners to cut their long braided hair queues, thereby humiliating them.

Violent attacks also increased. The anti-Chinese movement in California was further fueled by the August 1874 Chinese prostitution case, involving the women who had arrived on the Japan. The case was recalled and reported in the press throughout 1876, as the case worked its way from the California venues to the U.S. Court. The tenor of the coverage contributed to an attitude of racial superiority, touting the "superior law-abiding Anglo-Saxon, republican society."

Legal action against the Chinese followed in 1877, as the California Legislature petitioned Congress to end Chinese immigration. That year, violence against the Asian emigrants increased. Anti-Chinese riots were led by Anglo-Irish mobs that attacked laundries in Chinatown, beating Chinese workers. These were followed by anti-Chinese political agitation, led by former miner turned Teamster Dennis Kearney. Kearney organized huge sandlot bonfire demonstrations in San Francisco within view of City Hall.

"In the very shadow of Crocker's and Stanford's mansions on Nob Hill, he harangued the crowd: 'The Central pacific men are thieves and will soon feel the power of the working men.' Even more satisfying to the mob were his violent threats against the Chinese: 'The Chinamen must go. If they don't, by the eternal we will take them by the throat, squeeze their breath out and throw them into the sea.'"[120]

Congress tried to pass the first anti-Chinese immigration Bill in 1879. A bill termed the Fifteen Passengers Law that would have limited each incoming ship to fifteen Chinese passengers, effectively ending the emigration of a useful labor force. By 1881, Chinese immigration to the U.S. was avoided by U.S. politicians and business leaders. Negotiations began between the U.S. and China to revise the Burlingame Treaty's unlimited Chinese immigration provisions.

In 1882, after seven years of debate on the national level, begun with the Pacific Mail Steamship *Japan* and the "Chinese Maidens" incident, and leading up to President Grant's message to Congress on the China Question, the American Congress passed and President Rutherford B. Hayes signed into law the ten-year trial ban on the entrance of Chinese laborers into the U.S. The law represented the first time the U.S. had repudiated its policy of welcoming immigrants, regardless of race, religion, or national origin. It ushered in a period of intolerance against the Chinese in America.

The dramatic course of two decades, from 1868 to 1888, represents the start of the modern U.S.-China relationship. Things began optimistically in 1868 with the Burlingame Treaty, establishing the "Most Favored Nation" policy for the U.S. in exchange for "free emigration" for China. This was followed by the largest migration of Chinese overseas in history, leading to the completion of the trans-Continental railroad and the building of the California economy to new heights of trade.

This was followed by a complex sequence of economic downturns, political maneuvering, legal wrangling, worker conflicts, and ethnic friction. In the midst of it fell the fate of Captain Edward R. Warsaw and the last voyage of the S.S. *Japan*. The story of the *Japan* will hopefully rekindle interest in the beginnings of this important chapter of the modern U.S.-China relationship, while highlighting the enormous accomplishments of the Chinese emigrant pioneers, a group initially welcomed for their labors and eventually excluded as a race from emigration to the U.S.

Figure 56: A stern eagle

The last observation of the *Japan* was recorded December 30, 1877. Thomas W. Knox wrote in the *New York Times* that "the gilt eagle that ornamented the stern of the *Japan* lies on the dark sand of the bottom, and the Captain [Roberts] thinks that when his work on the treasure is ended, he will take this bird as a trophy." But he is now too busy with silver eagles to take any trouble with a gilded one."[121]

The lingering story of the *Japan*, one that has been invisible to modern readers, is not in the end about the loss of treasure in the form of silver coins or other valuable cargo. It is a tale of lives perished and dreams destroyed. The human beings whose version of this story would be perhaps the most fascinating are silent. Their voices remain at the bottom of the South China Sea. Thwarted in their hopes to return home to Guangdong, to their friends and family, the Chinese steerage passengers who died in the shipwreck tragedy deserve their memories to be honored. Perhaps, a deep-sea mission could even return some of their bones to better resting places, so that within Confucian tradition their souls may be released to heaven.

Their final resting place in the South China Sea is a time capsule. Shipwrecks have this special nature. They capture a moment in time, when a voyage is frozen for eternity, when all becomes entombed in a sudden

178

disaster. Though the remnants on the sea floor suffer some attrition, much remains on a shipwreck that can tell a rich story. In this case, the wreck of the S.S. *Japan* symbolizes the decade in which the modern U.S.-China relationship began to flower. Looking more closely at the story, we can see an international relationship in the 1870s between two powerhouse nations undergoing dynamic transformation. The remarkable history of the *Japan* contains instructive lessons about individual humanity and world politics – people yearning for a meaningful life, two countries yearning for a mutually beneficial relationship.

Historically, the loss of the *Japan* represented the greatest loss of Chinese steerage passenger life in modern history aboard the largest sidewheel passenger ship in the world at the time of her loss in 1874.

Some bodies were recovered but many remained at or around the wreck site.

As the living departed the wreck site, the floating bodies of the Chinese clung to the location amid the debris field as their countrymen still aboard the wreck continued to separate in distance and depth.

The sea and the wind were creating the final scene as the wreck of the *Japan* was about to be transformed into an offshore tomb-one that remains an ancestral sepulcher in sight of their China home.

By mid-day, the balance between the wreck above water and below the waves changed.

The *Japan* became heavy and down by the bow- tilting downward-reaching for the bottom. Her eagle adorned fantail rotated toward the sky, trying to indicate the final place with no-one watching.

The stern followed the bow downward in a short journey to the bottom.

The arrival against the dark sand of the bottom happened quickly.

The Chinese steerage passengers in their berthing area deep in the hull were now at last home. Others closer to the surface were jolted by the arrival on the bottom and released to the surface where they would float-some eventually picked up by passing junks, others making the longer journey to the shores of Tungao Bay.

In their new surroundings, the souls of the dead Chinese steerage passengers would now enter a restless period of concern-hopeful that their lives would still count and be honored while also hoping for a more peaceful sleep in the afterlife, but that could only happen if their ancestors knew where their final resting place was.

What remains for the story of the *Japan* has now been provided by this book.

She remains an American-flagged treasure ship in the Chinese Exclusive Economic Zone (EEZ) waters, originally with a ship's safe with $8,200 in gold, two unrecovered cargo holds, and a remaining $50,000 in U.S. trade dollars treasure worth an estimated $250 million dollars still to be found in the sunken treasure tank.

The ship also represents an extraordinary legal and diplomatic memorial to its famous transport of the 23 Chinese "Maidens" from Hong Kong to San Francisco in August 1874 which generated the case law ending in the landmark *Chy Lung vs. Freeman* (92.US.275) 1875 Supreme Court case which clarified the power of the states to regulate immigration, conveyed the rights of the Burlingame Treaty for all Chinese to freely immigrate and was the first case regarding the right of access to equal protection of the laws under the 14th Amendment to the constitution.

Finally, it is hoped that the sea hunters who read this story, and endeavor to locate the wreck sites, will do so not for treasure but to locate it in order for the two great peoples in America and China to hear the voices of their ancestors. As descendants, we might better understand the initial hopes of this generation of workers, merchants, politicians, and steamship captains, not only to prosper and to care for one's family, but to share a dream, that the oldest civilization with its yellow flag, emblazoned with the red-dragon and emblem of the 'Lord of the whole Earth and Brother of the Sun and Moon' and the newest civilization, with its starry emblem of sovereign people, 'By the Grace of God Free and Independent,' can live, prosper and understand each other in peace.

Acknowledgements

I began researching the *Japan* in 2006 after studying the China trade of tea, silk, merchandise, and Chinese laborers, and the transport of U.S. silver trade dollars to Hong Kong during the mid-1870s. While researching the San Francisco maritime components of this trade, I came across a San Francisco Maritime Museum posting on the loss of the Pacific Mail Steamship Company's steamer *Japan*.

The *Japan*'s loss of life by fire at sea with approximately $400,000 dollars in new trade dollars captured my attention and I began a hunt for the circumstances of her demise on the mid-watch.

The result of the search is this book.

I would like to thank Dr. Bob Dallek, my UCLA history Professor and the late Dr. Robert Pastor of American University for sponsoring my research. I would also like to thank Steve Yates, Kathy Lubbers, Kevin H. Baxter, James Stacy, Linda Cashdan at the Word Process and Phil Martin at Crickhollow Books for completing the initial readings, developmental edit and critique of the manuscript drafts each step of the way.

I would also like to thank the Huntington Library Rare Book and Photograph section in San Marino, California, the Library of Congress, the U.S. National Archives in Washington, D.C., Archives II in College Park, Maryland, the Mystic Seaport Library, the Mariners Museum in Newport News, Virginia, Harvard University's Widener Library, the Mississippi Department of Archives and History, Yale University's Beinecke Rare Book and Manuscript Library, the New York Historical Society, the Nevada State Historical Association, the Middlesex County Historical Society in Middletown, Connecticut, the University of California-Santa Barbara's Davidson Library, the San Francisco Public Library and the late John Haskell Kemble for his careful preservation of this important area of the U.S. and China trade.

The historical narrative has been pieced together from unpublished U.S. China Consulate cables, the official *Japan* Inquiry report, letters, and the official 1874-1877 correspondence from Hong Kong, Canton and Swatow to Secretary of State Hamilton Fish and Assistant Secretary of State John L. Cadwalader.

The official cables were then compared with the New York Times, Daily Alta California, San Francisco Examiner, Hong Kong Tribune, China Tribune, and New York Herald stories on the U.S. side-wheel steamer trade between San Francisco, Japan and China during 1868 through 1875.

Particularly insightful for the development of the narrative were Dr. Jonathon Haskell Kemble classic works, *Sidewheelers Across the Pacific* and *One Hundred Years of the Pacific Mail*, a collection of Shanghai Navigation Company photographs, the surviving Pacific Mail Steamship Company business records at the Huntington Library in San Marino, California, the Pacific Mail Steamship Company correspondence at the San Francisco Public Library, California Newspaper Project and Digital Library at the University of California, Riverside, the Pomona College Pacific Mail archives and log of the America (the Japan's sister ship), and the Yale University Beinecke Rare Book Library research notes from Kathryn Hulme's *Annie's Captain*.

Providing further imagination and insight on the *Japan's* sea service, Chinese steerage transport and tragic end were the Endicott and Company engravings of the *Japan*, stories of Chinese steerage passenger transit contained at the National Archives and Library of Congress, and the sole surviving trans-Pacific side-wheel saloon plans of the Japan from the Maritime Museum in Hampton Roads, Virginia and San Francisco Public Library.

The surviving photos of the *Japan* alongside the Brannan Street wharf in San Francisco, in the Hunters Point drydock and in Tiburon Bay as provided by the San Francisco Public Library and the Landmarks Society of Belvedere and Tiburon were also important in the development of the books narrative.

The story of the *Japan's* final hours of fire, abandonment, and death on December 18, 1874 are told using the actual first-hand accounts of over a dozen *Japan* passengers and crew.

Where possible, Captain Warsaw's trans-Pacific voyages have been used to capture the life aboard the ships of the Pacific Mail line and the *Japan*, Chinese steerage passenger conditions, immigration and emigration to and from the U.S. and China, and the commercial patterns and trade associated with Japan and her treasure cargo used for the China trades in silk and tea for exchange for coin silver, California wheat and quicksilver were pulled together from various voyages of the Japan and help reconstruct her 1868-1874 service life.

Locating the approximate resting spot of the *Japan* was accomplished by consulting the 1874-1876 National Archive U.S. Navy Asiatic Squadron ship logs from the USS *Yantic*, USS *Saco*, USS *Ashelot*, and USS *Monocacy*; the official U.S. Consul Hong Kong Inquiry record, and the 1875-1877 treasure salvage operations of American Captain John Pratt Roberts to determine the approximate locations of the separate remnants of the *Japan* wreck sites off the southeast coast of China.

The January 1876 letter from *Japan* salvager Captain John Pratt Roberts from Shanghai and an 1876 U.S. Consulate Swatow official map that recorded the whereabouts of the *Japan*'s final resting place helped correlate the official U.S. Navy log entries that used anglicized names for their navigation points along the China Coast in the 1870's.

A further refinement of the *Japan*'s and the Chinese steerage passenger's final resting place was deduced from a Google Earth and nautical chart comparison with the 1875 Coast Pilot of the China Coast that provided the landmarks and sailing conditions of December 1874.

Reporting in the New York Times and insurance business publications also told the story of historic open-sea deep dive salvage operations (that required U.S. Navy protection against pirates) and succeeded in recovering most, but not all, of the almost $360,000 in newly minted U.S. trade dollars.

The salvage recovery section of this book reasons that there is in addition to the existence of the bone remains of the Chinese steerage passengers, approximately $50,000 of unrecovered trade dollars, a ship's safe with $8,300 in gold and silver and an untold number of cargo chests in the forward cargo holds which could contain the returning silver and gold savings of the returning steerage passengers.

All told, the amount of unrecovered treasure could be conservatively valued at approximately $250 million dollars in San Francisco and Carson City trade dollars and Gold and silver coinage as valued by the 2014 Coinage "Red Book" among other market sources.

The search for survivors and the subsequent *Japan* wreckage, and salvage operation was reconstructed using the official records of the U.S. Consulate in Canton and Swatow, China.

More than the treasure or the story of the ship is the importance of discovering the final resting place of the Chinese steerage passengers. Their lives have a rightful place in the histories of two great people in China and America. Their labors helped America become one nation and solidified the reputation of the Chinese as a hardworking, industrious people.

Revealing the final resting place of the *Japan* provides a unique opportunity to remember them and hopefully provide a measure of comfort to their descendants in Guangdong Province and to their restless souls at the bottom of the South China Sea.

Appendix A

Captain Edward R. Warsaw - Life and Service

Captain Edward R. Warsaw was an extraordinary sea captain who began his career in charge of Yankee Clipper ships bound from New York for China, the Gulf Coast, and South America. He served in the Mexican War, and eventually became an acclaimed paddlewheel steamship captain for the new coal-burning steam-propulsion vessels used by the Pacific Mail steamers of the China line, based out of San Francisco.

During his clipper-ship service out of New York, Captain Warsaw was married in 1863 to Anna Weeks. In 1864, they welcomed the arrival of their daughter Hattie. Captain Warsaw listed his profession as shipmaster and maintained a home residence with his family at 126 State Street in Stratham, Rockingham County, near Portsmouth, New Hampshire.

After joining the Pacific Mail Steamship Company, Captain Warsaw served for over four years from 1868 through early 1873. He took the better part of 1873 off before returning to the line in August 1874, with his final assignment as the captain of the *Japan*. Based on the direct observations of tourism pioneer Thomas Cook, passenger observations on 1869-1872 voyages, personal notes of trust in the correspondence of the President of the Bank of California, and the testimony and evidence provided by the official Board of Inquiry for the *Japan* disaster, Captain Edward Warsaw was by all accounts a competent professional, an officer of great ability, integrity, compassion, and determination. He was well respected by the Pacific Mail line, his officers, the Chinese crewmen, and his passengers. By all accounts, he demonstrated heroic leadership in trying to save the lives on his last command, the *Japan*, during her final hours in the South China Sea.

A master mariner for 18 years, he had commanded all of the Pacific Mail's sidewheel steamers from 1868-1874. These included the *China* (1869), *Great Republic* (1870), *America* (1871), *Japan* (1871 and 1874), and *Colorado* (1872). In 1873, he took a year off before his fateful return to the Pacific Mail and the last voyages of the *Japan*. He received about $250 per month for service as a China-line steamer captain.

Sometime in 1867 and during a subsequent voyage from San Francisco to Hong Kong on the steamship *Colorado*, Warsaw had stepped up into command from being first officer when the ship's captain had been taken seriously ill on the return voyage.

Among his other noteworthy mentions during his years of service was the safe transport of U.S. naval officers and diplomats, Chinese and Japanese government officials, and thousands of European, American, and Chinese passengers between Hong Kong to San Francisco.

There are approximately a dozen voyage journals that contain actual reference to Captain Warsaw. The Mystic Seaport in Connecticut has an important memoir that captures in great detail some of Captain Warsaw's mannerisms. On the *China*'s January-March 1869 passage from Hong Kong to San Francisco, Captain Warsaw was described as an officer who "knows his business and needs no dictations."[122] On a *Great Republic* May 1870 voyage, Captain Warsaw was described as a "true and impartial lover of his fellow creatures,' as a flag which the Chinese gave him proved him to be."[123]

The most noteworthy cruise involving Captain Warsaw in command was the well-publicized November 1872 "Tour around the World" cruise of early tourism pioneer Thomas Cook aboard the *Colorado*. Just prior to the Cook voyage, Warsaw was in command of an October voyage of the *Colorado* which survived a typhoon. The incident was front-page news in San Francisco and carried a very complimentary story on Captain Warsaw and the crew of the *Colorado*.

The Pacific Mail was evidently quite proud of its *Colorado* crew and Captain Warsaw, and likely sensed that the fame of the world voyage with Thomas Cook might attract potential customers for an emerging tourist trade to Japan and China, along with helping to justify their new hard-won Congressional subsidy for the Pacific mail service.

"On the homeward voyage, about 800 miles northeast of the coast of Japan, she encountered one of the most severe typhoons on record, and those on board can never forget how worthily she fulfilled her trust. This is her sixth round voyage to China, and her prow has cleft through upward of seventy-two thousand mile of blue water, besides various voyages to Panama, without accident or delay. The Pacific Mail Steamship Company have newer and larger ships at their docks now, but they may be sure that none are better or more trustworthy than this good Colorado, and with such efficient officers at the fore, as Warsaw, Stuart, Harris, 'de langel, and Surgeon Burrell, they may always rely upon large patronage from their friends in the orient."[124]

185

In his book *Letters to the Sea and Foreign Lands*, Cook described his vision for world-wide tourism and the new opportunities for citizens in many countries to discover the world. Captain Warsaw was part of Cook's narrative, "Our good Captain Warsaw combines humanity with stern discipline, and every morning inspects every part of the ship with the keenest eye for dust and irregularity."[125] The November 1872 voyage of the *Colorado*, across the Pacific under his command, remains part of history that inspired Jules Verne and his imaginative novel, *Around the World in 80 Days*.

Captain Warsaw and the officers of the *Colorado* bid farewell to Thomas Cook in Hong Kong and began their return voyage to San Francisco on December 12, 1872. They arrived home on January 15, 1873. That was the final voyage of Captain Warsaw for 1873. In mid-1873, the U.S. District Attorney took the Pacific Mail to court for violating the Act of 1855, which governed the number of steerage passengers allowed for a trans-Pacific passage. In addition to Captain Warsaw, two other Pacific Mail Captains were tried and convicted of violating the maximum steerage allowed laws. The Pacific Mail Company appealed his case and got the fine reduced. "Two charges were lodged against Captain E. R. Warsaw, who's Colorado was entitled to carry a maximum of 828 in the steerage. On the two voyages in question, he carried 430 in excess on the first and 174 in excess on the second. The trial took over six months and the early 1874 judgment the original fine of $21,000 was reduced to $14,050."[126]

He would take a year off. In August 1874, he was re-instatement and allowed to return to the Pacific Mail. "Captain Warsaw, who formerly commanded the P.M.S.S. Colorado, in the China line, and who made himself very popular while in that capacity, received his appointment yesterday to the China. The many friends of this popular commander will be pleased to hear of his reinstatement in this company." [127]

One can imagine Captain Warsaw's anticipation in the weeks leading up to the *China*'s return to San Francisco from a run to Panama to pick up a spare sidewheel steamer shaft, when he could resume his duties as a ship's captain.

"Captain E.R. Warsaw, who has been six years in command of a Pacific Mail Company's steamer between this port and China, after a year's rest on shore has taken his old position in the line. Captain Warsaw will take charge of the steamer China on her arrival from Panama, and probably go to Yokohama and Hongkong. The Captain has been going to sea for thirty-four years, boy and man, and twenty years a Captain. The company may be congratulated on the return to active work of one of their most competent officers." [128]

But the China trade and the Pacific Mail's transport of Chinese emigrant was becoming fraught with controversy, as certain American political factions began to challenge the continued emigration of Chinese laborers. In August 1874, the *Japan* arrived in San Francisco with what was deemed a controversial population of Chinese prostitutes. The result was a legal summons for her Captain John H. Freeman, Freeman's reassignment from the Pacific Mail line later that year, and the reassignment of Captain Warsaw to the *Japan*.

Following the fire onboard and the sinking of the Japan in the South China Sea in December 1874, Warsaw was called to testify to the events of that fateful night. On December 24, 1874, je provided the following testimony to the Board of Inquiry at the U.S. Consulate in Hong Kong:

"The fire broke out at 11:25 P.M.

The first I knew of it was a confusion among the passengers on the main deck, which intimated to me that something was wrong. I was in the pilot house; a minute later I heard a noise - a cry of fire; upon hearing the confused noise, I sprang toward the pilot house, the door of which was open; when I reached the door-step, the second officer, who was the officer of the deck, cried out 'Fire!'

I rang the jingling gong to stop the engine, and at the same time sounded the fire alarm, and ordered all ventilators to be turned from the wind, ported my helm, and ordered the topsail halyards to be let go, in order to bring the ship to the wind.

At this time I had been running before the wind; my object was to prevent the smoke from being carried fore and aft the ship. I next went to where the fire was, right amidships. Fire was issuing from the fire room, ventilator, and ash shoot. I immediately ran to the stairs at the fore hatch, in order to descend to the main deck, the nearest point to the ash shoot, from which large volumes of smoke were issuing. This ash shoot was situated forward of the smoke-stack, and directly over the fire-room.

Smoke in large quantities was issuing from the fire room. Three streams were found to be issuing. All the available hose and connections were brought into use. We threw twenty-four streams from the main engines We could, however, only bring twenty to bear on the fire, in the places indicated and in the steerage, and they were all brought to bear within ten minutes from the time of the first alarm.

We cut holes in the steerage deck on the port side abreast of the engine and fire rooms. We directed three streams here, and covered the holes with blankets. I then instructed the officers who were with me to cut holes in the after steerage hatch, communicating with the freight deck.

I saw large volumes of smoke, but no fire.

About that time the fourth officer took off the fore hatch to see if he could make out the fire. He did not. The Chief Officer and myself went on the after freight deck to see if we could discover any fire. We did not, but saw considerable smoke. I returned forward to the place where the fire was supposed to be, in the fire room.

The first blaze I saw was issuing from the ventilator over the forward fire room. During this time all available hose and connections were laid, to bring all the hydrants to bear, fore and aft, making in all twenty streams. I now gave the order to my messenger to tell the chief-officer to detail men to swing out and clear all boats ready for lowering. That messenger is not here. I never saw him afterward. His name was Sutton, Quartermaster.

I went below again to the steerage, cut a hole abreast the foremast, through the deck, and saw fire. I applied a hose to it, and then went aft on the port side, pulled the butt out of a hole which we had cut before, and saw fire. This was directly under the ash-shoot.

Apparently, all the deck between, and the bulkhead between the engine room, fire-room, and wing bunkers, on the port side, were on fire. I inserted the hose again into the hole, covered it up, went up on the hurricane deck, and saw the third officer and a gang of men swinging the forward boats, and the second officer and another gang swinging the after boats.

During the whole of this time every effort was being made by the white men on board to extinguish the fire.

I advised Dr. Tindal then to make ready to leave the ship, and placed the women in his charge, telling him that I thought he would be compelled to leave. I then went back to the site of the fire, where my officers and men were doing their utmost to extinguish it.

At this time a man ran by me named Denham, an oiler, crying out "Every man for himself." I caught him and asked him who gave him that order? He replied, the Chief Engineer. I told him that if he repeated it I'd blow his brains out, and ordered him to work with the rest.

We fought the fire for about fifteen minutes after this. Finding that all efforts proved unavailing, and that the fire was rapidly gaining upon us, and that the water from the fire engines, caused by the fire and smoke issuing from the fire-room and engine-room, and that it would have been impossible for any man to enter the portion of the ship.

I then started with a view of saving life.

I went aft as far as the engine-room door on the port side, when the flames cut me off. I turned and ran forward passing through the some abreast of the ash-shoot, passing around on the starboard or weather side, aft through the store-room and pantry, and thence to the hurricane deck by the saloon stairs. I took a general survey of the weather side of the ship, on that side, the people forward apparently having life preservers on them. I passed along the port or lee side, abaft the social hall, and saw two boats hanging by their davits.

At that time I saw several Chinamen, together with Mr. Cropper, a saloon passenger, and the ship's storekeeper. These I advised to get into a boat. Not seeing anyone on that deck to assist me to lower a boat, I put Mr. Cropper at the forward tackle to assist, myself lowering the after tackle. When the boat was down, I sent him into it down the fall, cast off, and did not see him till next day when we picked him up.

A few moments afterward I saw a second officer standing by the forward tackle of the only remaining boat, abaft the wheel on the port side. I assisted him to lower the boat.

In the boat were all the Europeans and Chinese passengers abaft the fire, which was now right across the ship at the engine room. (I should have stated that when I escaped from below to the hurricane deck the flames took possession of the center of the ship and precluded any further communication with the forward part of the ship, even on the hurricane deck.)

I gave orders to the second officer to wait alongside the ship for me, and I returned to the weather side of the quarter deck, took a general survey of the ship, saw that the Captains gig was gone, that the non-pareil raft was gone, and that all the settees on the quarterdeck had gone.

I opened the engineer's room door, and called him. Receiving no response, I went aft, and lifting the sky-light called out to see if there was any more life on board aft, and, not hearing any response, concluded to leave the ship.

I went over the ship's side at 12:45 A.M. on the 18th

I shoved our boat clear of the ship, came round under the stern, and used every endeavor to save life, and picked up a number of Chinese, all of whom had life-preservers on and were on pieces of wreck, or hatches, chairs, etc. remained to windward of the wreck until daylight, when we went in search of the other boats.

I fell in with and engaged a Cape Chi fishing smack, in which I cruised about in the vicinity of the wreck material, and succeeded in picking up five boats and saving 117 souls from the boats and water.

At about 2 P.M. on the 18th, seeing no more life, I stood in for land. At 6:30 P.M., about a mile from land, communicated with the steamer Yottung. The Captain took us on board and conveyed us to Swatow, whence we took passage in the steamer Yesso for this port and arrived at 2:00 PM on the 20th."[129]

Timeline of Captain Edward R. Warsaw:

Circa 1827	Born in Montgomery, Alabama
1841-1845	China Trade
1846	Mexican War participation
1848	Retired from Mexican War Service
Sep 1849	Arrived in California
1849-1853	Miner
1854-1855	Stock raising in California
1856	Resumed Sailing
1856-1857	Command of sailing vessels
1857	Master mariner
Jan 19, 1861	Married Ann S. Weeks in New Hampshire; resides in Stratham town, NH

Sep 1863	Daughter Hattie born
Jun 07, 1864	Commanded *Marmion*, in NY. Sutton and Co., Pier 19 East River
Nov 07, 1864	Commanded *Marmion*, in SF. Pacific Street wharf. Wholesale toys/fancy goods
Jan 12, 1865	*Marmion* with Warsaw in Hong Kong enroute Whampoa
Jan 30, 1865	*Marmion* enroute from Hong Kong to Manila
Dec 19, 1865	Commanded *Marmion,* operating from New York (Pier 19) to New Orleans

1866	Captain Warsaw in New York
Apr 1866	Commanded *Marmion* from New York to New Orleans
May 1866	Captain Steamship *Marmion*; New Orleans to New York
Sep 22, 1866	Commanded *Ocean Express* from NY to San Francisco
1866-1867	Captain Warsaw resides at 126 State Street, Portsmouth NH with wife Ann and daughter Hattie

1866	PMSS Company China-trade steamers being built; *Great Republic* launched

1867	
Jan 16-17	Member of Newark, New Jersey Masons Lodge Number 7
Feb 25,	*Ocean Express* arrives in San Francisco. Discharges cargo at Howard St. Wharf
Mar 21,	Sailed *Ocean Express* to Liverpool
Jul 05,	*Ocean Express* arrives in Liverpool
Aug	*Ocean Express* and Warsaw sail from Liverpool to San Francisco

1868	Accepted a position as a PMSS captain
Jan 1,	Warsaw arrives in San Francisco on *Ocean Express*
Feb 1,	*Ocean Express* for sale in San Francisco
Spring	Warsaw begins at Pacific Mail in *Colorado*
Jun	Warsaw departs San Francisco in *Colorado*
Jul	Warsaw arrives in Hong Kong in *Colorado*
Aug 16,	Warsaw arrives in San Francisco in *Colorado*
Sep 02,	Warsaw departs San Francisco in command of *China*
Oct 06,	*China* arrives in Hong Kong
Oct 15,	*China* departs Hong Kong
Nov 23,	*China* arrives in San Francisco
Dec0	Departed San Francisco in *China*

Dec 30,   *China* arrives in Yokohama

1869

Jan 1,	*China* departs Yokohama
Jan 8	*China* arrives in Hong Kong
Jan 18	*China* departs Hong Kong
Jan 21	*China* passes Amoy, China
Jan 22	*China* passes the "White Dogs" of Foochow
Jan 27	*China* arrives Yokohama
Feb 08	Announces "good progress" to *China* passengers since leaving Yokohama.
Feb 20	Quelled Chinese "bobery" aboard *China*.
Feb 22	Arrived in San Francisco
Sep	In command of *China*; embarked AMCONSUL Yokohama Charles Shepard
Dec 30	*China* passengers present Warsaw with silver pitcher
Dec	Warsaw residing at Occidental Hotel, San Francisco, as CO, PMSS *China*

1870

Apr	In command of *Great Republic*
Apr 28	Yokohama
May 06	Hong Kong
May 12	Hong Kong
June 13	San Francisco
Nov 23	Depart Hong Kong in Japan
Dec 20	*Japan* collides with *Mermion* and *Caroline* in SF Bay; Warsaw exonerated
Dec 31	Depart San Francisco in command of *Japan*

1871

Jan 08	Communicated with America 29.58N/15601W
Jan 14	2:00 PM stopped at Midway for 90 minutes. Boat unable to land
Jan 27	*Japan* arrived in Yokohama 4:25PM
Jan 28	Departed Yokohama 5: PM
Feb 04	Arrived HK 0700
Feb 19	Arrive Yokohama 6:10AM
Feb 22	In command of *Japan*. Departed Yokohama to San Francisco.
Mar 10	Communicated with *Great Republic* at 30N/154.56W
Mar 15	Anna and Hattie arrive via train from Ogden

Mar 19	Arrived in San Francisco from Yokohama.
Apr	Warsaw family photo (Edouard/Cobb photography. Residing at Occidental Hotel
Aug 07	In Command of *America*; rendezvous' with *Japan* at sea.
Aug 23	Arrived in Yokohama from San Francisco in Command of *America*.

1872

Mar 01	In command of *Japan*
Mar 26	Arrive Yokohama
Apr 04	Arrive Hong Kong
Apr 12	Depart Hong Kong
Apr 23	Depart Yokohama
May 15	Arrives in SF in *Japan*
May 16	Departs SF in *Colorado*
Jun 10	Departs Yokohama in *Colorado*
Jun 17	Arrives in Hong Kong in *Colorado*
Jun 27	Departs Hong Kong in *Colorado*
Jul 07	Departs Yokohama in *Colorado*
Jul 28	Arrives SF in *Colorado*; 30,796 packages of tea
Aug 17	Depart SF in *Colorado*
Sep 10	Arrive Yokohama in *Colorado*
Sep 16	Arrive Hong Kong
Oct 02	Arrives Yokohama
Oct 23	Arrive SF
Nov 01	In Command of *Colorado* with Thomas Cook. Departs from San Francisco
Nov 28	Departed Yokohama
Dec 05	Arrived in Hong Kong
Dec 12	Departed Hong Kong enroute San Francisco
Dec 24	Entrusted with Japanese figurines in Yokohama.

1873

Jan	Arrived in San Francisco in *Colorado*
Apr 13	Arrived in *Colorado*
May 07	Warsaw arrested by U.S. Marshall in violation of Passenger Act (Mar 1855) 1,258 passengers on *Colorado*
Mid-1873	California state legal charges: Carrying excess steerage passengers
Sep 08	U.S. District Court SF finds Warsaw guilty; ordered to pay $30,458.

Dec 30	Humboldt Mining
Dec 31	Elected Board of Directors, Humboldt Mining

1874

Feb 09	Crown Point Extension Director, Comstock Lode in SF
Aug 6-7	Re-instated as a PMSS Captain after a year's leave
Aug 29	Departed in *Japan* from Yokohama; 23 Chinese Prostitutes taken off vessel
Sep 23-30	Yokohama, Japan
Oct 21	Arrive in *Japan* from Yokohama; U.S. Army delegation and Japanese students
Nov 14	Departs San Francisco in *Japan*
Dec 09	*Japan* arrives Yokohama; exchanges passengers and onload coal at anchorage.
Dec 10	*Japan* departs Yokohama for Hong Kong.
Dec 17	In Command of *Japan* off Swatow when midnight fire strikes.
Dec 18	Abandoned *Japan*
Dec 18	Landed in Swatow.
Dec 19	Departed Swatow
Dec 20	Arrived Hong Kong
Dec 24-28	Board of Inquiry, U.S. Consulate Hong Kong

1875

Jan 09	Presented memorial by Citizens of Hong Kong for Conduct
Jan 13	Departed on the *Alaska* for SF with Japan survivors
Jan 21-24	*Alaska* in Yokohama, Japan
Jan 28	Lower Comstock Mining Trustee
Feb 16	*Alaska* arrives in San Francisco
Feb 24	Inspector of Hulls Bob Waterman Board of Inquiry in San Francisco
Mar 2	Inquiry concludes
Mar	Retired from Pacific Mail
Mar 11	PMSS pays Captain Warsaw's Hong Kong boarding fee: $48.00.

1875-1876

Stock Operator in San Francisco

1876

May 17-21	Member of Mining Stock Oversight Board
June-July 8	Transcontinental railroad; Jul 7 in Carlin, Nevada outside Elko inbound
Jul 26	Director, Melbourne Mining Company
Aug 01	Vermont Consolidated
Aug 17	Meeting on Melbourne at 419 California St., SF
Aug 29	Vermont Mine Incorporated

1877

Feb 18	Vermont Consolidated claim survey
Mar	Merchandise or consignee on *Granada* from Panama

1878 Owner, Vermont Consolidated Mine in Virginia City, Nevada; SF President

Apr	Assessment levied against Vermont Mine Inc.
Oct	Suit brought against Consolidated Vermont, stocks illegally sold

1879

Jul 17	Vermont now Ophir Consolidated; debts paid
Jul 18	SF Board fraud
Sep 23	Vermont Consolidated now "Golden Gate"
Sep 27	Stock operator in SF
Sep 28	Warsaw SF deposition in Hill divorce case from SF

1880

Apr	Depression of Comstock silver stocks
Apr 09	Warsaw deeds to Robert Hewson 1,200 feet of the Crowley Lode, Virginia District-claim known as the silver wedge located Aug 1, 1880
Jun 01	Captain Warsaw commits suicide in San Francisco, 0540 AM
Jun 02	Coroner's Inquest Jury verdict: heart disease caused Warsaw to threaten to kill himself; ruling-suicide induced by severe physical suffering
Jun 03	Funeral at Captain Warsaw's home at #14 Oak Street, San Francisco
Jun 07	Wife Anna (Weeks) Warsaw states she's a widow in 1880 Census. Leave 16yo0 Hattie behind
Dec 13	Warsaw noted for having 15 shares delinquent for assessment

1893

Jan 01   Time Magazine Jubilee edition mention of Captain Warsaw, his whiskers and a romantic liaison

"Captain Edward R. Warsaw, well known in years past as a Commander in the service of Pacific Mail, and later as a prominent stock operator, committed suicide in San Francisco yesterday morning by shooting himself in the head. He was a native of Vermont, aged 53 years. He had been suffering from heart disease for a long time past, and is supposed to have been recently out of his mind." (Daily Nevada State Journal, June 2, 1880, pg1)

Appendix B

U.S. Consulate Hong Kong Cable 273
United States Consulate
Hong Kong, December 28th, 1874
Hon. John L. Cadwalader
Assistant Secretary of State, Washington D.C.

Sir:
I have the honor to enclose herewith a copy of a telegram forwarded be myself to the Hon. Hamilton Fish, Secretary of State, bearing the date December 19th, 1874 informing the Department of the loss by fire at sea of the P.M.S.S. "Japan"

Regarding this most fearful calamity, I have to submit the following facts; early on the morning of the 19th of December 1874 this community was startled by the intelligence that the magnificent Steamer "Japan" belonging to the Pacific Mail Steamship Company, had been completely destroyed by fire on the night of the 17th instant, off Breaker Point, distant only seven hours steaming from this port.

The news spread with the greatest rapidity, and at first little less than perfect consternation was felt, and the most anxious inquiries were made as to the passengers on board and for full particulars of the disaster.

The first news was brought by an open boat, which arrived at four a.m., containing the chief engineer, Miss Stott, a passenger, and seven Chinese. Later in the morning, namely about nine O'clock, a second boat arrived, containing the baker, stewardess, and six Chinese. This boat was picked up by a fishing junk, which took it on board, and brought it, together with the inmates, to Hong Kong. Finally yesterday, the "Yesso" arrived, containing Captain Warsaw and the remainder of those who were saved from the wreck.

On receipt of the intelligence, I at once communicated with Commander R.F.R. Lewis, commanding the U.S.S. "Yantic," Senior Naval Officer in port with a view of taking immediate steps to render assistance if possible to any of the shipwrecked men. Commander Lewis immediately directed that steam be got up, and in company with the "Saco" Captain Charles McDougall commanding, preceded to the scene of the disaster. The former vessel reached and continued to cruise about the neighborhood of the scene of the accident, following the prevailing currents for some thirty hours. They noticed many pieces of charred wreck floating about, a part of the hurricane deck, and other things which had evidently belonged to the ships stores and furniture, and succeeded in plucking up two metallic life boats, but seeing no life, returned to Hong Kong.

The latter vessel followed along the coast, at Tungao Bay obtained information that the Europeans had landed and left that same morning in a junk for Hong Kong. The "Saco" then started back and on the way overhauled the junk in question and took on board the missing gentlemen Dr. Tindall, United States Consul at Canton, Dr. Gates, the Surgeon of the ship and the rescued Chinese passengers. Subsequently they picked up and took on board a life boat, belonging to the "Japan" and finding no further sign of any of the survivors having reached the coast they returned to Hong Kong.

From what I can gather after repeated interviews with the survivors it would seem that the "Japan" under command of Captain E.R. Warsaw sailed from the port of Yokohama on the 11th day of December 1874 bound for the port of Hong Kong, with a crew including the Captain and officers of One hundred and twenty eight men, two cabin passengers, two Europeans, and four hundred and twenty five Chinese steerage passengers, making a total of five hundred and fifty seven souls on board. She had also six hundred and twenty tons of general cargo, one hundred and sixty eight boxes of treasure, value $358,508, and seven packages of mails. Pleasant weather was experienced up to noon on the 17th, when the wind freshened into a strong breeze from the north east, with a rough sea; at 9 P.M. passed Lammock Light, distant five miles, ship under sail and steam. At 11.25 p.m. Breaker Point bearing west half south distant twenty six miles; fire first discovered, the engines were immediately stopped and fire alarm sounded, ship headed in shore, ventilators turned from the wind; all fire engines working in splendid order; every effort was being made to subdue the fire, at the same time officers were detailed to swing out the boats, preparatory to saving life. Finding it impossible to subdue the fire, the ship was abandoned, the last boat in command of Captain Warsaw leaving at one O'clock a.m. on the 18th, the ship then being enveloped in flames amidships, directly in engine and fire rooms, all communication being cut off between the forward and after parts of the vessel. The Captain remained in the vicinity of the wreck until noon saving life; engaging a fishing junk to assist, and succeeded in saving one hundred and seventeen souls from boats and water, seeing no more life he stood in for Cap Chi Point. At 6.30 p.m. interrupted the English Steamer "Yottung" Captain Koch commanding, who kindly took the survivors on board and conveyed them to Swatow, they were then transferred to the Steamer "Yesso," and brought to Hong Kong.

I enclose herewith a statement giving the details of those saved and lost so far as is known up to this time.

In conclusion I will say that the statement of all clearly demonstrates the fact that the fire originated in the coal bunkers through spontaneous combustion. That everything was done possible to subdue the fire. Officers and men working manfully up to the last moment to save the noble vessel, and when finally compelled to leave her to her fate, with great calmness and self-possession the Commander Captain Warsaw directed the movements of all those remaining on board being the last man to leave the ship. All both officers and crew did their duty-nobly and well.

With regard to the action of Commander Lewis and McDougall I would most respectfully call the attention of the Department to the promptness displayed by them in responding to my suggestion and proceeding at once to sea in order that they might render such assistance as remained in their power to such poor unfortunates as might still be battling with the waves, or wandering upon the shore in the neighborhood of the scene of the disaster exposed to the anything but kind and hospitable treatment of the inhabitants of that locality.

In this connection I would also speak of the kind and human conduct of the Captain and officers of the British Steamer "Yottung," Captain Warsaw speaks very highly of the treatment and assistance received at the hands of these gentlemen, especially Captain Koch, the commander.

A Court of Inquiry is now setting at this Consulate and should any further facts be developed of importance I will acquaint the Department with same.

I have the honor to be, sir;
Your Obedient Servant,
H. Seldon Loring
U.S. Vice Consul

Enclosure:
Copy of a telegram to Hon. Hamilton Fish
Names of the saved, lost, etc, etc.

Copy
Telegram
Dec, 19th

Hamilton Fish
Washington, D.C.

"Japan" burned at sea, near Hong Kong, fearful loss of life, Mails lost.

Loring
Vice Consul

Tabular Statement giving the details of those saved and lost at the destruction of the Pacific Mail Steamship "Japan" by fire at sea on the night of the 17th of December 1874.

On board on leaving Yokohama:

128 Crew
2 Cabin Passengers (Dr. Tindall and Mr. Crocker)
2 Europeans steerage
425 Chinese, steerage

Total....557
Saved so far as known:

114 Crew
2 Cabin passengers (Dr. Tindall and Mr. Crocker)
1 Steerage (Miss Stott)
34 Chinese, steerage.

Total 151

Missing:
14 Crew
1 European, steerage (Mr. Gilder from Yokohama)
391 Chinese, steerage.

Total... 446

The saved include (Europeans) Captain E. R Warsaw, commander, F.W. Hart, 1st Officer, John Cosgrove, Chief Engineer, John Rooney, Purser, V.B Gates, Surgeon, C.L. Gorham, Freight Clerk, H.H. Andrew, 2nd Officer, J.P. Gallagher, 3rd Officer, Charles Sengfelder, Painter, J Kennedy, Carpenter, William Blanchard, Quartermaster, Edward Murdoch, Quartermaster, Emil Gullicon, Deck-watchman, David Fulton, 2nd Assistant Engineer, James Hackett, Water Tender, Edwin W. Tucker, Oiler, James

Dremon, Oiler, Peter Graham, Oiler, John Dalton, Engineers storekeeper, O.N. Clarke, Chief Steward, William Ray, 2nd Steward, Augus S. Leslie, Steerage Steward, L.W. Tose, Butcher, Thomas Green, Baker, Joseph Spavona, Pantryman, W.B. Korn, Storekeeper, Frank Christy, Saloon Watchman, Harry Lester, Steerage Watchman, Kelly Noble, Stewardess, Barber (not on the Articles.)

The missing includes (Europeans) Mr. Bennett, First Assistant Engineer, Quartermasters Harris and Sutton, Martin Cussack, Cook, and Mr. Gilder, a steerage passenger from Yokohama.

Appendix C

U.S. Consulate Hong Kong Cable 274
United States Consulate
Hong Kong, January 7th, 1875
Hon. John L. Cadwalader
Assistant Secretary of State, Washington D.C.

Sir:

With reference to my dispatch to the Department No. 273, bearing date December 28th, 1874, regarding the loss by fire at sea of the P.M.S.S. Company's steamer "Japan," I have the honor to submit herewith enclosed for the information of the Department, a copy of the Decision of the Court of Enquiry held at the Consulate at the request of Captain E.R. Warsaw, late commander of the ill-fated steamer, as to the facts attending the loss of the above named vessel.

I have the honor to be, Sir;
Your most Obedient Servant
H. Freelen Loring
U.S. Vice Consul

> Enclosure
> Copy
> Decision

We the undersigned composing the Court of Enquiry assembled at the United States Consulate, on the 24th day of December, 1874, to enquire into the cause of, and circumstances attending the loss of the P.M.S.S. "Japan", Captain E.R.Warsaw Commander, after hearing and carefully considering all of the testimony adduced in the case, do find as follows:

That the P.M.S.S."Japan," of 4351 21/100 tons register, registered at the port of New York, sailed from the port of Yokohama, on the 11th day of

December 1874, at 4 O'clock p.m. fully manned and equipped in every particular,- bound for the port of Hong Kong.

That on the night of the 17trh of December, when off Breaker Point, at the hour of 11:25 or thereabouts, an alarm of fire was sounded, the approximate position of the ship being Latitude 22.45N Longitude 116.36E.

That the fire in our opinion originated in the forward bunker immediately under the freight deck.

That the fire was caused by spontaneous combustion of the coal placed there when coaling in the harbor of Yokohama, the coal having been taken on board during a violent rain storm, and consequently stowed in a wet and damp condition.

That at the last inspection previous to the fire, the engineer on duty failed to inspect the bunker, although he did inspect all others containing coal, the reason assigned being that no coal had been used from the bunker since 5p.m. on that day.

That at the last inspection of the vessel at 8 p.m. the inspecting officers failed to detect any evidence of the presence of fire.

That such was the condition of affairs at 11:25 p.m. when the first alarm was given and smoke seen to issue from the vicinity of the coal bunker referred to.

That at this moment no flames were seen only a dense volume of smoke.

That immediately the engine was stopped, a general alarm sounded, ventilators turned from the wind, and in fact, the rules and regulations of the Company, made and provided for such an emergency, strictly complied with, and that the officers and crew at once put forward every effort in their power to subdue the flames.

That under the direction of Captain Warsaw all available streams, some seven or eight in number, were brought to bear in the immediate vicinity of the fire, located in the engine and fire room at that time.

That all the available fire apparatus was brought to bear on the fire within about 10 minutes, some 21 streams in number.

That the fire apparatus was in excellent condition and was used to its utmost capacity, until increasing heat prevented the pumps from working.

That everything was done on the part of Captain Warsaw and the officers and crew generally under his command, to save the vessel.

That After all human efforts had proved futile, as shown by the evidence to subdue the fire and save the ship, she was abandoned by all on board at 12:43 on the morning of the 18th, the commander being the last man to leave the ship, but we find in abandoning the vessel there was an evident lack of organization in lowering and manning the boats properly, although they were properly equipped and provisioned.

That we are of opinion that there should have been established a Boat Station Bill upon this Steamer, providing for the emergency of abandoning the ship, with a view to the greater security of the lives of the passengers as well as the ships company, and to prevent confusion and disorder, as well as the lowering of the boats unauthorized by the commanding officer.

That a more rigid inspection of coal bunkers, a greater care in regard to burning surplus coal first, and a more careful supervision of the condition of the coal when coaling should be exercised, and that the temperature of the coal bunkers should be taken at least once every four hours for the purpose of preventing and detecting any incipient signs of combustion going on in them.

That from all the evidence, we gather the Captain was cool, calm, and collected, that he did his duty nobly and well, and exerted himself to the fullest extent to save the vessel under his command, and after her abandonment, in remaining by the vessel until all hope of saving further life was gone.

That we consider the conduct of the chief engineer reprehensible, both in passing an unauthorized order calculated to dispirit the persons engaged in subduing the flames, and in allowing the largest boat, in which he was the only male European, to leave the ship only partly filled, without endeavoring to save the lives of those remaining on board and in the water, although, from the evidence, he appears after reaching the boat to have been suffering from inhalation of smoke, and not to have been actually in command of the boat.

That we consider the great loss of life among the Chinese passengers arose from the communication between the fore and aft ends of the ship (at which latter end most of the boats were placed) being cut off, their paralysation by fear preventing any efforts to save their lives, the roughness of the sea, and darkness of the night, and the weight of the money in many cases slung upon their persons, although the life preservers were abundant, and were extensively made use of.

(Signed) H. L. Loring
Vice Consul in Charge and President of the Court.
(Signed) R.T.R. Lewis
Commander, U.S.N. and Senior Officer present
(Signed) W.W. Gillpatrick
Lieut. U.S.N., Member
(Signed) Benj. P Cloug,
Master American Ship, "Malay"

Appendix D

Japan Wreck – Salvage Timeline

Nov 16, 1874	Captain Roberts organized to refloat *Alaska*; $35,000-$50,000 contract signed
Dec 19, 1874	Consul Hong Kong cable to Secretary of State Hamilton Fish on *Japan*'s loss
Dec 21, 1874	Consul Swatow dispatch #186 to State on *Japan*'s loss
Dec 23, 1874	Captain Roberts successfully refloats the *Alaska*
Dec 24, 1874	Court of Inquiry assembled at Consul Hong Kong by Vice Consul Loring
Dec 26, 1874	Vice Consul Loring drops cable #273 off at PMSS for *Aloma* voyage
Dec 28, 1874	Consul Hong Kong cable #273 provides results of concluded Court of Inquiry
Dec 30, 1874	Vice Consul Loring dispatches auditor letter to Swatow on *Japan* loss
Jan 07, 1875	Authorities for salvage effort begin to emerge and become established
Jan 12, 1875	Court of Inquiry results posted in cable #274
Jan 16, 1875	Augustine Heard issues letter introducing Capt. Roberts to Consul Swatow
Jan 18, 1875	Consul Swatow receives Military magistrate letter on *Japan*
Jan 19, 1875	Magistrate results sent from Consul Swatow
Jan 28, 1875	Russell & Co. cables Macondray and Co.; treasure probably to be saved
Jan 29, 1875	Consul Swatow letter fm Captain Holcomb and *Scotland* on *Japan* salvage
Jan 30, 1875	Reply to Captain Holcomb – *Scotland* letter from Consul Swatow
Feb 17, 1875	Steamer *Aden* sails from Hong Kong to scene of wreck
Feb 27, 1875	Chinese bodies taken from wreck with money belts on
Mar 10 1875	Scotland anchors over *Japan* wreck; dredging and diver confirms wreck.
Mar 13, 1875	Battle and Co. sends salving *Japan* letter - protection request for *Scotland*
Mar 17, 1875	Battle and Co. letter reply from Consul Swatow on salvage of Japan

Mar 19, 1875   Captain Roberts finds one of the paddlewheels

May 17, 1875   USS *Yantic* communicates with American schooner *Scotland* on wreck

Jun 14-5 1875   USS *Yantic* communicates with Little Orphan - schooner *Loitens* on wreck

Jun 16, 1875   *Great Republic* passes Little Orphan on the wreck of the *Japan*

Jul 31, 1875   *Japan* wreck discovered by Captain Roberts, 11 miles southwest of wheel

Aug 5, 1875   Salvage of *Japan* too deep; Danish divers and Scotland depart for Hong Kong

Aug 15, 1875   USS *Ashelot* guards recovery efforts of salvage party on *Japan* wreck

Aug 21, 1875   Consul Swatow visits USS *Ashelot* at anchor off Swatow

Sep 12, 1875   Treasure tank reached, divers recover $24 trade dollars; NE monsoon begins

Oct 14, 1875   Captain Templar and the English divers return to Hong Kong for season

Mar 1, 1876   Captain Roberts departs Shanghai for Hong Kong and 1876 salvage effort

Apr 17, 1876   Work is progressing by the English submarine divers on the wreck

Jul 18, 1876   USS *Monocacy* communicated with steamer Rajah recovering treasure

Jul 30, 1876   USS *Monocacy* arrived in Swatow and remained in vicinity for wreckers

Oct 1877   Augustine and Heard report *Japan* treasure of $47,000 to be recovered

Oct 31, 1877   Thomas W. Knox interviews Captain Roberts on the wreck

During the summers of 1876 and 1877 about $175,000 of the treasure was recovered. Thomas W. Knox indicates that Captain Roberts stated that almost $300,000 recovered by 1878.

Compiled from a combination of Consul Hong Kong and consul Swatow official cable and correspondence logs, official U.S. navy logs of the USS *Yantic*, and reports from, reporter Thomas W. Knox, and the *New York Times* and *Alta California* newspapers.

Appendix E

Captain John Pratt Roberts and the *Alaska*

A direct descendant of Connecticut's Pratt family, Captain John Pratt Roberts was also a seafaring officer bringing Irish immigrants from Liverpool to New York in the 1850s as a sea captain on the vessel *Underwriter*. As relations between Britain and the U.S. became more belligerent during the beginning of the Civil War, he made the decision to join the American Russell and Company trading agency in Hong Kong. The opportunity had been presented to Captain Roberts to join that company's effort in establishing sidewheel steamboat capability on the Yangtze River to increase the China trade to America. Captain Roberts agreed to captain the sidewheel steamer *Huquang* from New York to Hong Kong, traveling around the Cape of Good Hope in South Africa on May 28, 1862. After his arrival, he joined the Russell and Company agency and became the most well-known American marine engineer in China.

During the late 1860s and early 1870s, Captain Roberts established the shipping concerns in Shanghai, became a co-founder of China's first navigation company – the Shanghai Steam Navigation Company, and was directly involved in the important Anglo-American steamship rivalry with China's treaty ports to secure market share in the rich cargo carrying trade along the Yangtze River. He would live for the remainder of his life in Shanghai until his death in 1906.

Captain Roberts is an important part of the *Japan*'s final voyage in two ways. The first role was as a marine engineer hired by the Pacific Mail Steamship Company to refloat the company's steamer *Alaska* from the rocks. The new contract for refloating the vessel was taken by Roberts on November 28, 1874, as the CMSN Superintendent.

The second role is the most important: his selection to salvage the wreckage of the *Japan*. Through his extraordinary efforts, Roberts and his salvage teams located the final two sites of the *Japan*'s wreckage.

In the fall of 1874, the *Alaska* had suffered several rounds of damage in close succession. A week after dropping the U.S. Transit of Venus delegations in Yokohama on August 23, the *Alaska* broke one of her shafts just before entering Hong Kong and had to be docked and re-coppered at the Kowloon dock across from Hong Kong. The repair work was completed in about three weeks. As a substitute to take up the gap, the Pacific Mail had chartered the *Vancouver* to cover the San Francisco – China runs.

Then the typhoon of September 22-24 struck Hong Kong. During what some considered the most violent storm ever to hit Hong Kong, the *Alaska* was grounded on the rocks.

"After getting to her wharf on the 22nd, the storm burst with terrible fury. Her new hawsers parted like threads. She dragged her anchors and struck on the opposite shore with her living freight. She was carried bow on to the rocks with terrible force, at first pounding greatly, then listing to starboard and resting quietly."[130]

The Pacific Mail Company's original attempt to get her off the rocks was unsuccessful. Following that, a new contract was signed with the China Merchants Steam Navigation Company (CMSNC) out of Shanghai to refloat the vessel.

"Poor old Alaska! A week or so after we left her she broke her shaft , on her way down to Hong Kong, and while lying in the harbor there, repaired and nearly ready to sail, she was caught by the typhoon of September and driven ashore upon the rocks, from which she is hardly likely to get off."[131]

The CMSNC was set up in 1872 as China's first joint-stock company. The company was originally established in 1862 when the American trading house, Russell and Company, put up a third of the required capital to establish the Shanghai Steam Navigation Company. As part of the deal, Chinese merchant officials began to acquire steamships of their own, employing "westerners" as captains and engineers.

"It is, of course, generally known that among the numerous shipping disasters caused by the recent typhoon, at Hongkong, was the driving high and dry, on the beach, close to the Kowloon Dock, where she had just been overhauled and re-coppered, of the Pacific Mail Company's magnificent steamer Alaska. It is also known that efforts were promptly made to get her afloat, but the difficultly of doing this had proved greater than was anticipated, and the steamer still remained on the most undesirable berth to which –not the harbor master-but the harbor invader and destroyer had consigned her. Letters received by French mail, from

Hongkong, inform us that our fellow resident, Captain John P. Roberts, has, to the astonishment, to say the least of it, of the denizens of the crown Colony, entered into a contract to have the steamer afloat within sixty days-his compensation for doing so variously stated at from $36,000 to $50,000. To form some idea how arduous a task Captain Roberts has thus undertaken and which, we are told, he declares himself certain to accomplish satisfactorily, bearing death or serious accident-it must be keep in mind that the Alaska is a vessel registering 4011 tons, being 360 feet long, 48 feet beam and 40 feet depth of hold from the hurricane deck. When she left the dock just before the catastrophe, she was drawing 17 feet 8 inches, and when the storm subsided she was found lying in line with the beach, listed off the shore, and at low tide her port bilge is out of the water. We may here mention that in a most interesting collection of photographic views of the effects of the typhoon, which may be seen at Messrs. Lane, Crawford, and Cos, the position of the steamer may be seen from two points of view, the two combining to give a very impressive idea of the extent to which she had been driven "out of her element." At the same time, the fullness with which her hull can be seen at the bottom of the ebb, gives satisfactory assurance that she has not suffered the slightest strain-that there is not even a wrinkle on her copper. She is a very strong and heavy ship, her sides and bottom being for the most part four feet thick, while her double planking is sixteen inches through. Altogether, he hull and machinery are estimated to weigh 8,000 tons, and it is this enormous mass that Captain Roberts has undertaken to move into water deep enough to float her. It was generally thought that the contract would be secured by the Hongkong and Whampoa Company, which had the enormous advantage of a great part of the men and means required ready on the spot. But we understand that the Company's plan of operations was not approved, while their terms were much higher that Captain Roberts' tender. Certainly, there is that in the antecedents of Captain Roberts which makes him worthy to be entrusted with the arduous task he has undertaken." [132]

The *Alaska* had been launched from the same Henry Steers yard two months after *Japan* in September 1867. The *Alaska* had carried the scientific parties sent out by the U.S. Government to observe the Transit of Venus in Nagasaki, Japan, Vladivostok, Russia and Peking, China. Then, she was marooned in Hong Kong. As the *Japan* departed San Francisco and passed through the Golden Gate on the afternoon of November 14, the salvage effort to refloat her sister ship, the *Alaska*, from the rocks across from Hong Kong was entering what many hoped would be its final phase. As the *Japan* loaded coal in Yokohama, Captain John P. Roberts was placing ten pontoons around the *Alaska* in order to begin a series of attempts to refloat her on the high tide.

The stories of the *Japan* and the *Alaska* were fatefully joined again one last time. After the loss of the *Japan*, the *Alaska* would be home to the survivors of the *Japan* tragedy and return the survivors home to San Francisco after the first of the year. After successfully refloating the *Alaska*, Captain John P. Roberts would then take on a new task of recovering the treasure from the wreck of the *Japan*.

A Hong Kong Snapshot – A Picnic on the *Alaska*, December 2, 1874

The Brisbane Courier in their Hong Kong Letter column of December 2, 1874 captured the post-typhoon sentiment in Hong Kong and an interesting slice of contemporary life in Hong Kong society, which viewed the Alaska tragedy as a social destination for conversation and a destination for amusement.

"We have not yet recovered from the ravages of the typhoon. Lots of houses are still surrounded with scaffolding, and the bricklayers are having a splendid time of it, whilst tiles are still much dearer than they used to be...Several of the sunken ships are still blocking up the harbor. The Government ordered them all to be removed before November 15, but it was no use issuing such an order, as at present the owners can do nothing with them....The Pacific Mail steamer Alaska is a case in point. As I told you in my former letter, she was blown ashore at Aberdeen, in the typhoon, and has remained there ever since. She is close to deep water-only a few feet from it, but yet they have not succeeded in getting her off. She has been the great topic of conversation for a long time. Numerous bets have been made about her chances of coming off uninjured-so far, she has been very lucky, as no damage has been done to her bottom. Any amount of picnics have been organized to go round and see her, and I should think everybody in Hong Kong had been several times.

Whenever a lady feels inclined for a little amusement, she at once suggests a trip to the Alaska, and, as there are lots of steam launches in this colony, no difficulty is experienced in borrowing one and going round to Aberdeen, which is only a few miles off. There have been numerous disappointments connected with the unfortunate ship. Several times large parties have gone round, learning she was coming off, but, so far, she has not moved. About six weeks ago we heard positively that an attempt was to be made early next morning. Of course a picnic party of about five and twenty was at once organized. The P. and O., with their usual liberality, lent us their steam-tug, the Sanda, which is much more comfortable than any one of the launches. We were obliged to get up very early, as we left the wharf before seven, and naturally there were a few sluggards who were left behind. We reached Aberdeen in excellent time, and our hopes were raised considerably by seeing the Oregonian (another large Pacific mail steamer), with steam up, and several huge hawsers attached to the stem of the Alaska. However, we were again doomed to be disappointed. The tide did not rise so much as expected, and after waiting an hour in anxious expectation, we were informed that no attempt would be made that morning. We went aboard the Alaska and wished them better luck next time in a real American cocktail, which consoled us somewhat and made us look more hopefully on things in general than we had heretofore. After all we had a capital outing, and enjoyed it immensely. The next excursion was, by no means, so pleasant; the ship was to come off at 12 o'clock at night this time, and a party of ladies accompanied us, as this was supposed to be a bona fide attempt. However, after hanging about the ship for a couple of hours, and everybody growling horribly at the cold, the tide again failed to do what was expected, and we returned very much sadder, if not wiser men. The Pacific Mail Company now began to feel that something else must be done besides waiting for a high tide and finally they engaged Captain Roberts (a surveyor), from Shanghai., who has had some experience in raising ships. He was to make all necessary preparations, and get the steamer off, for $35,000. Captain Roberts at once set to work and had ten large pontoons constructed, each capable of raising a great weight; the ten cost about $20,000. These were placed round the Alaska, and shears fixed up on top of them against the ship's sides; a great many nautical experts asserted that these shears were too weak to support the weight of the vessel as she rose, but Captain Roberts and the Captain of the Alaska were quite confident about it, and as usual in China, bets were made for and against her getting off at the first attempt. On Sunday night, everything was ready and placed in position, and as the tide rose the pontoons were observed moving; but, unfortunately, the experts were justified in their prediction about the weakness of the shears. Directly these felt the weight of the vessel, they began cracking up in every part, and the result was a dead failure, and the Alaska remained undisturbed. However, the pontoons did their duty as well as could be expected, and the Americans are not discouraged. They are hard at work on much stronger shears, and when these are completed, the same plan will be tried, and there is every reasonable probability of its being successful. It is a most unfortunate affair for the Pacific Mail Service Company, as the Alaska has been idle so many months, besides all the expense of getting her off."[133]

After accepting the assignment to refloat the *Alaska* on November 28, 187, it took Roberts and the CMSN less than a month to achieve the desired results. On December 22, 1874, the steamship was finally back in the water.

"I have just received from Shanghai a telegram announcing that the Pacific mail steamer Alaska was floated at Hong Kong, by Capt. Roberts, on the morning of December 23d. It will be remembered that the Alaska was blown ashore in the great typhoon there on Sept 28th last, remaining upright, but in shoal water. Captain John P. Roberts took the contract for getting her afloat, and succeeded in doing so, to the no small astonishment of the Hong Kong folks, who never expected to see her off again. The achievement is considered by all a great credit to his engineering ability, which is already well known in China. Hong Kong is a British colony, and Capt. Roberts' success was in the face of no little national prejudice, and reversed the opinion of the best English engineers. Ten floating pontoons, immense levers, and full-moon tides did their business."[134]

After succeeding in lifting the *Alaska* from the rocks at Aberdeen, Roberts's next challenge would be the salvage of the *Japan*. Coincident to the dispatch of the Navy ships to search for the wreck, the underwriters of the *Japan's* cargo (the PMSS, Hong Kong and Shanghai Bank, A. Heard, and the China traders Insurance Company) immediately gave notice of their intention to attempt the recovery of the coin and engaged Captain Roberts for this undertaking. "A dispatch from Hongkong says: 'the steamer *Alaska* is afloat. She makes no water and shows no strain. We must change her shaft and can dispatch her January 6th.'[135]

Appendix F

The PMSS Japan's Service Life 1868-1873

The sidewheel steamships of the late 1860s were considered some of the finest specimens of naval architecture afloat. The *Japan* was the third of four of the world's largest sidewheel steamers ever built. She was one of the three steamers built by shipbuilder Henry Steers at the Green Point shipyard in Brooklyn, New York. Green Point was located at the foot of Huron and Green streets and, at that time after the Civil War, was regarded as the heaviest shipbuilder outside of government during the Civil War.

Japan's keel was laid on January 1, 1867, and the vessel was launched on September 17, 1867. She was beautiful.

"The Japan is one of the finest ships of the fleet to which she belongs. She measures 4351 tons, is 370 feet in length, 79 in breadth; he depth of hold is 31 ½ feet, and, as we are sailing, she is 20 feet out of the water. Her cylinder is 105 inches in diameter, and her smoke-pipe 36 feet in circumference-not a very small chimney, reminding us of the big trees in California."[136]

The *Japan*'s hull was made of wood, and subdivided by bulkheads into water-tight compartments. "Constructed of white oak, live oak, back matack, and red cedar. Her doors and furtocks were made of white oak, the "tops" of live oak and red cedar, and the half tops of hack matack. She had two thicknesses of planking-the inner layer of yellow pine and the outside layer, from the bottom of the bilge of yellow pine."[137] Her engine rooms were an important part of her service life, and the naval architects had designed temperature and ventilation improvements in order to improve the suffocating hot conditions that were common on other seagoing steamers.

"Should fire break out, thirty two streams of water from force pumps, worked by engine, may be put in play in two minutes."[138]

Mr. W.W. Vanderbilt of PMSS insisted on temperature improvements in the engine room, and because the sidewheel steamers were to be used in the China trade, design measures to avoid coal gas, bilge water, drainage and sweating would protect the cargoes of silk, teas, sugars, and provisions.

The engine rooms were said to be "kept as cool as the saloon deck."

The maximum speed with favorable weather and sea conditions would approach 17 knots.

The *Japan's* marine engines were manufactured by the Novelty Iron Works and were considered to work as smoothly as any marine engines. The Novelty design consisted of steam pumps and siphon pumps by Woodward that could discharge 6,000 tons of water in 6 minutes, a prodigious amount greater than the ship's own weight.

The accommodations were also designed to be first class and were considered as good as any hotel of the day. The cabins were designed to have running water in each stateroom, bathrooms would adjoin the staterooms, and the room appointments offered every convenience found in a first-class hotel.

The staterooms are large and comfortable, the cabins as wide and ornate in finish as the drawing rooms of a first class hotel. [139]

Throughout every part of the ship, even to the staterooms, in the second cabin, and the lower decks and in the steerage and the hold of the vessel; fresh and steady currents of air were folded in. Her fastenings were exposed to water were of what is known to shipbuilders as yellow metal which is copper and brass united and elsewhere with iron, her planking being bolted edgewise and laterally. Her decks were made of 4-inch white pine."[140]

"The action of the Pacific Mail Company in adopting side-wheel vessels, when all European companies are building screws, has been criticized; but the company looking to the transportation of Chinese emigrants as the chief source of revenue, chose a model which would give room for a large number of steerage passengers."[141]

Index

217

219

- role with Chinese worker remains-22
- promise to return bodies-22
- recruiting workers in Guangdong with Central Pacific-13
- regional houses-16
- counting emigrant population-63
- employment of steerage passengers-64
- and railroads-64
- petition to President U.S. Grant-70,72

Stacy, James-181

Steamers

- meeting in the Pacific-51-52

Stott, Mary-90

- as passenger-90
- in the fire-128
- in the lifeboat-134
- Hong Kong arrival-136

Sunday services

- aboard S.S. *Colorado*-49

Swatow, China

- arrival of S.S. *Japan* survivors-139-140
- as hub of S.S. *Japan* salvage operations and U.S. Asiatic Fleet piracy protection of the salvage vessels-155

T

Tindall, Robert

- nomination by President Grant as U.S. Consul to Hong Kong-83
- biography and Mississippi background-85
- as S.S. *Japan*'s most distinguished passenger-85-86
- letter to Secretary of State Fish-87
- in the fire-128
- in the lifeboat-128-129

Twain, Mark

- in San Francisco July 1868-24
- as Samuel Clemins-25
- working on *Innocents Abroad*-25

225

Endnotes

Chapter 1: The Central Pacific Railroad Needs Workers!

[1] Stephen E. Ambrose, *Nothing Like It In The World-The Men Who Built the Transcontinental Railroad*. (New York: Touchtone-Simon and Schuster, 2001), p243 as cited in William Deverell's *Railroad Crossing: Californian's and the Railroad, 1850-1910* (Berkeley: University of California Press, 1994), p14i.

[2] Ibid. Ambrose, p298.

[3] Corrinne K. Hoexter, *From Canton to California-The Epic of Chinese Immigration*. (New York: Four Winds Press, 1976), p82.

[4] Mr. Anson Burlingame's Mission as Envoy of China to the Treaty Powers, *Daily Alta*, March 22, 1868, p1.

[5] The Chinese Embassy Banquet, *Sacramento Daily Union*, May 1, 1868, p1.

[6] The Chinese in California, *Daily Alta California*, Chih Tajen remarks at the Grand Banquet, Apr 30, 1868, p3.

Chapter 2: The Chinese Emigrants

[7] Corrinne K. Hoexter, *From Canton to California-The Epic of Chinese Immigration*. (New York: Four Winds Press, 1976, p.xii.

[8] *"The Six Chinese Companies,"* *The Overland Monthly*, October 1868, p222.

[9] William C. Bunner, *Pioneering the Pacific-A Saga of Sixty Years of Steamshipping*, unpublished 1926 manuscript in the possession of Professor John H. Kemble, Pomona College and transcribed by Kathryn Hulme for ***Annie's Captain***. The Bunner manuscript copy is at the Beinecke Rare Book and Manuscript Library, Yale University, New Haven, Connecticut. Mr. Brunner was the Oriental Agent of the Pacific Mail Steamship Company in San Francisco from 1867 until the 1890's.

[10] Ellen H. Walworth, *An Old World Seen Through Young Eyes*, (New York: D&J Sadler and Company, 1877), p297

[11] Thomas Woodbine Hinchcliff, *Over the Sea and Far Away*, (London: Longmans, Green and Company, 1876), p313.

[12] Ibid., Bunner, pp11-12

[13] Iris Chang, *The Chinese in America-A Narrative History*, (New York and London: Penguin Books, 2003), p80.

Chapter 3: Mark Twain and a Perfect Palace of a Ship

[14] Please see Mr. Mark Twain's *Letter to Mary Mason Fairbanks*, 5 July, 1868, page 1. The *SS Japan* had just completed her maiden voyage from New York to San Francisco and coincidentally, Mark Twain was spending his last time ever in San Francisco negotiating the contract for the release of his letters from the *Alta* that were generated from his voyage on the *S.S. Quaker City* to the Holy Land. A frequent voyager and passenger on Pacific Mail steamships, Mark Twain greatly admired the *Japan* and knew the First Engineer aboard, "Engineer Harris" who was also on the *Quaker City* voyage. Twain's letters would be published as *"Innocents Abroad";* his first book. The original Mark Twain 5 July letter citing the *SS Japan* is at the Huntington Library, San Marino, California.

Chapter 4: Captain Warsaw and the S.S. Colorado

[15] Let Merchant Captain's Command Our Mercantile Marine, *Daily Alta California*, Aug. 29, 1874, p1.
[16] Thomas W. Knox, The Coming Man, *Leslies Illustrated Newspaper,* May 7, 1870, p122.
[17] Ibid, TWK, p122
[18] Benjamin Robbins Curtis, *Dottings Around the Circle*, 1876, p76.
[19] J.F. Campbell, *My Circular Notes*, (London: Macmillan and Co. 1876), p153.
[20] James Brooks, *A Seven Month's Run*, (New York: D. Appleton and Co., 1874), p26.
[21] Frances B. Thurber, *Coffee from Plantation to Cup*, (New York: American Group Publishing Association, 1881), p260.
[22] Thomas Woodbine Hincliff, *Over the Sea and Far Away*, (London: Longmans, Green, and Company, 1876), p315
[23] Rev. O. Gibson, AM, *The Chinese in America,* (Cincinnati: Hitchcock and Walden, 1877), p14.
[24] The Chinese in San Francisco, *The Friend-A Religious and Literary Journal,* Vol. XLIX, Number 22, Jan. 15, 1876, p1.
[25] The Six Chinese Companies, *Overland Monthly*, Oct. 1868, p221-222.
[26] Ellen H. Walworth, *An Old World Seen Through Young Eyes*, (New York: D&J Sadler and Company, 1877), p307
[27] From the Orient Direct, *The Atlantic Monthly*, November, Volume XXIV, (Boston: Fields, Osgood and Co., 1869), p546.
[28] Arrival of the "Colorado" From China and Japan, *Daily Alta California*, August 17, 1868, pg1.

Chapter 5: John Chinaman and Chinatown 1868-1874

[29]Corinne K. Hoexter, *From Canton to California-The Epic of Chinese Immigration.* (New York: Four Winds Press, 1976), pps.96-7
[30] Stephen Powers, California Saved, *The Atlantic Monthly*, November 1871, p597.
[31] John Chinaman in San Francisco, *Scribner's Magazine*, March 1876, p862.
[32] Ibid, Powers, p598
[33] Ibid, Powers, , p600
[34] *Chy Lung vs. Freeman et al*, Supreme Court of the U.S., Oct. 1875, p275.
[35] Ibid, Iris Chang, *The Chinese in America*, p72. Ms. Chang notes that the "Chinese formed the backbone of western farm production. They sowed crops, plowed the soil, and ended up producing about two-thirds of the vegetables in California....As the Chinese poured into farm work, grain swiftly surpassed mining as the largest source of revenue for the state. By the 1870's, California had become the wheat capital of the United States."

Chapter 6: 1874 A Turning Tide

[36] Herbert Asbury, *The Barbary Coast: An Informal History of the San Francisco Underworld*, (New York: Thunder's Mouth Press, 1933), P144. Mr. Asbury describes in sordid detail the rise of the ill treatment toward the Chinese in the 1870's, the social conditions in Chinatown, the riots at the Pacific Mail piers and the 1874 letter Memorial from the Six Companies to President Grant which categorically denied the violent city and state official harangues and petitions against the Chinese presented at an April 1874 mass meeting attended by more than 20,000 in San Francisco.

[37] Ibid, Herbert Asbury, *The Barbary Coast*, p146.

[38] Ibid, Herbert Asbury, *The Barbary Coast*, p147.

[39] The fate of the "Chinese Maiden" habeas corpus case secured front page news each day in the *Daily Alta California* for the better part of the week from August 24-31, 1874 and as occurring news from their trial in the California Courts occurred in 184 through the eventual U.S. Supreme Court trial and ruling on (Chy Lung v. Freeman et al. . For the Chinese Maiden articles see the *Daily Alta California*, August 26-30, 1875, p1.

[40] The Twenty Two Chinese Maidens, *Daily Alta California*, August 28, 1874, p1.

[41] The Chinese Maidens, *Daily Alta California*, August 26, 1874, p1.

[42] The Chinese Maidens, *Daily Alta California*, August 30, 1874, p1.

Chapter 7: Captain Warsaw Returns to the Pacific Mail

[43] For Captain Warsaw's re-emergence as a Pacific Mail China steamer Captain in August 1874 see *Daily Alta California*, August 7, 1874, p1.

[44]Thomas Cook organized the first around-the-world cruise in 1872 after the opening of the Suez Canal. At the time of the advertisements for the cruise on the Pacific Mail steamer **Colorado** in the New York Herald, Captain Warsaw was already scheduled to be the Captain for the cruise. Thomas Cook's world cruise inspired the world, is said to have been the catalysts for Jules Verne's *"Around the World in 80 Days"* and was chronicled in Cook's " *Letters From the Sea and From Foreign Lands-Descriptive of a Tour Around the World"* by Thomas Cook. Captain Warsaw's mannerisms on the voyage were captured in the second and third of Cook's 18 letters. Pps 17-29.

[45] Alleged Violation of the Passenger Act, *Daily Alta California*, May 2, 1873, p1.
[46] Robert J. Schwendinger, *Ocean of Bitter Dreams: Maritime Relations Between U.S. and China 1850-1915,* (Tucson: Westernlore Press,1988, p84
[47] The Chinese Maidens, *Daily Alta California*, August 30, 1874, p1.

[48] *Note.* The case would eventually be decided by the U.S. Supreme Court in October 1875 (Chy Lung v. Freeman et-al) under the 14th Amendment to the Constitution, that no state shall deny to any person within its jurisdiction and that the state law was unconstitutional because it was in conflict with the treaty relations between China and the U.S. The case was also the catalyst of a broader petition from San Francisco's Six Companies to President Grant. See *"The Chinese in America"* by Reverend O. Gibson A.M 1877 p315 *"A Memorial from the Representative Chinamen in America to His Excellency U.S. Grant, President of the United States of America."*

Chapter 8: The Final Voyage-Preparations

[49] *"The Six Chinese Companies,"* The Overland Monthly, October 1868, p233.

[50] Kathryn Hume, *Annie's Captain,* (New York: Little Brown, *1962),* p156.

[51] Testimony: 1876 California Senate Committee on Chinese Immigration
[52] Francis B. Thurber, *Coffee: Plantation to Cup,* (New York: American Grocer Publishing Association,1881), p258.

[53] J.F. Campbell, *My Circular Notes,* (London: Macmillan and Co. 1876), p150
[54] "The first voyage of the Colima" *New York Times*, July 31, 1874, p1.

[55] Harold S. Williams, *Burning of the S.S. America* from *Shades of the Past: Indiscreet Tales of Japan,* (Rutland, Vermont: Charles Tuttle, 1959), p.150.
[56] On the *Colima* voyage see the A Voyage To Yokohama; Incidents on Board The Steamship Colima. How The Passengers Amuse Themselves. John Chinaman Returning to His Native Land-A Fast Voyage *New York Times*, September 5, 1874, p5.

[57] John Chinaman in San Francisco, *Scribners Magazine*, 1876, p.865.
[58] From Lucius A Waterman's Journal, 1869, *Library of Congress.* Mr. Waterman's Journal is an insightful record of an actual voyage with Captain Warsaw in command of the Pacific Mail Steamship China. The voyage describes the passage along the China coast, the mannerisms of Captain Warsaw, the Chinese passengers, the arrival in San Francisco and the lodging accommodations of passengers as they prepare for follow-on transportation on the new transcontinental railroad. Captain Warsaw's post-voyage courtesy and stewardship is also accounted for by Mr. Waterman during his visit to the Occidental Hotel after the China's arrival. According to the 1869 San Francisco Directory, Captain Warsaw's residence was described as the Occidental Hotel (See the San Francisco Directory for the year commencing December 1869-Warsaw, E.R., captain P.M.S.S. China, dwl Occidental Hotel.)

[59] James Brooks, *A Seven Months' Run*, (New York: D. Appleton and Company, 1874,) p.25.

Chapter 9: The Final Voyage-Crossing the Pacific

[60] J.F. Campbell, *My Circular Notes*, (London: Macmillan and Co. 1876), p195.

[61] The America Disaster, *New York Times*, September 4, 1872, p1.

[62] Benjamin Robbins Curtis, *Dottings Round the Circle*, (Cambridge: University Press-Welch, Bigelow and Company 1876), p55.

[63] Baron de Hubner, *A Ramble Around the World*; London: Macmillan and Company, 1878), p193.

[64] Thomas Woodbine Hinchcliff, *Over the Sea and Far Away*, (London: Longmans, Green and Company, 1876), p312.

[65] Colonel J.P. Sanford, *Letters of travel from Different Lands*, (Marshalltown: Marshall Printing Company, 1887) p12, from an actual voyage of the *Japan*, March 1872.

[66] A Voyage To Yokohama; Incidents on Board The Steamship Colima. How The Passengers Amuse Themselves. John Chinaman Returning to His Native Land-A Fast Voyage, *New York Times*, Sep 5, 1874, p5.

[67] William H. Seward, *Travels Around the World*, (New York: D. Appleton and Company, 1873), p32.

[68] J.F. Campbell, *My Circular Notes*, (London: Macmillan and Co. 1876), p156. Recording an October 1874 voyage of the *Great Republic* to China.

[69] Baron de Hubner, *A Ramble Around the World*; London: Macmillan and Company, 1878), p186.

[70] Familiar letters From Japan, *Putnam's Magazine. Steamer Great Republic in the Pacific, December 15, 1867, NY 1868, p 631.*

[71] Charles Coffin *Our New Way around the World*, (Cambridge: University Press-Welch, Bigelow and Company, May 1869), p465.

[72] A Voyage To Yokohama; Incidents on Board The Steamship Colima. How The Passengers Amuse Themselves. John Chinaman Returning to His Native Land-A Fast Voyage, *New York Times,* September 5, 1874., p5.

[73] Ibid, *Coffee.* Francis Thubee, 1881, p 258.

[74] E.D.G. Prime, D.D. *Around the World: Sketches of Travel Through Many Lands, DD (*New York: Harper and Brothers, Franklin Square, 1874) p.78.

[75] Ibid, Prime, *Around the World,* p78.

[76] Ibid, Prime, *Around the World,* p78.

[77] The Burned Steamer, *Fitchburg Daily Sentinel*, December 21, 1874, p1. The initial report on the sinking of the *Japan* indicated that there was "973 tons of freight and $8300.00 in treasure when she sailed from San Francisco." This would be in addition to the $358,858 in treasure tank trade dollars. The safe value amount of $8,300 could be a combination of silver and gold. The 1874 passenger rates for cabin and steerage was $200 cabin and $100 steerage in Gold. Gold coin would have been necessary for change and exchange for passenger and freight transactions in Japan and China and also serve as working capital at the Pacific Mail agencies in Yokohama and Hong Kong. Silver treasure for the Hong Kong logistics transactions would also be necessary and there is evidence that Purser John Rooney dispensed silver trade dollars to rescue junks in the aftermath of the Japan's loss ("The Purser on leaving the ship had some coin in bags, that were in his room, which he saved, though the Chinese

fishermen had a peculiar liking for the dollars." *From the Burning of the Steamer "Japan",* Daily Alta California, February 19, 1875, p1). The gold pieces in 1874 would likely have consisted of a combination of San Francisco and Carson City mint coinage including 1874 S Double Eagles worth (all 2014 Red Book figures for uncirculated coinage) $3,250-$28,500 each; 1873 S and 1873 CC worth $43,500 each; 1873-74 S Eagles worth $8,000-22,000 each; 1873-74 S half Eagles worth $7,000-20,000 each; 1873 S Quarter Eagles worth $2,750-7,000 each; The 1873 CC Eagles would be worth considerably more-upwards of $30,,000-65,000 each. A conservative estimate on the value of an $8,300 safe value at $10,000 per coin would place its worth at $83 million dollars. There is no direct evidence from the Roberts wreck recovery notes or the 1875 discovery of the initial sidewheel and the recovery of some of the steerage bodies to suggest that the ship's safe was ever recovered and most likely remains at the bottom of the first wreck site adjacent to the port sidewheel and the debris from the engineer's store room. The depth of water in this region is 14 fathoms-84 feet.

[78] Benjamin Robbins Curtis, *Dottings Round the Circle,* (Cambridge: University Press-Welch, Bigelow and Company, 1876), p60.

[79] Ibid, E. Mowbrey Tate, *Transpacific Steam,* p237.

[80] Colonel J.P. Sanford, *Letters of Travel from Different Lands,* (Marshalltown: Marshall Printing Company, 1887) p11. From an actual March 1872 *Japan* voyage from San Francisco to Yokohama, Japan.

Chapter 10: The Final Voyage-Into the South China Sea

[81] The passage from Hong Kong to the White Dog islands "may be considered as the most difficult portion of the coast that a vessel has to contend with in the N.E. monsoon, and it is believed there are few men who know the coast of China but will allow that Turnabout Island is well named." The China Sea Directory, Vol IV, London, 1873, page 197.

[82] Russell H. Conwell, *Why and How-Why the Chinese Emigrate, and the Means They Adopt For the Purpose of Reaching America,* (Boston: Lee and Shepard, 1871), p117.

Chapter 11: Fire on the Mid-Watch

[83] The "Japan"-Full Particulars in the Burning of the Steamer, *The Daily Alta California,* January 31, 1875, p1.

[84] Ibid.,The "Japan, *Daily Alta California,* January 31, 1875, p1.

Chapter 12: Misery at Dawn

[85] The Burning of the Steamer "Japan", *Daily Alta California*, February 19, 1875, p1.
[86] The "Japan"-Full Particulars in the Burning of the Steamer, *Daily Alta California*, January 31, 1875, p1.
[87] George Anthony Peffer, *If They Don't Bring Their Women Here, Chinese Female Immigration Before Exclusion*, (Urbana and Chicago: University of Illinois Press, 1999), p43.
[88] Reports of De B. Randolph Keim to the Secretary of the Treasury, relating to the Condition of Consulates of the United States 1871. p74.
[89] *Hong Kong Dispatch number 273 dtd December 28th, 1874*. U.S. National Archives, College Park, MD.
[90] The "Japan"-Full Particulars in the Burning of the Steamer, *Daily Alta California*, January 31, 1875, p1.
[91] The "Japan" Confirmation of Her Loss, *Daily Alta California*, Dec 21, 1874 p1.
[92] The Burning of the Steamer Japan, *Daily Alta California*, Friday February 19, 1875, p1.
[93] William Kooiman, *Invitation to Disaster: The Burning of the S.S. Japan*, Sea Classics, July 2009, pps57-8.
[94] The Burning of the Steamer "Japan", *Daily Alta California*, February 19, 1875, p1.
[95] *Hong Kong Dispatch number 273 dtd December 28th, 1874*. National Archives, Hong Kong Dispatches. Note: On Thanksgiving Day one year later, Captain Koch was commended for his gallantry and service during the rescue of the *Japan* passengers. Captain Koch would not accept compensation for the rescue saying that he was only doing his duty and received with gratitude from the U.S. Government and the Pacific Mail Steamship Company a gold chronometer and massive watch guard and a telescope. The U.S. Consul in Hong Kong, Mr. Bailey, said "It is a pleasant duty I have to perform, under instructions from my Government, in presenting a testimonial of its very high appreciation of your conduct in rescuing the passengers and crew of the American mail steamer Japan. You rendered a notable and important service, at a critical juncture, on that occasion, and you did it with vigour, judgment, and courtesy. But that conduct does not need to be recapitulated by me now, for it is well known, not only here but in America. Your response in declining compensation saying "I only did my duty," cannot be forgotten. But as duty always win, so is your case, for the head of the nation pays you this tribute of respect. On behalf of the President of the United States, I now hand you this gift, with the inscription engraved on it:-"Presented by the president of the United States to Captain Koch, of the British steamer Yottung, for his humane services in rescuing the passengers and crew of the American steamer Japan." The spyglass presentation was likewise presented to Captain Koch "in recognition of the service rendered by him to the survivors of the Co.'s S.S. Japan, off Cupchi Point, 18th December, 1874."

[96] USS *Yantic* deck log dtd Sunday, December 20, 1874, National Archives.

[97] Ibid, The "Japan", *Daily Alta California*, Jan 31, 1875, p1.

[98] Excitement Over the Loss of the Japan, *Morning Oregonian*, Sunday, December 21, 1874, p1.

[99] *Daily Nevada State Journal*, Sunday, December 20, 1874, pg 1.

[100] The Steamer Japan Burned Near Yokohama, *New York Times*, December 20, 1874, p1.

Chapter13: Inquiry

[101] The Burning of the Steamer "Japan", *Daily Alta California*, February 19, 1875, p1.

[102] The "Japan", *Daily Alta California*, January 31, 1875, p1.

[103] *New York Times* and *Daily Alta California*, January 31, 1875, p1.

Chapter 14: Salvage

[104] *Morning Oregonian*, page 1 Dec 21, 1874 and *New York Times* Dec 19, 1874)

[105] *Report of the Commercial relations of the United States in Foreign Countries for the Year 1875, China (Swatow) p-312, Washington 1876*

[106] William Kooiman, *Invitation to Disaster: The Burning of the S.S. Japan*, Sea Classics, July 2009, p.58

[107] The Japan Disaster, *Sacramento Daily Union*, March 3, 1875, p.3.

[108] China and Japan, *New York Times*, March 29, 1875

[109] *China Overland Mail*, Dec 19, 1874

[110] R.M. Ballantyne, *Under the Waves or Diving in Deep Waters*, (London: James Nisbet and Co., 1876), pp 188-190.

[111] Thomas W. Knox, The Celestial Empire, *New York Times*, Dec 30, 1877

[112] Charles B. Whittelsey, Letter from John Pratt Roberts, Shanghai, China in *"The Ancestry of John Pratt and His Descendants of Hartford, Conn."* Pps119-120.

[113] *New York Times*, Nov 21, 1875.

[114] *Journal of the North Sea branch of the Royal Asiatic Society*, Shanghai, 1877 pviii.

[115] Thomas W. Knox, *Frank Leslie's Monthly*, pp726-727 and "A Close Shave" Thomas W. Knox, *A Short Trip Around the World*, (New York: Saalfield Publishing, 1900), pp129-30.

[116] Ibid, Celestial Empire, TWK, *New York Times*, Dec. 30, 1877.

[117] Thomas W. Knox, *Adventures of Two Youths in a Journey to Siam and Java*, (New York: Harper Brothers, 1882), p 260.
[118] Ibid, The Celestial Empire, TWK, *New York Times*, Dec 30, 1877.

Chapter 15: The Tragic Aftermath

[119] The Pacific Subsidies, *New York Times*, May 1876, p1.
[120] Corinne K. Hoexter, *From Canton to California-The Epic of Chinese Immigration*. (New York: Four Winds Press, 1976), p108.
[121] Thomas W. Knox, The Celestial Empire, *New York Times*, Dec 30, 1877.

Appendix A: Captain Edward R. Warsaw Life and Service

Endnotes

[122] Please see Lucius A. Waterman *"Journal"*, Library of Congress Mystic Seaport American memory, Volume 467, Jan 19-March 23 1869 p1-39. The Journal chronicles an entire voyage of the Pacific Mail steamer China from Hong Kong to San Francisco via Yokohama. Captain Warsaw's mannerisms, the ship's routine, and the behavior of the passengers and the Chinese steerage passengers figure prominently.

[123] Major William Morrison Bell, *Other Countries*,, (London: Chapman and Hall, 1872), p154.
[124] *Daily Alta California*, Oct. 24, 1872, p1.

[125] Thomas Cook, *Letters from the Sea and Foreign Lands*, (London: Thomas Cook and Son, 1876), p23.

[126] Robert J. Schwendinger, *Ocean of Bitter Dreams*-Maritime Relations Between China and the United States, 1850-1915., (Tucson: Westerlore, 1988), pp 84-85.

[127] *Daily Alta California*, August 6, 1874, p1.

[128] The Pacific Mail Steamship Company's Steamer "China", *Daily Alta California,* August 7, 1874 p1.

Appendix F: The PMSS Alaska

[129] *New York Times* and *Daily Alta California,* January 31, 1875, p1

[130] Awful Catastrophe, *The Janesville Gazette,* Nov 14, 1874, p1

[131] *Letter from the Transit of Venus U.S. delegation member Professor C.A. Young, NYT, p1 December 31, 1874*

Appendix E: Captain John Pratt Roberts and the Alaska

[132] The Raising of the Pacific Mail Company's Steamship "Alaska", *Daily Alta California,* December 23, 1874, p1.

[133] Our Hong Kong Letter, from *The Brisbane Courier,* Saturday, January, 9, 1875, p6
[134] *The Ancestry and Descendants of John Pratt of Hartford, Conn, Charles Whittelsey, 1900, p118.*

[135] The Japan and the Alaska, *Daily Alta California,* December 24, 1874, p1.

Appendix F: PMSS Japan's Service Life Endnotes

[136] E.D.G. Prime, D.D. *Around the World: Sketches of Travel Through Many Lands, DD (*New York: Harper and Brothers, Franklin Square, 1874) p.69.
[137] The Steamer Japan Burned Near Yokohama, *New York Times,* December 20, 1874, p1.

[138] Charles Coffin *Our New Way Around the World,* (Cambridge: University Press-Welch, Bigelow and Company, May 1869), p466.

[139] Ibid. Coffin, *Our New Way Around the World,* p466.

[140] *New York Times*, Dec 11, 1874.

[141] Ibid., Coffin, *Our New Way Around the World*; p466.